MILES FRANKLIN

Marjorie Barnard (1897–1987), born and educated in Sydney, graduated in 1920 with honours in history from the University of Sydney, and worked as a librarian during various periods of her life. Barnard's literary collaboration with Flora Eldershaw under the joint pseudonym "M. Barnard Eldershaw" produced five novels, numerous critical essays, histories, short stories and a play. Barnard's independent publications began in about 1937, including short stories and historical monographs. Her distinguished literary reviews included the first thorough evaluation of Patrick White's fiction. Among Barnard's most notable achievements were her entry on Australian literature for *Chambers's Encyclopedia* (1950) and her study of Miles Franklin. Towards the end of her long life, Barnard began at last to receive the acclaim she deserved.

By the same author

The Ivory Gate
The Persimmon Tree and Other Stories
Macquarie's World
A History of Australia
Australian Outline
The Sydney Book
Sydney: The Story of a City
Australia's First Architect: Francis Greenway
Lachlan Macquarie

"M. Barnard Eldershaw" (with Flora Eldershaw)

A House is Built
Green Memory
The Glasshouse
Plaque with Laurel
Tomorrow and Tomorrow and Tomorrow
Philip of Australia
The Life and Times of Captain John Piper
My Australia
Essays in Australian Fiction
The Watch on the Headland

MILES FRANKLIN
The Story of a Famous Australian

MARJORIE BARNARD

University of Queensland Press

First published 1967
Published 1988 by University of Queensland Press
Box 42, St Lucia, Queensland, Australia

© Estate of Marjorie Barnard 1967
Introduction © Jill Roe 1988

This book is copyright. Apart from any fair dealing
for the purposes of private study, research, criticism
or review, as permitted under the Copyright Act, no
part may be reproduced by any process without written
permission. Enquiries should be made to the publisher.

Printed in Australia by The Book Printer, Melbourne

Cataloguing in Publication Data

National Library of Australia

Barnard, Marjorie, 1897–1987.
    Miles Franklin.

    1988 ed.
    Includes index.

    1. Franklin, Miles, 1879–1954. — Biography.
    2. Authors. Australian — Biography.
    I. Title.

A823'.2

ISBN 0 7022 2146 5

To

Stella, Miles and Brent

Contents

Foreword *xi*

Preface *xv*

Chronology *xvii*

1. Who was Miles Franklin and What was she? *1*
2. Pioneers O Pioneers! *5*
3. Childhood at Brindabella *20*
4. Stella and Miles *34*
5. Thirty Years an Exile *62*
6. Miles Goes to War *70*
7. Brent of Bin Bin Steps out of the British Museum *73*
8. Miles Takes up her Other Pen *106*
9. A Mixed Bag *122*
10. A Homestead in the Suburbs *140*
11. Everyone has a Philosophy *147*
12. Farewell and Hail *156*

Notes and References *159*

Selected Bibliography *169*

Index *171*

List of Illustrations

following page 78

1. Sarah Lampe, Miles's grandmother
2. Susannah Franklin, Miles's mother
3. Old Talbingo homestead where Miles Franklin was born
4. Miles, aged 4½ months
5. Brindabella homestead where Miles spent her childhood
6. Miles Franklin, aged 4 years
7. Miles with long hair, taken in Sydney
8. Miles, aged 17 years
9. Miles on horseback
10. Joseph Furphy who corresponded with Miles for several years
11. "Merry Maid Miles." Miles worked as a maid in Sydney and Melbourne
12. Miles in London with Percy, the monkey in her book *Bring the Monkey*
13. Miles (second from left) as a suffragette in Chicago
14. Miles Franklin in middle age
15. Miles at Grey Street, Carlton, holding sunflowers
16. Miles in later years in her "homestead" at Carlton, Sydney
17. Miles in old age

Foreword

Marjorie Barnard, writer and historian, was born at Ashfield, Sydney on 16 August 1897. Educated at Sydney Girls High School, she won a bursary to the University of Sydney, graduating with first class honours in history in 1920. She then trained as a librarian, having been prevented by her father from pursuing graduate work at Oxford. Success as a writer came in 1929 with *A House is Built*, a historical novel written in collaboration with Flora Eldershaw, a friend from student days. In 1935 she resigned as head librarian at Sydney Technical College to devote herself full-time to writing, returning to library work for a time in the 1940s. Her writing career spanned over fifty years, from the 1920s to the 1970s. During this time she published fifteen major works of fiction, history, and criticism, either in collaboration with Flora Eldershaw as M. Barnard Eldershaw, or in her own name, as well as numerous minor works and a great deal of occasional writing, the last especially after her retirement from paid employment in 1950. In 1983 she received the Patrick White Award to honour undervalued older writers, for the final and most impressive M. Barnard Eldershaw novel *Tomorrow and Tomorrow* (1947; reissued in full as *Tomorrow and Tomorrow and Tomorrow* in 1983). In 1986 she was awarded an honorary Doctorate of Letters by the University of Sydney for her early and sustained contribution to Australian history, for example *Macquarie's World* (1941) and *A History of Australia* (1962). She died in Sydney on 8 May 1987, aged eighty-nine. Marjorie Barnard was by then a great survivor and a legendary figure in Australian letters.

In 1955, a year after Miles Franklin's death, Marjorie Barnard published a critical essay on the writer and her work in the literary quarterly *Meanjin*. Twelve years later in 1967, her book length account was published by Twayne's (New York) and Hill of Content (Melbourne). The first substantial account of the writer and her work, and the only one to date, it was also Barnard's last major work and her only literary biography. It has not previously been reissued.

Miles Franklin appeared as the fifteenth title in Twayne's World Authors Series, an authoritative and extensive series surveying major writers in many countries which today includes a number of Australian writers. (An excellent study of Marjorie Barnard and M. Barnard Eldershaw by Louise E. Rorabacher appeared in the series in 1973.) The author's brief for the series, stated in each volume, is to offer a critical analytical study of a writer's works, with relevant biographical and historical material, written in a clear, concise yet scholarly style. Marjorie Barnard was admirably equipped to fulfil this brief. She sticks to the literary aspect, casting a cool and critical eye across what was then understood to be Franklin's entire oeuvre. She insists, correctly in the opinion of many, that "Miles writing is indivisible from Miles living". True to the biographer's craft, she aims to present "a living personality". Her historical skills are especially evident in the opening chapters on the pioneering ethos, her authoritative approach to the then vexing, not to say tiresome, problem of Franklin's main pseudonym "Brent of Bin Bin", and in the final summation of Franklin's claim to immortality.

In this book Marjorie Barnard, critic, biographer and historian, is also, perhaps especially, a witness. She knew her subject well, though only in Franklin's later life. Miles Franklin was eighteen years old and had just drafted *My Brilliant Career* when Marjorie Barnard was born. Franklin left Australia shortly after, in 1906, to spend nearly thirty years in America and Britain; but when she finally returned home in late 1932, she re-entered the Sydney literary world with zest. It was Marjorie Barnard's world too. Barnard and Franklin first met in the mid-1930s; and although they later fell out (see page 3 of the text), they worked together on several literary projects in subsequent years and they shared many hopes for Australian culture. Tucked into the text are telling firsthand observations, such as those on Franklin's secretiveness. It should be noted that tension between the two was virtually inevitable, considering among other things Franklin's mythic status and her rich international experience compared with Barnard's superior professional qualifications and literary sophistication.

Louise Rorabacher has suggested that Barnard's *Miles Franklin* was not only the first study but very likely the last, as if to say Barnard had captured the essential Franklin. Maybe she had. Kylie Tennant reviewing *Miles Franklin* in the *Sydney Morning Herald* thought so (2 December 1967). Barnard certainly strongly conveys *her* Miles Franklin. There are very few people still alive who actually knew Franklin and it is unlikely that there will be another "witness" biography. But as Barnard recognised in Verna Coleman's *Miles Franklin in America: Her Unknown (Brilliant) Career* (1981; a study of a period not covered by Barnard's work), there's always more, in Franklin's case much more.

That there are limits to Barnard's work detracts not a whit from her significance and achievement as the first Franklin scholar. Her book is based mainly on literary sources. It seems to have been written in the early 1960s. (*Childhood at Brindabella* which appeared posthumously in 1963 is extensively cited in the opening chapters.) This was well before the release of the voluminous Miles Franklin papers willed to the Mitchell Library, Sydney. The papers, yet to be assimilated, consist predominantly of correspondence and manuscripts. They cast a flood of light on Franklin's driving concerns, especially with feminism, and they have already yielded two novels from her Chicago years, *On Dearborn Street* (unpublished until 1984) and *The Net of Circumstance* (published pseudonymously in 1915, to be reissued shortly), years previously thought to be barren of literary endeavour. As the terms of Miles Franklin's will were made public in 1957, it may seem strange that Barnard accepted the story that the relevant papers had been accidentally destroyed when Franklin moved from Chicago to London in 1915. However Barnard is known to have been concerned about individual privacy — it is notable that she eschewed psychologism and made little comment on the significance of gender — and apparently she felt protective of Franklin, a vulnerable figure on many counts. When questioned by Louise Rorabacher, Barnard replied "I was careful not to touch on things she kept hidden. I could have found out a lot of things". Very likely she was also concerned about Franklin's family and friends. In any case, her author brief encouraged her to concentrate on published writings, and the papers were simply not available at the time. Up-to-date discussion which utilises the Franklin papers includes the collection *Gender, Politics and Fiction: Twentieth Century Australian Women's Novels* (1985; edited by Carole Ferrier), Drusilla Modjeska's *Exiles at Home: Australian Women Writers 1925-1945* (1981) where Miles gets "a chapter of her own" and the entry in the *Australian Dictionary of Biography* (vol. 8, 1981).

In a letter to me of 15 February 1982, Marjorie Barnard wrote "Did you know Miles? Her personality was most intriguing and enigmatic — best advertisement her books could have had. If still alive she'd have loved the publicity whilst maintaining her inbred secrecy". (This letter is also the source of her response to Verna Coleman's book, referred to above.) A balanced assessment of what Barnard with characteristic modesty called "my little book on Miles Franklin" should also note that while the puzzle of personality endures, perspectives change over time. When Marjorie Barnard tackled "the riddle that was Miles Franklin", it was in the context of concern for cultural nationalism. In the 1960s, Miles Franklin's star waned, along with cultural nationalism which had been in the ascendant since the 1930s. Those who remembered the critic A.G. Stephens's verdict that *My Brilliant*

Career was the first genuinely Australian novel and who welcomed Miles Franklin's return to Australia in the 1930s as evidence to the potency of "the legend of the nineties" — that is the 1890s, seen as the seedtime of an independent Australian culture — were bemused and defensive. By and large they shared Miles Franklin's mistrust of what she dubbed "the garrison", meaning academic criticism, but the more complex and sophisticated culture coming into being could not be so easily summed up. On the other hand the legacy of cultural nationalism could not be denied. In the swinging sixties, memories of Miles Franklin were fading and she seemed set to become a puzzling museum piece. Literary critics found little to say about her work, and the rising generation was sceptical of her values. It was in this context that Marjorie Barnard, who, historically and intellectually, occupied a midway position began writing. In her firm and perceptive way she addressed the main question at the time. Chapter 1 asks "Who was Miles Franklin and What was she?" That Miles Franklin was a spent force by 1933 was a helpful perspective, still worth considering (chapter 9).

Time has yet to redeem cultural nationalism, but thanks to the revival of feminism in the 1970s, it has begun to work for Miles Franklin. The screen version of *My Brilliant Career* (1979) was an international success and her name is now as well known in Australia as Dame Nellie Melba's. Now feminist perspectives predominate. But perspectives of both nationalism and feminism are needed to comprehend the life and work of Miles Franklin, as are considerations of class. Though the equation has yet to be worked through, Barnard covers an essential aspect with style, skill and the unique authority of a witness. Franklin may have not thought so, but she was fortunate in her first biographer. *Miles Franklin* is not only a fundamental reference; it is also a minor classic.

Jill Roe
June 1988

Preface

In writing this short book, which is both a biography of Miles Franklin and a critique of her writings, I have not divided the two phases. Miles writing is indivisible from Miles living. Experiences and memories, especially those stemming from childhood and youth, form the substance of her novels. Their background is that against which she grew up. I have tried to present her life and writing as one organic whole and hope that by so doing. I have been able to bring her before you as a living personality.

How angry Miles would have been if she had been chopped up and crammed into a series of academic pigeonholes!

Thanks are due to The Permanent Trustee Company Ltd., Sydney, Trustees of the Miles Franklin estate, for permission to quote from her books.

To Mrs. Nettie Palmer for her generosity in lending me her file of private correspondence with Miles Franklin and allowing me to quote from it and from Vance Palmer's *Legend of the Nineties*.

To John Tierney for the gift of an unpublished manuscript describing Brindabella.

To C.B. Christesen, editor of *Meanjin*, for allowing me to use again part of an article on Miles Franklin which I wrote for his journal in 1955.

To Ian Mudie, the poet, for permission to quote a lengthy description of Miles Franklin in her latter years.

To Douglas Stewart, dramatist and poet, for permission to quote from his article on Brindabella in *Meanjin*.

To Mrs Bruce Pratt (Pixie O'Harris), the artist and close friend of Miles Franklin, for allowing me to quote her.

To other authors and critics to whom I am beholden and to whom acknowledgment is made in the notes.

To Miss A.M. Moore for valuable assistance in an editorial capacity.

MARJORIE BARNARD

Chronology

1788 Edward Miles (Miles Franklin's maternal great-great-grandfather) landed from first fleet
1815 Joseph Franklin, grandfather, born in Ireland
1831 Sarah Lampe *nee* Bridle, grandmother, born
1839 Joseph Franklin migrated with wife to Australia
1841 Altmann Lampe, grandfather, migrated to Australia from Germany
1847 Joseph Franklin took up land at Brindabella
      John Maurice Franklin, father, born
1850 Sarah Bridle married Altmann Lampe, grandparents
      Margaret Susannah Eleanor Lampe, mother, born
1852 Joseph Franklin went to the gold fields
1854 Joseph Franklin returned from the gold fields
1857 Alice Henry born
1863 Joseph Franklin purchased Brindabella
1878 John Franklin married Susannah Lampe
1879 Stella Miles Franklin born
1884 Miles visited Sydney
1885 Mary Franklin, grandmother, died
      Una Vernon Franklin, sister, died
1889 Franklins moved from Brindabella to Stillwater
1898 Joseph Franklin died
1901 Miles published *My Brilliant Career*
1904 Miles in Sydney writing for *The Bulletin*
      Met Joseph Furphy in Melbourne
1905 Miles left for America
1906 Miles met Alice Henry
1909 *Some Everyday Folk and Dawn* published
1912 Sarah Lampe, grandmother, died

1915	John Franklin bought house in Sydney Miles left United States for England
1916	Miles went to Balkans with Scottish Women's Hospital Unit
1917	Miles returned to London
1924	Miles visited Australia
1928	*Up the Country* published
1930	*Ten Creeks Run* published Miles visited Australia
1931	John Franklin died *Old Blastus of Bandicoot* and *Back to Bool Bool* published
1933	Miles returned to Australia to live *Bring the Monkey* published
1936	*All That Swagger* published and won Prior Memorial Prize
1937	*No Family* (play) published
1938	Susannah Franklin died
1939	*Pioneers on Parade* published First draft of *Joseph Furphy* won Prior Memorial Prize
1944	*Joseph Furphy* published
1946	*My Career Goes Bung* published
1947	*Sydney Royal* published
1950	Miles gave Commonwealth Literary Fund lectures at University of Western Australia *Prelude to Waking* published
1954	*Cockatoos* published Miles Franklin died
1956	*Gentleman at Gyang Gyang* published *Laughter, Not for a Cage* published
1963	*Childhood at Brindabella* published

CHAPTER 1

Who was Miles Franklin and What was she?

THERE is a simple answer to this question. Miles was the eldest child of Margaret Susannah Eleanor and John Maurice Franklin, pioneers in the Monaro, and she became a distinguished Australian writer. But that tells us very little; nothing, you might say, of importance. Throughout this book I shall try to unravel the riddle that was Miles Franklin, who she was by descent and upbringing, the influences that shaped her writing and the uses to which she put her talents.

I knew Miles in her later years. She was a small, slight woman who held herself very straight. Her hair was dark brown and had been luxuriant, so long and thick that when she sat on a stool it fell around her like a curtain to the floor. Her eyes behind their spectacles were hazel and very bright. Her nose, of which she was too conscious, was small and snub, a curiously undignified nose, "Pure aboriginal," she called it. It was, to mix metaphors, a thorn in her side. It mattered to her but to no one else. What all her friends remember is her smile. Radiant, quick and gay, it transformed her. It was irresistible and in her old age still charming and youthful.

Henrietta Drake-Brockman, the novelist, writes of Miles's "almost solemn expression breaking readily into a wide smile that not only turns up the corners of her lips but also turns down the corners of her eyes, so that she smiles with all her face. She has a repertoire of smiles, often impish, sometimes mocking, I have yet seen a sweet almost diffident smile; as when she recently concluded a quite brilliant series of lectures on Australian literature, folded her hands, hesitated, and said suddenly, simply and humbly: 'That is all.'"[1]

Miles cared nothing about fashion. She dressed neatly, never went out without hat and gloves or mittens. Her appearance was always a little prim and more than a little old-fashioned. Her close friend, the artist Pixie O'Harris, gives this revealing picture of her:

She wore a hat which she said had been stuck in a box years ago and had the acquired shape now that one would pay money to get. It was yellow straw with wild flowers, poppies, cornflowers, and wheat. She wore a black short-sleeve dress and long white gloves, black stockings and black shoes such as a child might wear. At home she wore ballet shoes. These black shoes were strapped around the ankles. She carried a red plaid shawl and her eyes were shining.[2]

Not everyone found Miles engaging. A recent picture from memory was anything but flattering: "The long, truculent upper lip, the scorn for make-up and dress, the earnest, domineering voice propounding—such an aggressively unvarnished personality I found forbidding. A little artifice would have helped humanize her. Still she conceals more effectively than any artifices. Only the inveterate crossness of tone, the assumption of infallibility points to a something concealed—the thorn in the lion's paw."[3] This brought a spate of angry denials from Miles's friends.

Miles was an individualist and she was thrifty. Her heart was in the past. For these reasons it mattered not at all to her that her clothes were unfashionable. Possibly she took a secret pride in it.

This was the visible Miles. To present her character is a more difficult task. She was not an ordinary woman. She was full of complexities and contradictions and quirks of character.

Her most endearing quality was generosity and she showed this particularly to other writers. She was always ready to help beginners with advice and encouragement and, something more, with her complete attention and sincere interest. To those writers who had already arrived she was neither competitive nor jealous. She was quick to praise and, if a book, a poem or an article pleased her she would at once write to or telephone its author. She gave her warmth and gaiety to all her friends.

She was gay, full of wit and laughter but she was also sad. This sadness may have sprung from the Celt in her or it may have had a more reasonable explanation. The world she loved, the world of her youth, had gone. She was scornful of so-called progress and always filled with nostalgia. She had been an ardent crusader for various causes such as the franchise for women, equality of opportunity between the sexes and the protection of female and child labour. She had seen the reforms she fought for realized and discovered that the world was no happier, the millennium as far away as ever. She grew up in a large family, she ended her life alone.

The mingling of gaiety and sadness gave Miles an air of gallantry. In her youth she was a daring horsewoman and feared nothing in her bush environment. Her physical courage was later to be tested under fire. She was spirited and provocative in conversation but her audacity smacked of the 1890's. All her daring had an antique air. She was, and remained, an *enfant terrible*. She might have shocked people by her forthrightness fifty years ago. She obviously thought that it would shock them still and felt a little snubbed when it did not.

However spirited Miles was she could still be reduced to quivering nervousness when she found herself at a disadvantage or coping with something of which she had had no experience, such as broadcasting. In truth Miles was extremely vulnerable for all her dash and her robust contempt for fantods, vapours, tantrums, broken hearts, repinings, declines, neuroses and taking to drink. She took any unfavourable criticism of her writing very much to heart. I had an unfortunate experience over this! I was giving the Commonwealth Literary Fund lectures in Australian literature at the University of Sydney. Miles, somewhat to my horror, arrived to listen to my lecture on her work. I am a sincere admirer of her writing and gave a fair, even enthusiastic account of it, but when I read some passages in illustration the students were convulsed with laughter. This so hurt and angered Miles that she refused to sit down to lunch with me and for a time diplomatic relations were broken off. However, the crisis passed and the hurt healed.

Because she was vulnerable, Miles was secretive. There were other reasons too. She loved a mystery and used it partly as display and partly as cover. Even her name is a minor mystery. She herself told me that she was christened Stella Mary Miles Franklin. The Mitchell Library of Australiana gives Stella Miles Lampe Franklin. Another authority, Professor E. Morris Miller,[4] uses Stella Maria Sarah Miles Franklin. They are all, except Stella, family names which she may have added or substituted as the mood took her. This is only symptomatic.

In many other ways Miles showed a tendency to mystification. She submitted a novel for a competition. When the accompanying sealed envelope was opened it contained no name or address, only the words "Christopher Columbus." Authorship had to be sheeted home to her. If you telephoned her she usually pretended to be someone else and went off to "fetch Miss Franklin." Examples of these half playful deceptions could be multiplied indefinitely.

The game went deeper when Miles took a *nom de plume* for her most important work and when, by silence and evasion, she cut off and hid the thirty years she spent away from Australia. This all points to some deep hurt.

She loved Australia yet she voluntarily spent the heyday of her life in America and England. Loyal to her family, she rebelled against it. Affectionate to her friends, she could be malicious. Did she not threaten us all with her diary, to be published when she was safely dead? Her belief in the value of the franchise was only equalled by her contempt for politicians. A pacifist she was by nature a fighter—for her ideals, for causes, for the books which were to her like children. She was fiercely virginal yet even to the end of her life she was habitually flirtatious. She was gay, she was sad. She wanted to cut a figure in the world of literature, she wanted to hide.

I am tempted to say that, like the spoilt child she was once, she still wanted everything her own way. The child lived on in the woman and was bitterly hurt by life. She forfeited her place in the world into which she was born, the world of the bush, and the pioneers, and for this reason felt herself an exile. She was perpetually homesick. It is as if her books were written in an effort to allay that gnawing pain. Idealism fought with disillusionment and she was the casualty.

Of Miles's intellectual attainments it is even more difficult to speak. Brought up in the bush she had few educational advantages but she made up for this by omnivorous reading and an overplus of mother wit. She had an amazingly long and exact memory for places, people and idioms of speech and a truly Irish facility with words. These were her chief literary stock-in-trade. She was no philosopher, displayed little skill in constructing her books and not much originality in plot. It is the feeling for life in the novels that gives them their very special quality.

Miles Franklin was a legend in her own lifetime. That legend had two roots, one in her background and the other in her character. For many she stands for the old Australia of the pioneers. The nostalgia that so many feel for that lost world is wind in Miles's sails.

CHAPTER 2

Pioneers O Pioneers!

I *Pioneering in Australia*

THE WORLD moves very fast now. Only seven generations ago the continent of Australia was a *tabula rasa*, untouched since the beginning of time. The Malays had called it the Land of the Dead. The finding of Australia was a postscript to the Great Age of Discovery. This newest world lacked the riches of the Spice Islands to the north and the idyllic peace of the Pacific islands to the east. It was neither for Tom Tiddlers nor for lotus eaters. The thing that it had in plenty was distance. It was very big and very far away from the western world. For that reason, and that alone, it was colonized by England in 1788.

A penal settlement was planted on the east coast, a tiny point of light in a great darkness. The continent was as reluctant to receive the settlers as they were to come to it. It did not offer even sustenance. Everything had to be brought into the country; only air, water, wood and a small supply of fish were available.

The country was not dangerous except for its silence, which drove men mad, and the monotone of the bush in which they so easily became lost. The animals were strange enough but gentle. The aborigines were shadows flitting through the land. They and it had evolved together. They did not cultivate the soil, not because they were too stupid or backward but because in their long journey from the north, many centuries before, they had brought nothing with them. They had no seed to plant—no animals, except the dingo, to domesticate and use. They came to terms with the continent and lived off it by nomadically following food sources round the year. They left only the faintest traces and they never ate out the country.

In all the quiet centuries of isolation an almost perfect pattern of evolution had worked out. Men, animals, vegetation and earth were in a curiously perfect accord. Neither men nor animals took more than the country could afford to give them. Plants were adjusted by nature to the rainfall. They conserved moisture just as the aborigines conserved food. It is important to recognize this pattern, this scarcity economy, as the background of pioneering.

The continent is very old and, a thing not easily recognized because of its vastness, very delicately adjusted. It had a hoarded surplus fertility which could be tapped, but woe to them who squandered it.

Australia has no artificially drawn frontiers either between the white men and the indigenous inhabitants, the aborigines, or between one pioneer and another. The continent is self-contained and separated from the rest of the world by sea. It follows that no frontier spirit has grown up, defensive, assertive, fearful.

The little settlement on Port Jackson grew, became healthy and expanded only as the settlers were able to bring in and acclimatize plants and animals and techniques from overseas. Since the eastern and southern parts of the continent lay in the temperate zone, the trees, fruits and flowers of England flourished together with the maize, corn, wheat, barley and vegetables of the northern hemisphere generally. Animals were imported—sheep, cattle and horses. The sheep was the greatest pioneer of all. There was a market in wool. The looms of England were hungry for it. The suitability of Australia for wool-bearing sheep raised the colony from a penal settlement to the status of a useful and profitable dominion. The increasing flocks needed space and still more space; in their interest the country was explored and opened up.

It took twenty-five years for the settlers to find a way across the main Dividing Range, the mountain barrier which roughly parallels the eastern coast from north to south. The section nearest to Port Jackson, to Sydney, was early named the Blue Mountains for they stand grape-blue against the sky. They were not very high but they were difficult because the conventional approach up the valleys was useless. Only by following the waterless crest of the range did a small party at last make its way into the interior. The flocks fanned out on the plains. After the sheep came cattle as a separate pastoral industry, and horses were the answer to the distances and the terrain.

The flockmasters, the herdsmen, the horsemen were the pioneers. They pushed out into the wilderness, felled trees, built rough homes and pastured their stock. The stock needed room and so the holdings were widely spaced. The greatest enemy of the pioneers was loneliness. It bore most heavily on the women who followed their men up the country. There was no resistance—only silence, loneliness, strangeness.

Pioneering was no simple victory of man over nature. The settlers had to learn, eventually, to live with the land and not simply to belabour it into submission. Mistakes were made in good faith.

Trees were treated as enemies to be felled and burnt so that the grass might grow. Denuded country was eroded by wind and rain. Rainfall was affected, and water was the most important factor in a country with only one large river system and subject to cyclical dry spells.

The land was without disease. It was pure and uncontaminated, its waters wholesome and clear. All pests from rabbits to fruit-fly, from prickly-pear to skeleton weed were brought into the country by carelessness or misjudgement.

The pioneer created and destroyed. He broke into a delicately balanced pattern of evolution without understanding or restraint. He wasted the timber because it was in his way; he slaughtered the fauna because it competed for grass with his stock. He, or his grandsons, suffered the consequences.

Before he claimed it the land was adjusted to semi-aridity, to bushfires, to wet spells. They did little harm to native vegetation and animals. To his imported crops and stock they could be, and often were, disastrous. The aborigines conformed to the land, the white pioneer ignored it. He gave the world a new granary but despoiled a continent. There was between the pioneer and the continent this love-hate complex, generally unconscious but real.

To pioneer a continent was a Herculean task. It still, in one form or another, goes on. The bush was always waiting silently to take back the country won from it, as many a stone chimney, or hardy quince tree, memorial to lost endeavour, signifies in country gone wild again.

The word "bush" is significant. The whole interior of the continent is "bush" whether it is scrub country or gibber (loose stone) desert or rain forest. It is a belittling word. It has that touch of inverted affection dear to the Anglo-Saxon heart. It is a secret word, half-magic, half-disparagement, used by Australians to express a shame-faced love of something they consider to be uniquely theirs.

The pioneers made a selection of words from the English language to suit their new environment. There was, of course, nothing concerted about this. It fell out that way. They chose the harsher words *paddock* not *field*, *creek* not *stream* or *brook*, *timbered* instead of *wooded*, *brumby* for wild horse and so on.

A pioneer needed above all endurance, for far from help, he must face whatever came. He must be hardy, for he had no comforts and few necessities. He must be a bushman, able to find his way in the trackless wilderness, and a good horseman. He must be inventive, adapting whatever was at hand to his purpose, for supplies as a rule came only once a year brought by pack-horse or bullock wagons over mountains and rivers with infinite effort. In his lonely world mateship was of first importance in survival. A fire, a flood, a lost child was everybody's responsibility. Every society has its canons and they tend to be most rigid where every man, however scattered, is a neighbour.

The Pioneering Age crystallized into the Pastoral Age. Holdings, out-stations, or stations, as properties were called, became fixed points; families took root and a way of life adapted to the country began to take shape. The Pastoral Age lasted roughly from about 1821 until the discovery of gold in 1851. This was a time when Australia was preponderantly pastoral, when there seemed to be no other destiny for her.

Pioneering still goes on, for the continent is large; the country is still pastoral, but it is many more things as well. The all-enveloping Pastoral Age with its enclosed spaciousness and its biblical flavour has gone. You may wonder at the words "enclosed spaciousness" but they are carefully chosen. Distance was an all-important factor. Stations in the bush were remote from the coast and the towns, neighbours were distant from one another. England, Scotland, Ireland and Wales, the homelands of most settlers, were very far away. Transport was by horse and later by bullock wagon and to recross the sea took months in a sailing ship. The great distances made it difficult for the squatters, and almost impossible for their families, to move about. The animal life-line, the pack-horses or wagons bringing supplies, only accentuated the sense of being far, far away from all centres of communal life.

A limitless landscape of mountains or plains surrounded the squatter. Or he was walled in by bush. He had space and space was his prison. His freedom was immense, his restriction intense. He must not only subjugate the land to his purpose but he must create a life for himself. He must learn to live with the country. He must put away all he remembered of another world and take Australia as his partner. The Pastoral Age, biblically simple, was a time of consolidation for the gains of the pioneers. It was thirty years thrown clear of outside influences.

I have used the word *squatter*. It means literally "one who sits down." He went out into the primeval bush and sat down, but only figuratively. There was little ease in his life. The ugly belittling words *squatter* and *squattocracy* were, like *bush*, adopted into Australian usage. Now you more often hear *grazier* or *pastoralist* because the age of the squatter, the man who went out and made a place for himself, has passed and the big properties are largely inherited, bought or turned into companies.

II *The Franklins and the Lampes*

Miles Franklin was born into the squattocracy. That was an accident over which she had no control. She was of the fifth generation of a pioneering family. When she was born there had been only four generations of white Australians living in the continent. So Miles's forebears were in at the very beginning of colonization.

It happened like this: Edward Miles came to Australia in the first fleet, that small convoy which brought about one thousand souls to a completely unprepared and scarcely known destination at Botany Bay, a little south of the future site of Sydney. The first fleet has little in common with the *Mayflower*. It sailed, not in the interests of liberty but to extend servitude. Most of those aboard were convicts bound for an open air prison from which there was no escape. Adventure and pioneering were thrust upon them. Some survived and some did not. For some Australia even provided splendid opportunity. What Edward Miles's status was I do not know. If he was, as he may have been, a convict, that is not important.

At one time Australians were very sensitive about their country's early days as a penal settlement. It was a fact almost too painful to mention. This was followed by a burst of sentiment in which felons were passed off as the victims of a cruel society and savage laws: men who had stolen a loaf of bread to feed their hungry children, farm labourers on a starvation wage who had snared a rabbit, little girls who had ridden a neighbour's horse as a high spirited prank, or straight-out victims of a miscarriage of justice. This was, of course, quite unrealistic and has been superseded by a saner approach.

Crime is not a congenital disease. We all probably, in the thickets of our family trees, have saints and sinners and are little the better or worse for it. Some of the convicts proved excellent colonizing material. The convict-descended element in the population is in any case very small and can scarcely have left a trace on the modern Australian population.

You may think that this is a digression. It has bearing on our story. Not only did this first Australian ancestor give Miles one of her Christian names, suggesting that he became an honoured member of the family, but Miles herself shows again and again in her novels that she thought the reformed lag, to use the slang expression of the day, and his children were as good as anyone else. It was part of her egalitarian attitude. In her stories of the past the problem of convict versus free man comes up several times.

Edward Miles married Susannah Smith in 1802 and in 1807 a daughter was born to them and christened Martha. She grew up and married William Bridle. Their first home was at Macquarie Fields near Sydney. Later, in 1848, they moved to the Monaro, where William had a station at Talbingo near Tumut. It could not have been a happy marriage, for in 1837 Martha ran away from her husband. He declared publicly that she had left him without reasonable cause and that he would not be responsible for her debts. She returned to him. There were at least three children of the marriage, Elizabeth, William and Sarah. Sarah, born on 21 November 1831, was Miles Franklin's dearly loved grandmother.

In 1841 a young German from Bremen named Altmann (or Oltmann) Lampe landed in Sydney. He was tall and handsome and was said to come from a good family, one of the *Herrenvolk* as he liked to boast. He became a naturalized British subject in 1853 and took up ten thousand acres of land in the Cooma district. Cooma is now the centre for the Snowy Mountains project in New South Wales. It is somewhat to the south of Brindabella but in the same sort of mountainous country. Altmann met Sarah Bridle and they were married at Gundagai on 12 February 1850 when Sarah was nineteen years old. Altmann took over his father-in-law's property already called Old Talbingo. This consisted of thirty thousand acres of grazing country for which he paid the government £24 a year. We must remember that money did not have the same value then as now and that a man might have wide lands but still find difficulty in raising even a few pounds.

The Lampes had a very large family of whom Miles's mother was the eldest. Her name was Margaret Susannah Helena (or Eleanor) according to the records but she turned it round and became Susannah Margaret Eleanor.

The 1850's were unsettled years. Gold was discovered with the consequent big influx of population. Wages rose sharply and even at high wages it was difficult to find anyone willing to work on the land. We do not know how the Lampes managed.

When Susannah was fifteen tragedy struck the family. Her father, as the result of an accident in which he injured his back, became a helpless cripple. He also went blind. Susannah had to be brought home from school to help nurse him. Her brothers, John aged nine and William aged six, had to work very hard on the property. John was dubbed "the working manager" and earned the title.

John drove the bullock wagon and tended the cattle. William "was given the lighter task of going to town, twenty-four miles distant, with a pack-horse on errands or to supplement supplies in the winter when the unmade tracks were impassable for drays or carts. The horse he rode would also be loaded. My great-aunts have told me that his head could just be seen above the rolls on the pommel. It was difficult to mount among such impedimenta. In uncle's words: 'I had to get the old nag beside a fence and first climb it and then clamber on from there.'"

Tales remain of his heroism in days of storm and boggy roads when the packs would slip and he had to walk in tall, thick bush to some distant settler to have them replaced. "I never forgot the confounded old pack saddle. It wasn't properly balanced and would always roll. Mother got it cheap because we had no money and she would never go in debt."[1] That was pioneering.

Their homestead at that time was what Miles later described as a "pig wallow." The Lampes had moved into a shack that had been a port of call on the way to the diggings, as the goldfields were called, when Altmann was stricken. The floors were of earth, doors hung off their hinges. The place was both dirty and dilapidated. Susannah and her mother worked like men to make it not only habitable but gracious. They succeeded. Sarah Lampe was indomitable.

Miles has left a picture of her beloved grandmother and of the home she created, which to Miles was the dearest place on earth. "She was not quite five feet tall and composed of energy, determination, generosity, common sense, honesty, and courage. She believed God to be a fixed identity as defined by the Church from the Bible. She never owed a penny or turned a tramp from her door without replenishing his tucker bags or giving him care if he were ill. She mothered the 'godwits' by patching their clothes, giving them boots and admonishment. She was ceaselessly industrious, had a head for business and was known as a 'good manager.' Her hay sheds and other store houses were always well stocked for winter with the yield from her orchards, potato and pumpkin paddocks, her fowl houses, her dairy and vegetable garden. She grew and cured her own bacon as well as her own beef. Her streams were full of native trout and Murray cod. Order, plenty, decency, industry and hospitality were in the home I loved."[2] Old Talbingo was Miles's Garden of Eden.

Susannah left Old Talbingo when she married John Maurice Franklin in November 1878. For her, pioneering began again.

John was the third son and sixth child of an Irishman, Joseph Franklin, who came to Australia in 1839 with his young wife Mary and a baby daughter. Joseph was the son of a school master in County Clare. On the voyage out in the *Orient* the young couple became friendly with Dr. Allen, Mr. Williams and Mr. Smith. Smith was a man with capital and purchased a property called Walgrove near Yass, a town on the main route between Sydney and Melbourne. The Franklins lived with him in the Red House, Joseph was his overseer and Mary was his lady housekeeper. (Mary, by the way, was always called Maria and it was from her and for her that Miles had this name.) The arrangement lasted until 1847. Mr. Smith's son, who lacked his father's agreeable qualities, paid Mary unwelcome attentions so that she was anxious to leave. Joseph had always hoped to own land. So they decided to make a break.

Joseph had seen and been strongly attracted by the green valley of Brindabella on the Goodradigbee River in the High Monaro. Now he squatted there. The house he built was burnt down and, discouraged by this and tempted by the search for gold, he left Brindabella but did not forget it.

For eighteen months from 1852 Joseph tried his luck on the gold diggings. Fortune apparently smiled on him for in 1854 he was able to buy a property called Oakdale on the Murrumbidgee River not far from Yass. Nine years later he returned to Brindabella and bought the station from its owners, Hill and Webb, leasing additional land at Brarina and Bin Bin. This property passed to the three sons George, Thomas and John. John brought his bride to Brindabella. The stage was set for the remarkable little girl who was to be their first born.

III *The High Monaro*

Miles Franklin, as we have seen, was born into the squattocracy, of the fifth generation of a pioneering family. Even that might not have influenced her writing very strongly. Her youth spent at Brindabella and with her grandmother at Talbingo in the High Monaro country marked her for life.

She learnt early to love the bush; she drew in with her very breath the attitudes and ways of her large family circle; she fell in love permanently with the mountain country. For her the time, the place and the loved ones were all there in Monaro before the turn of this century.

To read Miles's novels with sympathy and understanding you must know something of the country in which she was born, the times she grew up in and her bush background. Pioneering was her theme, the Pastoral Age her stage. When she writes from her heart it is always about the country and times she knew so well in youth.

The Miles Franklin country, as it is often called, the Monaro or Manaroo in the old spelling, lies about thirty miles west of the capital city of Canberra. Here the main Dividing Range coils itself into a great knot of mountains rising to 5,000 and 6,000 feet. They are not quite as high as the more famous Snowy Mountains to the south-west, where the great hydro-electric scheme has taken shape, but they are still high and snowy in winter.

It is cattle country, with some sheep. The cattle and the sheep too are taken up the mountains to the snow leases for the summer, much as they are taken up to the "seaters" in Norway, and brought down again at first snowfall in the autumn. There too were bred hardy and sure-footed horses, the whalers, which Australia used to export to India as Army remounts. It is certainly horseman's country and the well-known ballad "The Man from Snowy River" might have been as well set in the High Monaro.

The country is well watered, alive with rivers whose names have a music of their own. There are the Murrumbidgee (the young Murrumbidgee near its source) and its many tributaries, Bramina, Micalong, the Flea, the Yarrangobilly, the Eucumbene. The most often praised is the Goodradigbee. Douglas Stewart, poet and playwright, has described it.

The stream itself was a wild little creature, the loveliest and wildest of them all; crystal and silver in the sunlight, dark under the granite in the gorges, green and yellow in the pools with the reflections of the wattles and the ribbony-gums; fierce as a snake in its sharp and frequent floods. In the valley it ran sparkling under willows, bubbling over rocks and shingle, moving in that ever-enticing progression of rapid and run and pool, rapid and run and pool, sinuous, lithe and musical as it turned down out of the mountains, it was the very model of a trout stream.[3]

The music of these rivers, or creeks, flows through Miles Franklin's novels. John Tierney talks of "the song and the sigh" of the Goodradigbee, and of the place names of the Miles Franklin country in general he says: "Most, if not all, of the names . . . are of aboriginal origin. Old, old names they are, and in them all, buried for ever, endless pages of unrecorded and forgotten history.

Most of them . . . have the strange wild music that aboriginal names so peculiarly possess . . . Our tongues still caress them and that much at least of a forgotten music is still ours."[4] Miles was attuned to their music and gives it back to us. Their song runs through her novels like a thread of magic. Creeks and rivers and waterholes are most precious in a dry country.

Miles loved to string together place names, some taken from this countryside, some invented by herself in the same rhythm. Here she describes sheep coming down from the snow leases:

The exodus proper was in full swing. The roar of the motor lorries distributing hay and chaff was loud in the land. Streams of little quadrupeds like breaking dams belched forth from the snow leases on the great stock routes that connected Monaro and Riverina and poured silently all day long as sheep can with the rhythm of grey waters in level country, their voices raised only as they descended upon the feed camps. By Talbingo and Tumut, Cooloolink and Bool Bool, Neangen, Mungee, Broken Cart, Yellow Boy and Tumbarumba from Monaro to Riverina and farther out and lower down they went . . .[5]

IV *Brindabella and Old Talbingo*

In the heart of the ranges there is a long, fertile, well-watered valley, so surrounded by mountains as to be an almost secret place. This is Brindabella.

As one who loves it describes it: "a gracious valley, not so very wide, green and fertile, undulating in its little dimpled hills, jealously guarded and rightly held—as a precious thing should be—by the high ranges. And through its whole length flows the clearest of the little rivers—the Goodradigbee."[6]

The Brindabella range encloses it in a great V. There is a peak called Mount Franklin. The Murrumbidgee River follows the line of the range and beyond that the main Dividing Range curls in something like the shape of a Z.

The valley is very well guarded by nature and to this day is difficult of access. The roads in are better for horses than cars. They are narrow, flanked by precipices and with a slope towards the drop. In winter they are deep in snow and even more dangerous. If the valley is difficult to enter it is harder to leave. There is only a bridle track over the mountains. Looking at it, Douglas Stewart thought that to the first settlers "it must have looked like the end of the world."[7] He shows us its peculiar character:

I have never, elsewhere in Australia, felt that impression of the extreme antiquity of the land which so many people have recorded; but here at

Brindabella, and particularly when looking at that grey granite bluff across the river from the shack, I did indeed feel the weight of the centuries. It was something to do with the bulk of that great bluff, like the back of an elephant, a mammoth more likely, curving above the tree-tops; and its greyness; its stoniness; its smoothness. It intruded among the trees like a creature of stone, patient, immobile, worn smooth. It was old, worn-down country ...[8]

Here is Miles Franklin's own picture of Brindabella, its name changed to Burrabinga for the purposes of fiction.

Unconquerable longing assailed him[9] each time he came up from the chasm through which the Murrumbidgee elbows its way to the great plains. As he would rein-in to pick out the notch in the ramparts that led to Burrabinga, he would fall into worshipful contemplation of the ranges, thrown one upon another like storm waves petrified when the world had cooled. The foreverness soothed and inspired. The dignity of permanence lay on a view superb as that from Edessa in Old Greece down the valley of the Vardar towards Olympus. But the view towards Salonika is bearded with legend reaching back to the dawn of human history. The spoliation and squalor, the desecration and degradation of which human history is compounded equally with glory, had been cleansed from Delacy's province since eras lost in time.[10]

Miles saw the secret valley as a place of purity, uncontaminated by human sinfulness, a new world. Brindabella was full of wildlife. There were many birds, most particularly magpies and kookaburras, but there were also eagles, pelicans and the beautiful shy lyrebirds who, when times were hard, would sometimes eat with the domestic fowls. Beside the wild birds there was every sort of poultry even to guinea fowls and peacocks. Wombats tunnelled under fences and echidnas, small spiny ant-eaters, made charming playthings. It was not rare to find a platypus in the creek. This strange creature, an egg-laying mammal that lives in water, is a rarely seen link in the evolutionary chain. The rivers were full of fish, trout and Murray cod, and there were snakes in the bush. Miles was not afraid of them but could not bring herself to touch them even when they were dead. One snake seen in childhood became for her a sort of familiar. The whole passage describing it is worth quoting:

One day ... my youngest aunt yielded to my plea to go for a walk to pick flowers. I had not outgrown the greedy desire of children to grab flowers suffocatingly in their fists. No native flower was then used in house decoration. Their elfin grace could not compete in favour with the imported riches of the garden plots. The cattle paddocks were bright with bloom, and, seeking variety, we followed one of our swiftly running home creeks, lovely as a fountain, through several fences to the hills. A big black snake lay full-length at his ease beside the water in the thin fringe of maiden-hair ferns that were sprouting after winter's retreat. The creature's forked tongue flickered rapidly in and out, his new skin gleamed blue-black with peacock tints, a little of his underside was showing like blended scarlet and pomegranate. I stood a fascinated moment and fled to my aunt. She went back seeking the snake but it had dissolved leaving no trace.

The experience was not startling, merely surprising. Then why should that snake have persisted in my consciousness for over thirty years? As I have sat in some great congress in one of the major cities, or in a famous concert hall, or eaten green almonds on a terrace in Turin in the early morning, or worked amid the din of the Krupp guns on an Eastern battle front, or watched the albatrosses in stormy weather off Cape Agulhas, or have been falling asleep in an attic in Bloomsbury, that snake has still been stretched in the fern beside the creek, motionless except for the darting tongue.[11]

It was, I feel, Miles Franklin's first artistic experience, one of those ineffable moments that come to the creative artist unheralded and that nourish his art. Perhaps they come to all men but generally go unrecorded. They have a deep inarticulate meaning, they are one step over the threshold of the unknown. They become a touchstone that separates reality from unreality in a personal and secret way. Common sense may say that such moments do not exist. There are many things that common sense does not understand. Her beloved bush gave Miles this experience—the first of how many?—while she was still a child.

Life does not usually live up to its ineffable moments. There is always an antidote at hand. But for Miles it did. She found her snake again long after in her middle age and caused its death.

There came a day when the bone-ache for my birthplace was being sunk in the rapture of return. It was the last time I was to see the old place in family ownership with my uncle and aunt and some of his family in residence ...

I sought the spot where the snake had laid in my memory for so long. The dense grove of the quick-growing brittle acacia, with a broad leaf, that loves watery ground, was gone. Brambles and underbrush had been cleared away ... The place was bare and flat and unrecognizable: the creek was stripped of its exquisite shrubs but it had not changed its course. That was the same as when it had turned the mill put on it by some of the forebears who otherwise had to grind wheat for their bread in a quern in the evening when they desisted from felling and grubbing and fencing to establish agriculture. But the spot I sought was actively in my mind and the new rabbit-proof fences followed the old lines so that I could be sure of it. And there was the snake! He lay in exactly the same position full-length in the sunlight on the right bank in the short grass, headed up-stream, motionless but for his forked tongue. His blue-black coat glistened in the sun, his carmined underside was partly discernible. It could have been the same creature lying there bewitched while I had travelled in far places from infancy to middle age. I was smitten to timelessness by something beyond my groping powers of expression. He lay supine. His fellow long ago had disappeared when I turned my back. I reined-in to consider him. There was no coverage as of old, the stream was naked. I sat. I could have sat till the snake thought fit to depart. But Uncle . . . came on to see what was detaining me. The snake did not depart as I had expected, as I had hoped. Uncle drew a girth from his saddle and dismounted.[12]

And that was the end of the snake. This is curiously like a parable of the disillusionment that figured so largely in Miles's life.

It was not at Brindabella but at Old Talbingo that the incident of the snake happened. Miles was born there in her grandmother's house and could write, more than seventy years later, "No other spot has ever replaced the hold on my affections or imagination of my birthplace." [13]

There is some doubt as to the exact location of this homestead. It is in the same country as Brindabella, the High Monaro, but on the western side of the range, near the Tumut river. There is Mount Talbingo and a region called Foot of Talbingo. The homestead may have been on top of the mountain but I think that unlikely. A creek ran in front of the homestead. It had a most splendid orchard. "Fruit trees," wrote Miles, "were respected and loved . . . Each tree was a personality like members of the family themselves." [14] Two big apple trees were grown from the pips of an apple brought by bullock dray from Prospect near Sydney, two generations before Miles was born. There were also apricots, plums, cherries and quinces. Of these trees the quinces are the most persistent and hardy.

Despite the big families of the nineteenth century there are no Franklins or Lampes left at Brindabella or Talbingo. As Miles herself suggested it took more avarice than either the Franklins or the Lampes possessed to make money from the land, enough money to hold on through bad seasons. Even in Miles's lifetime they had left and the land had passed into other hands or gone back to nature. You have only to turn your back and the bush returns and only a few fallen chimney stones and a gnarled stick or two of quince trees show where a homestead used to be.

V *A Bride Comes to Brindabella*

Both the Franklins and the Lampes seemed to be securely settled on their holdings at the time Susannah Lampe married John Franklin and continued her pioneering at Brindabella. The bride was not only used to hard work and well trained in all the domestic arts but had as well the accomplishments of a young lady, fine sewing and piano playing amongst them. She came riding her blood horse Lord Byron, bringing with her not only her house linen but a sewing machine and a rosewood piano. The piano came by bullock wagon and was handled so reverently that there was not a scratch on its surface. In the language of today that piano was indeed a status symbol. Susannah was a fluent pianist with a large repertoire of "pieces" but was not really musical. Her daughter was to write of her parents long afterwards:

My mother was the wonder of her region. She was beautiful and accomplished, clever as a hostess and in all departments of home-making. My father's pride in her was a poem and a triumph combined, and sustained him to the end of his days. There was open expression of surprise as to how he could have carried off such a prize, but he too must have been irresistible with his slim straight height, his equestrian fame, his blue eyes, dark hair and sharp classical profile, his exuberant and witty though unbarbed humour, his boundless generosity. He was prized by all his contemporaries as "white throughout." [15]

Susannah was more fortunate than many bush brides of her time. She was not isolated or cut off from the company of other women. George and Thomas Franklin had homesteads on Brindabella. They were already married with large families. Thomas's house was only about a mile distant, not far at all when everyone, men, women and children rode horseback.

Susannah too had, for its time and place, a very comfortable house. It was built of slabs of timber with a high pitched roof with shingles of well seasoned mountain ash. The attic so formed was used for storage. This was very necessary as supplies generally came in only once a year and the sugar, tea, rice and flour must be stowed in a dry place safe from ants. The kitchen fireplace, the size of a small room, was of stone or of bark lined with stones cemented with mud. "Beams across it carried the hams and sides of bacon, spiced beef and bullocks' tongues preserved by slow smoking, and protected from the weather by a hooped sheet of bark. Lower beams would support the kettles and camp ovens and three-legged pots for cooking." [16] The kitchen was always separate from the rest of the house because of the danger of fire.

The rest of the house was built on the "add-a-pearl" system. It began with a bedroom and living room with a lean-to at the back for nursemaid and baby. As the family increased another room could be and was added, then another, as many as were needed all opening onto a verandah. The end room was traditionally the visitors' room, probably because it was quieter.

A house with floors and kerosene lamps may have been better than the lot of many young wives in the bush but just once Miles raises that rose coloured curtain that covered most of her early recollections. Susannah's life was not, after all, one of satisfied rectitude and triumphant virtue. "My mother's technique," wrote Miles, "remained unflawed through all the grinding and tragic vicissitudes of a long, impecunious, unrewarded existence. She loathed the early hardships, restrictions and often complete isolation [of Talbingo]; to be removed to [Brindabella] even more secluded, and wilder, with all its amenities to be introduced and maintained by herself, with the cruel burden of unrestricted childbearing added, was too much." [17]

This is an isolated passage in Miles's account of her childhood. For her everything was perfect in those far-off days. The only "tragedy" occurred when her sovereign rule was threatened by the teasing of a boy cousin. The death of a baby sister not yet a year old passed over her head, though she remembered the funeral cortège, her father and neighbours carrying the tiny coffin across the paddocks, and the fenced grave with an elm planted in it. For the first and perhaps the last time she saw her mother weep. There are many things beyond the grasp of even the brightest child.

CHAPTER 3

Childhood at Brindabella

I *Journey in the Snow*

TWO months before Miles was born Susannah went on horseback seventy miles over the mountains to her mother at Talbingo. No matter what the circumstances Susannah would never yield a jot to convention. She rode now, sidesaddle (and a stiff new saddle at that) on the spirited Lord Byron. He had his own troubles, for the snow collected in balls of ice on his hoofs and he had to shake them off as best he could to the discomfort of his rider. She was jolted and shaken all day long and a tight-fitting boned habit made her even more uncomfortable.

After the first day's journey she was utterly exhausted. She had travelled more than thirty miles. There were, of course, no inns or hotels but hospitality is a strict law of the bush. Susannah and her escort, probably her husband for she would never have been allowed to make the journey alone, came to a selector's hut. Selectors were usually poor men who had taken up land under the Robertson Land Laws which aimed to open up the country. They were not of the squattocracy with big runs and well-filled store rooms but travellers were welcome to share what they had and when it was a woman who came the selector's wife was happy indeed. They were all starved for feminine company.

So Susannah received a warm welcome from Mrs Dan Herlihy who put her to bed in her own bed, probably the only one, and laid her baby at her visitor's cold feet to warm them. (I have heard of cats being offered in lieu of hot water bags but never before of a baby in this capacity.) Susannah stayed three nights with the Herlihys and then continued her journey.

Susannah remained for five months with her mother and in the peace and order of that house with her sisters to wait on her it must have been a happy and restful time. When Stella Mary Miles Franklin, to make a selection from her names, was three months old it was time to take her home, "by a different route over the daisied plains by the sparkling rivulets where some of our longest creek-rivers began."[1] The baby was carried on a purple sateen cushion on her uncle William's pommel. "Thus," wrote Miles,

CHILDHOOD AT BRINDABELLA 21

"straight from the bed in which I was born to the back of a horse with no perambulator in between."[2]

II *A Galaxy of Relations*

Miles—it is easier to call her Miles consistently though she was Stella in her childhood and ever after to her family—Miles had a great many relations and grew up amongst them. They were a community in themselves, a clan, and they constituted the little girl's world. It was not quite a homogeneous clan perhaps because the Lampes thought themselves superior to the Franklins and Miles, sensing the feelings of her elders even when no word had been spoken, as children do, looked down on her Irish grandfather. This was something for which she was to make amends later.

The child leant towards her mother's family, the Lampes. Susannah was the eldest child and Miles the first granddaughter. The homestead at Talbingo was full of young aunts and uncles most of them still in their teens, and all willing to play with and entertain the little girl. She claims that she was not spoilt. Neither her mother nor her grandmother would have tolerated that. They had too much good sense. But she was very much a pet and not at all slow to realize her importance. Her ego was well fed as she admitted herself.

. . . I reigned alone among six young uncles and aunts with my grandmother at their head. I grew up with pride in and unwavering affection for my grandmother, aunts and uncles. My satisfaction in them assumed a different character with maturity but it never waned, never was wounded. In my estimation my grandmother equalled God, with beneficent resources and powers, and my aunts and uncles ranked as seraphim and cherubim.[3]

It is not unkind to suggest that the love lavished upon her and her obvious importance to all these delightful people coloured with rosy light her grandmother's house and all its inhabitants. At home there were as time went on, six brothers and sisters to share her limelight. She always had a share of attention but she was not unique. Nearer at hand were the households of her father's two brothers, each with large families of boys and girls all older than Miles but very much a part of her life. Her schooling began in her uncle Thomas's house, sharing a tutor with her cousins.

The firmament was filled with relations. Her maternal great-grandmother was still alive in her childhood and there were her grandmother's brothers and sisters and their families, all numerous.

In addition to Grandma I had the equivalent of seventeen other grandparents in her eight sisters and brothers and their spouses all of whom I knew and remembered...

On my father's side were two grandparents and ten uncles and aunts. All these relatives had the same tribal status. Not till we young fry were grown-up did we know the difference between blood aunts and uncles and their in-law spouses. There were also squads of Mother's cousins and some of Father's nephews and nieces in the age bracket of uncles and aunts and just as affectionately regarded, and all of whom lived up to their status in affection and kindly interest.[4]

Such a thing as losing touch with relations simply could not happen. It was unthinkable. It was no ordinary environment in which Miles grew up. Practically everyone she knew was related to her, felt a special affection for and knew all about her. It was, from her point of view, a safe world and she was an important person in it. This network of family life was to be repeated in her novels sometimes to the reader's confusion. The close ties of her childhood, however valiantly she might declare they never loosened, only underlined the loneliness of later life. It is difficult, too, to imagine how anyone living as she did in her formative years could grow up as secretive as Miles did. That is all part of the story; the family tapestry is important to the understanding of the girl Stella and the writer Miles.

III *A Bush Childhood*

Miles Franklin's childhood is well documented, much better than any other time in her life. In her seventies she wrote the story of her first ten years, published after her death and called, not by Miles but by the publishers, *Childhood at Brindabella*. The events, places and people of those years are candied in memory. That is natural. Miles was looking back to the happiest days of her life. That is a cliché but in this instance true. She was remembering in old age bright days that were not only lost to her but lost from the world.

One of her reasons for writing her memoir of childhood was to record her golden age, to set happiness in amber. In a paper found after her death with the manuscript of *Childhood at Brindabella* she wrote:

For a long time I have been intending to write down earliest memories to discover how many I retain clear-cut before my memory is too motheaten. I meant to do this as a diary for myself alone, as sailors in the doldrums erect full-rigged ships in bottles just because the mind is an instrument that sanity cannot leave idle. I must find some kind of exercise for a mind unused except on chores or with the triffle-traffle of housewives.[5]

She decided to publish it for two reasons: one was to refute the legend of unhappy childhood that she met so often in autobiographies and found so depressing; the other was to please a close friend, Pixie O'Harris (Mrs. Bruce Pratt), a well-known artist and author of books for children. Pixie O'Harris had for years urged her to put her memories on paper and at last persuaded her. It is a simple, cheerful record to the point of guilelessness, idealized but not, I think, distorted. No doubt some things were left unsaid, others gently tinted, but the picture of a bush childhood towards the end of last century comes through clearly.

Miles had an exceedingly long and clear memory. Her first memory, of a red nightdress, a dipping candle flame and her father carrying her along the homestead verandah, belonged to her tenth month. At a year old she could talk and walk and was, in the colloquial phrase, "into everything." She was constantly with her father and the men on the station and was observant of everything.

She was a great conversationalist and a believer in the stark truth. So greatly did her parents reverence the truth that Miles was never punished for telling it, however inopportune her remarks might be. Thus when a visitor asked why she would not give him a kiss she could say with impunity: "Because you are a nasty old man and smell of rum."

The bush was Miles's wonder book, animals and birds her friends. "I was infatuated by animals. I preferred them to children."[6] She was particularly fond of the pigs. "They are companionable creatures and will always respond with almost human grunts to their familiar friends."[7] Many were her pets, including a snake-killing cat who used to bring her trophies to the child's bed and ended by terrifying her, and a chicken she accidently hurt and tended for the rest of its life with passionate care.

She could ride almost as soon as she could walk, and wrote: "The rhythm of horses came to me earlier than walking."

In those moments—rare with me—when the sense of actuality has been slightly loosened by over fatigue or a high temperature, there recurs for ever like the movement of a stream or the pattern of leaves flickering in a zephyr, the sensation of a well-bred horse being released, or about to be released, into action. Unforgettable are the pleasant odour of the warm, satiny skin and the noble animal's every sensitive gesture as he waited a-tingle . . . Then off, the instant the weight was on him, settling to the required gait as he cleared his breathing with a ruffle of goodwill and good going in his skilled responsibilities.[8]

Her mother made Miles a riding habit.

It had a tidy square-cut jacket, braided, and the regulation skirt trimly to floor length . . . At the right side the skirt was enlarged for the knee to go over the pommel or horn exactly like the smartest models for grown-ups. This had to be held up with the right hand when dismounted. I was such an exact replica of Mother that my appearance to take place on a full-sized horse never failed to excite astonished admirration from strangers.[9]

Small creatures like lizards or echidnas were her toys. She had no others. Books she was taught to treat with reverence. But they must be sensible books; no fairy tales were allowed on the grounds that they were too sad, Little Red Riding Hood and The Babes in the Wood for instance. Fantasy was next door to lying.

There is a photograph of Miles at the age of four, a sturdy well-cared for child in a long-sleeved dark frock with a sash and, at her neck, a white ruffle. Her hair is parted in the middle and brushed back. The thing that singles her out is her assurance and maturity.

She was a healthy child, except for the trouble with her back, and rarely had a cold or any other ailment—even the dreaded sandy blight, a type of conjunctivitis of the eyes, which at some time or other afflicted most bush children and was highly infectious. Of course, in those days, with so little contact with the outside world, children had few opportunities of contracting measles, mumps and the rest. Even as a baby Miles could not or would not sleep until after midnight but made up for it by sleeping late in the morning. This in later life became a persistent insomnia.

There were not many events in such a childhood. Visits to her grandmother seventy miles away were the highlight. At about five years old she was brought to Sydney and the thing that impressed her was the Zoo. Trains were major wonders but neither Sydney nor locomotives were part of her life.

At six years old her parents began to think of her education. Her mother had begun to teach her, or should I say train her? The first and most important lesson was self-control: no tantrums, no fantods, no tears, no arguments. Truthfulness and cleanliness ranked very high. No member of the family was demonstrative and the children were rarely kissed. The mother thought it was repulsive for old people to kiss babies.

Religion does not seem to have figured very largely in their lives. Miles as a little thing dabbled in prayer. When she did not want to leave her grandmother she prayed that something would happen to delay their departure. It did. An axle broke and the party was forced to return. Later Miles prayed for her doll's arm to be mended. Nothing happened. She lost faith. Her grandmother had regular prayers which she conducted herself but Miles was more interested in the rewards for being quiet, generally a little jelly from a pomegranate, than in the religious exercise.

Education in pioneering days in the bush did not present the problems one would expect. It was possible to engage a tutor, for there were, in those days, a number of remittance men in the bush. They were often of good family and well educated but had a weakness, usually for alcohol, and for that reason had been shipped off to the colony by their families and paid an allowance or remittance so that their aristocratic relations were free of the shame of them. They were better off in the bush than in the towns because there was less temptation. Apart from their addiction they were generally pleasant and well-mannered men.

Miles's uncle Thomas Franklin secured the services of such a man to teach his children and the six-year-old Miles would walk the mile, "a very small girl, mostly sunbonnet, moving at a pace scarcely perceptible"[10] to her uncle's house every day. Her mother could watch her progress for half of the distance and the tutor for the second half. His name was Mr. Auchinvole. Or you may be sure that was not his name but one that Miles invented for him. She describes him:

In his gentleness, his unbreachable good breeding, he was an example of how ineffectual English Public School education could be in fitting a man for life. He belonged to the school who couldn't so much as boil an egg or sew on a button. He would have starved amid tins of food if stranded without a tin-opener, or have gone thirsty beside the purest running water for lack of a drinking vessel. In his superior upbringing one thing he had not been taught was to abstain from alcohol. So, he was on a remote cattle station hidden in the ranges instead of playing golf with upper middle-class lairds in Scotland.[11]

The child was quick to learn.

I could learn all the allotted tables of weights and measurements in a twinkling. I revelled in the old spelling book and absorbed pages of words in the time allotted to master a column. Everyone was tired of examining my prowess in that line. There was not enough talent in the teachers to make the piano interesting. I would go through the five-finger exercises and scales and then make up more of my own. This strumming could be heard and was forbidden.[12]

She grew bored because she could not progress in any direction as fast as her intelligence would let her.

IV *Stillwater*

Life ran smoothly for Miles until she was ten years old. Then everything was changed. Her father left Brindabella, presumably for financial reasons, and took his family to a much smaller property at Thornford, north-east of Canberra and a little south of the cathedral city of Goulburn. The new property was christened Stillwater by Mrs. Franklin because of the many waterholes or lagoons.

Our new home was in the flatter, more lightly-timbered country. Its situation near to schools and railways and town had advantages, but I never forgave it for its inferiority to my birthplace. Its first sight filled me with a sense of desolation. The trees were not so majestic. The ranges were low and ragged without gorges and mighty rocks like castles and cascading streams draped with tree ferns and maiden-hair and flowering shrubberies along their banks. No lyrebirds gambolled across the track to flute in eucalyptus aisles across a big singing creek. . .[13]

Miles hated the change. Perhaps the most bitter pill was that a pretty young sister was left behind in Grandma's care enjoying the love and the privileges that Miles had always thought of as hers.

Miles missed the horses of Brindabella, for Thornford was not horseman's country. Only men rode and then, as she said, on "mokes." But there were other animals to hold her interest, particularly the gentle koalas that could be cuddled like babies and the fierce wild cats who were not cats at all but marsupials. They were a menace to the poultry and were trapped and shot. Mrs. Franklin made the girls tippets and muffs out of the soft dark fur with its white spots.

Miles went to the local school and had to try to be an ordinary little girl. Womanliness was being thrust upon her and she resented it bitterly. She did not like children of her own age. They were rough and often untruthful. She disliked babies because she thought them stupid. Later in life she was to develop a great tenderness for children of all ages and became a success with them, but not in her Thornford days.

The limitations of the company of infants and toddlers now confronted me again in restriction to the women's domain. The artificial bonds called feminine were presented to my understanding. I must become genteel as befitting a young lady. A good deal was attributed to God's will, and did not turn my heart any more warmly to that gentleman. It was the humbug in "womanliness," the distorting and atrophying of minds on a sex line, the grinding superstition that all women must be activated on a more or less moronic level, the absence of fair play between men and women when the masculine and feminine issue arose that was at the root of the trouble, though I did not know so much in my first decade. I was more bewildered and tormented and rebellious in my second, when preoccupation with sex was discovered to be in excess of all needs for perpetuating the species, and banished logic from human behaviour.[14]

This was to be Miles's perpetual cry often expressed in her writings. The sudden cramping of a spirited child and the well-meant efforts to press her into a conventional mould had far-reaching effects on her life. She rebelled and her grandmother called her "froward" a biblical word she did not understand but felt as an insult. "Grandmother would look over her specs to say 'Your froward heart will bring you trouble. You must pray to God to cure you of it.' It was the exact word, and Grandma's prophecy was to come true in much heart-burning."[15]

Miles often in letters and conversation referred vaguely to sorrows and disappointments but her recorded life does not enumerate them. It was not necessary for a calamity to befall her for her to suffer. A small thing could cut her to the heart. Sometimes I think we all suffer according to our capacity and without much relation to the tragedies that may befall us.

Miles concludes her last book on a note of pain. Her happy childhood ended when she left Brindabella and Talbingo.

I was leaving Uncle Hil and my young uncles and aunts and Grandma. I was exchanging their protective aura for real trials, disappointments and deprivation, and inner gropings and turbulence and furious and agonized beatings of wings of a bird not knowing where to fly.[16]

V *The Girl is the Mother of the Woman*

In considering Miles Franklin and her writings this last of all her books *Childhood at Brindabella* is a keystone. It is a very revealing piece of work and explains the enigma of Miles as clearly as it will ever be explained.

It is curious that Miles reveals so much of herself in this book when she is at the same time being particularly secretive. Nowhere does she mention names; she either invents one or talks of Aunt A, or my father's second brother, or Mrs. M. G. She even refers to her father as F, a transparent disguise. She changes most place names; Brindabella becomes Bobilla and Talbingo, Ajinby and the town of Tumut masquerades as Gool Gool. Only Stillwater at

Thornford wears no mask. It is difficult to understand why she does this. There is no vestige of scandal in the book, no character is aspersed and no reader deceived. To be mysterious was with Miles a sort of nervous tic. It had become a meaningless habit. Behind this again there is a deeper reason. Miles treasured privacy not only for herself but for others. She would never conceivably have written an autobiography. That she wrote the story of her childhood was a concession, and she seems to have approached it with a faint sense of guilt as if she were revealing something too personal to be made public.

There is no end to the paradoxes in which Miles's biographer becomes involved. She was secretive, given to mysteries, and yet she was from a very young child outstandingly truthful. Not only did she never lie but she told the exact truth, which is something that even the most scrupulous people are not always able to do. Miles had a clear mind and an excellent memory. She was never vague about any place, person or event. Her truthfulness often took the form of outspokenness. Looking back she frankly analyses this trait in her character:

Truth-telling, for which I was noted and which stood tremendous wear and tear before it began to have threadbare patches, was not—I have come to feel through adult self-analysis—due so much to virtue as to exceptional gifts of observation, supported by a turn for clear and accurate reporting. I revelled in exercising my faculties and was contemptuous of noodles who could not see exactly what had happened and how. To tell a thing straight was part of a love of order. Failure to do so was irritating to me.[17]

Here was the budding writer with "exceptional gifts of observation" and her "clear and accurate reporting." Nothing had yet happened, as it was to happen before another decade had passed, to undermine her confidence. There is no suggestion that the little girl at Brindabella, who was not allowed to read fairy tales or indulge in fantasy, was ever secretive or invented mysteries. That was to come later and there was another reason, besides a reverence for privacy.

If her ability to remember and report was already a part of her equipment in childhood, Miles lost, somewhere along the way, the orderliness she claimed. Her books are not orderly or well planned. They straggle, they wander, they are discursive and wordy. If they were not they would lose half their charm. It is as if two gifts cancelled one another. The good memory and clear recording undermined the orderliness, for orderliness can only be achieved by editing, shaping, omitting what is extraneous. Miles loved her memories so much that she could not bring herself to clip them into shape.

Many of the pictures of places and patterns of life that we find in her novels date back to childhood days. In book after book she uses the Monaro as her background. Its creeks and rivers sing through her books. The Goodradigbee lives again "singing the G Minor Ballade over its great boulders"[18] or with "a song that charmed the night"[19] or again a "velvety Monaro song."[20] We hear the sigh of the Murrumbidgee "as it ran from out eternity into eternity, crying Hussssssssssssssh!"[21] The Monaro is for Miles's nobler novels; for the lesser ones she uses Thornford or its equivalent. She never wrote of a place she did not know, and usually she goes back to those she knew in childhood.

In her childhood Miles imbibed the pioneering attitude. This is a way of life covering the relationship of man to the soil, to his family, his neighbours, and a set of values not founded on money or possessions. The foundation stone of the pioneer's life is survival. He must begin at the beginning and build a new life. In the great loneliness the family is of enhanced importance and its members interdependent. Neighbours are valued, whatever they are like.

Only in her earliest years was Miles herself an active part of this pioneer way of life. She inherited the pioneers' feeling for the land, enhanced and made articulate by her literary gift. She accepted their code. This was egalitarian rather than democratic. Flood or fire was everyone's concern. If a child were lost every man for a hundred miles turned out to help in the search. No one was turned away from a homestead without food or refused lodging for the night for which there was never any payment. There were grades of society certainly ranging from the hatter, or half-crazed wanderer, to the owner of a large station, but all were judged on their capacity to cope with their environment. Pretension was never enough.

Miles was not, I think, truly democratic in outlook. A benevolent despotism such as she had lived under as a child was more to her liking. In some small ways she was even a snob but she was a strong believer in human worth wherever it was found. For her the brave, the truthful and the kind were equals wherever they were born or how they were reared.

Miles has given us many portraits of pioneers great and small: Danny Delacy, the Mazeres of Three Rivers, and McEacherns of Gowandale, the Brennans of The Gap, the Pools, convict taint and all, right down to Old Blastus of Bandicoot. This is not just the genteel squattocracy but the whole spectrum from Teddy O'Mara to Oswald of Cooee. Loneliness and isolation fostered individuality. Men were themselves without artifice or pretension; only on women were conventions clamped tightly down.

Miles as a child must have observed many "characters." She laid in a store of them in her retentive memory and drew on them later. They were too much in the picture for pure invention and could be rooted in no other part of Miles's life. She transfers to her novels the big family groups such as surrounded her own childhood. Kinship bulked large in her books and she never hesitated to lead her readers through a maze of family relationships. Her novels were family tales just as surely as they were rooted in the squattocracy. The pattern was stamped on her mind when young.

Even from reading *Childhood at Brindabella* you can see how she uses figures and incidents from her childhood in her novels. Her grandmother was the prototype of Mrs. Mazere in *Up the Country* and *Ten Creeks Run*. Mr. Auchinvole, the tutor with a weakness, appears again as Mr. Eustace Blenkinsop[22] and the "beautiful young Aunt who died before I knew her" may have suggested Emily Mazere, who was beautiful, died young and became a legend.

Incidents were sometimes picked straight out of her own background. Charlotte Mazere's journey to Three Rivers for the birth of her baby harks back to Susannah Franklin's return to Talbingo. "Philip accompanied his wife on the journey. She stayed the second day in bed at the rude hut of a stockman on the Jenningningahama and on the third pressed on again on horseback over snow-covered precipitous peaks and slippery sidelings, though her time was distant only a matter of weeks."[23] This is only an example to show how early experiences and family tales wind through her work. Miles acknowledged that *All that Swagger*, the longest and most impressive of her novels, was based on her grandfather's pioneering experiences and character.

One trait that Miles developed early and which was not necessarily a part of the pioneering world was her love of animals. Horses were part of her life from earliest childhood and she has left many portraits of them: Merrie Monarch, The Waterfall, Romp, the blue roan, Black Belle, Sweetheart and, on a less romantic level Splodger, Suck-Suck and Flea Creek. She had her own blood horse called Zephyr, scorning ponies as "dunkies." For working bullocks she had a great respect.

In a country that draws its wealth very largely from animals there has been too often, and there still is an utter disregard for their suffering. Sheep and cattle starved to death in bad seasons on runs overstocked out of greed. Miles castigated this callousness with all the strength of her bitter anger:

"But the books show" said the big syndicates, "that it is cheaper to let the sheep die and breed up again in a few years, than to spend perhaps more than their value in labour and fodder sustaining them in lean years." This course was pursued in the interests of dividends regardless of consequences to the face of the earth, and free of control excepting such as the trade unions could impose. The torture of frail dumb animals, in their failing strength left by crows with bloody vacant eyeballs for the last agony, did not show on the big land syndicates' ledgers—yet. It showed in the register of man's stupidity, which in cycles leaves thousands of himself mutilated on some field, no more considered commercially than the sheep and cattle fallen in drought.[24]

The pain of animals went deep in Miles. In her first book *My Brilliant Career* she drew a heart-rending picture of drought-stricken cattle and in *Ten Creeks Run* thirty years later the poignancy is no less.

The drought continued. The bodies of sheep falling as they reached the promised land punctuated the Route even as the earlier beeves, whose hides were now dry and empty. The crows and dingoes had a good season, the drovers and their employers a hard one. The employers had shattering losses. The drovers had plenty of work with all the world of shifting stock but it was in a world of shifting sand and stinging flies, and disheartening to crawl all day long tortured by sandy blight behind weak suffering animals on a route already littered with stinking carcasses, to the accompaniment of a devil's chorus of crows, to deliver half the flock with which they started.[25]

Of cows she wrote, "How could men rear these creatures to such trustfulness and then slaughter them?"[26]

There was the other side of the picture too. Miles thought it was very nice of animals to be friendly to people when you thought what people were like. Here is a charming and whimsical picture of one of her characters:

Labosseer was gifted with the faculty for personal, spiritual friendships with animals, which rendered him comfortable under physical contact. No cat was too disreputable to be free of his shoulder, no cockatoo could annoy by trying its beak on the best pieces of furniture; should cocky extract the eyelets from his best boots it never failed to amuse him and did not prevent him wearing the boots. He never complained of the personal odour of dogs or kept them at a distance for fear of fleas. He dipped them for fleas and apparently accepted the odour. When he had a dog passenger in the car it was a lesson in high breeding to see them start. He would take a nervous cringing little kelpie, inquire her name with the same care as he would that of a human, and apply it. "Wait till I make you comfortable" he would say, spreading his own overcoat or mackintosh, if no bag were available, and the look that dog would give him as she settled down in confidence and comfort was something to be tabulated among the beautiful contacts on the earth's plane.[27]

Birds were a constant delight to Miles, the song of magpies in the early morning, the laughter of kookaburras, "flocks of black swans and pelicans at least three miles wide . . . clouds of green and red and purple and rose parrots."[28] The wild sad call of the curlew was near to her heart, like the voice of her own homesickness. The mopoke was one of the voices of Australia.

Like all members of her family Miles was a passionate gardener. She began early.

I was first given a packet of balsam seeds. Dear beautiful balsams, amenable to grow in pots and quickly blooming for impatient childhood. Next I had a yellow pansy with a dark face to tend. I was an assiduous and obedient pupil and as a reward was to have a flower of my very own, different from any other.

Mother brought out the seed catalogue, one of those magical magazines which after half an hour's browsing leave one in an Eden of burgeoning flowers, vegetables and fruit. Away went the order on packhorse by bridle track through gullies and streams and mountain gaps to some mysterious other world. Mother's choice was an out-sized bulb. She showed me how to set it . . . To see the first leaves of plants or seedlings break from the earth is an enchantment that never stales. I used to sit and watch for the tulip's appearance like a cat near a mouse hole.[29]

The tulip when it bloomed was a miracle in her life.

It got on with its job in privacy and one day when I was strolling around the path playing some inner-life game with myself there was the *Tulip!* Something wonderful, something new! It is the only one I remember to have seen in Australia; nowhere have I seen another exactly like it. The new soil, space and natural fertilizer may have helped. It stood on a noble stem nearly as tall as myself, a big dark reddish bell.[30]

Miles never forgot a tree or even a bough in her grandmother's orchard, and all the homesteads in her novels are endowed with orchards and gardens. Flowers spring up everywhere in her pages

CHILDHOOD AT BRINDABELLA 33

and vegetables are neither scorned nor forgotten. Here is a passage describing the gardens of one of the Milford ladies:

> Mrs Bob had a bed of Prince of Wales feather as tall as maize with streamers feet long, and borders of double English daisies and anemones, others of wall flowers, of pinks and carnations that smelt like heaven, and wide borders of sweet-william that the bushmen rode miles out of their way to see and smell, and all who ever saw those borders of sweet-william were unanimous that they never saw any to equal them. She had also a laburnum-tree like a rain of gold, and purple lilacs, and honeysuckle over an arch at the entrance, and a hedge of pink roses all round the enclosure, and two strips of fleur-de-lis, purple and white, and bushes of rosemary, and daffodils growing in a lawn of rye-grass, which Mr. Blenkinsop said always reminded him of England.[31]

This has the air of a garden seen and loved and not of one merely imagined.

The bush too had its flowers and Miles wrote of "eighty miles of blossoming snow gums or blackthorn or ti-tree spreading a perfumed canopy of bridal lace."[32] In her love of these things—animals, birds, flowers, trees—Miles was giving back to life some of the love lavished on her as a child.

Miles's life falls into well-defined periods. The first ten years, her childhood at Brindabella and Talbingo, was a time of safety and happiness, of love given and received, of confidence. The next decade, from her departure to Stillwater till the publication of her first book and its consequences, was a time of rebellion. After this came thirty years of exile, seeking and homesickness. The last twenty-one years are more difficult to label. She was home again but she had stopped writing. She was disillusioned and still homesick for a lost world. Who knows exactly what Miles felt—even when she told you?

CHAPTER 4

Stella and Miles

I *A Time of Ferment*

THE FRANKLIN family's move to Stillwater had far-reaching consequences for Miles. She was thrust, all unprepared, into a different sort of life. She went to school for the first time and amongst children she did not know and whose backgrounds were quite different. This would be an ordeal for any child.

Mr. Auchinvole's lessons, though more cultured, were unlikely to be on the same lines as those in a State school. She would have known more in some ways and less in others than her school mates. This could only produce alternations of superiority and humiliation. She may even have begun to suspect that she was not the clever little girl she had been led to believe she was.

We know little of her prowess, or lack of it, at school. Only small fragments of fact remain: that she worked a sampler with the words "Thornford Public School 1890. SM. SM. Franklin;" that her teacher was Mary Ann Elizabeth Gillespie; that Miles won first prize in open competition for darning at an agricultural show. Well, naturally, her grandmother had taught her to darn. There is not much in these fragments to construct a picture of her life.

Miles had other things to distress her than possible difficulties at school. The family had come down in the social scale, and no one realizes a thing like that more quickly than a child. The Franklins were no longer station folk, they had become small farmers—cockies as they are called in the local idiom, for were they not like cockatoos scratching in the ground for a living? They were no longer surrounded by their relations in a closely knit community. Even Miles thought there was no one to talk to, and in her early books when she portrays cockies and their families it is with scathing wit. Later she was to come to a better understanding of their difficult lives.

In her childhood Miles was an important person. She liked being important. Her small, but not undeveloped, ego was satisfied and fulfilled. Although the eldest of seven children it is significant that Miles scarcely mentions her brothers and sisters. When she tells the story of her baby sister's funeral it is Miles who is the most important person, though not the chief mourner. There is another slightly acid reference to a pretty sister who was eclipsing her, a situation which she was to use for her novels.

Miles much preferred the company of adults to that of other children; she could not stand up to teasing and caused a family crisis when a cousin, Donald Franklin, tormented her in schoolboy fashion. She had more success with adults but there was also another reason why she preferred them. A curvature of the spine made rough play painful.

Childhood at Brindabella was happy, almost too happy for Miles's good. It did not prepare her for the struggles and reverses that are an inevitable part of life. All members of her family were, apparently, famous for their rectitude. This was like a wall around her. When she discovered deceit in others it was a shock to her. The first time she met this particular serpent was at a picnic when a strange child took her tot, as a mug was called, from her under pretext of washing it and did not bring it back. In her small closed world her mother's firmness with her gave her the feeling that so long as she was good she was absolutely safe. The discovery when it came that the world was not run on those lines left a lasting scar. To it I attribute, and I think that I am right, her vulnerability, her defensiveness and her half-hidden sense of neglect.

For three years Miles did not see her grandmother and, worse still, a sister, younger "and prettier" as Miles points out bitterly, took her place at Talbingo. By doing this Grandma was probably trying to relieve the strain on her over-worked daughter and by caring for one child to help the family financially. It could not be Miles, for she was of an age to profit by schooling and also, it was hoped, to be of assistance to her mother. The child did not realize this and felt herself passed over and cast out. It rankled.

Then again Miles and her mother were out of tune with one another. Mrs. Franklin was a practical woman, of sturdy common sense, a good mother and a good wife. No matter what reverses the family suffered she never lowered her standards. Displays of emotion were quite out of bounds. She herself was stoical and uncomplaining. She expected her children to be the same. She lacked imagination and thought any sort of fantasy was nonsense and lies. She was certainly not without tenderness or understanding but in many ways she was rigid, perhaps taking after her German father.

Miles gave lip-service all her life to her mother's rules of self-control and reticence but their root was not in her. She was half-Irish and the Celt was strong in her. She was sensitive, imaginative, gay, spirited, even with a streak of wildness which led to mental adventures rather than actions. She was nearer to her father, the tall handsome man who was never very successful in material things. Being a girl it was for her mother to bring her up. There was friction.

Miles was a romantic however she might try to disguise it, or to conform in the family, or drive it underground. She fell into fantods however much she might decry such things. *Fantod* was a favourite word of hers. The dictionary tells us that it means a burst of nervous irritation.

This is not an excursion into psychoanalysis, which would be suspect. When Mrs. Franklin died in 1938, at a great age, Miles was overcome by grief and remorse. She felt that she had never understood her mother or valued her sufficiently, that as a rebellious girl she had caused her sorrow. She grieved, not because she loved her mother but because she had not.

Miles was fast becoming a rebel. She felt deprived and misunderstood and the victim of a hard fate. The awful realization dawned on her that she was a girl in a man's world; that all the best things were reserved for men and boys; that she was an inferior creature through no fault of her own. She had nothing to look forward to but marriage and housework and babies and the perpetual frustration of the talents she felt burgeoning in herself.

As a child she had had great freedom; she was always out and about on the station with her father and the men. No muster was complete without her and she used to "help" her uncles with the harvest. At Stillwater everything was different. She was no longer amongst her relations. Schooling was important and might not be interrupted. Also she was older and must learn to be a genteel young lady.

She looked at the women she knew, the cockies' wives, and saw how utterly dull their lives were. She looked at the men and boys of the district and saw their lack of education, of refinement, of spirit. As husbands they would be impossible; to be inferior to such creatures was galling in the extreme. The young girl who was Miles, was revolted by the scheme of things and the part she was obviously expected to play in it. The day of careers for women had not yet dawned. Out in the great world there were singers and actresses but what could a little girl in the bush do? Feminine as she was, Miles revolted against being a woman because they were "cabin'd, cribb'd, confin'd" and the best they could hope for was to put Mrs. in front of their names by grace of some man. This attitude remained with Miles all through her life. She maintained her identity and her privacy. The *enfant terrible* became a rebel and the rebel became a campaigner for the cause of woman's rights.

At seventeen Miles was attractive but far too spirited to accept advances from the opposite sex. She was petite with a trim figure, a thick plait of softly curling dark hair, steady questioning eyes and a rather sad little mouth. There is a portrait of her in a gem hat and leg-of-mutton sleeves, a jabot, and a tasselled umbrella held at an elegant (and dangerous) angle.[1]

Her life, of course, was not all gloom and frustration. In a big family there is always activity and fun. Miles became intensely interested in music and wanted to make it her career. She read every book she could lay hands on and the sight of a shelf full of new books was an intoxication. There was not very much Australian literature for her to read but what she could find she enjoyed, particularly the poets and Henry Lawson's short stories. Long after she was to write:

It is hardly possible to overstate how much indigenous ballading and versifying meant in the nineties to those in and below their teens, and on up to grizzled old men too. Each fresh expression of the land and its activities had the stimulation of news. Lawson, Paterson and Ogilvie ably filled the places of the film's favourites today, being of handsome physical appearance and winning personality. The poems of these men and others were recited by everybody, whether he had gifts that way or not. Around camp fires or in huts rival self-expressionists grew truculent as to who should come first with "The Man from Snowy River" or "When the World was Wide."[2]

She read Thackeray and Dickens—something of Dickens's approach and style clung to her mind—and the popular authors of the day like Hall Caine and Marie Corelli. At least La Corelli suggested that women could write and make a success of it.

Stillwater was not the family's last move. From there John Franklin went to a property of much the same kind—except that here he was probably growing fruit—Chesterfield out of Penrith, a sleepy town on the Nepean River thirty-four miles from Sydney. They were out of the Miles Franklin country and further away from Brindabella and Talbingo. Here one of the children died at the age of eleven. I have not been able to find the date of this move. It is not important in the Miles Franklin story except that Penrith under the name of Noonan provided the setting for her second published book, *Some Everyday Folk and Dawn*.

Place contributed to Miles Franklin's rebellion; so also did time. Born in 1879 her teens were spent in the 1890's. In this last decade of the century there was a quickening of new life in Australia, an awareness of identity. There was ferment and turmoil.

No one has described the nineties as well as Vance Palmer. The first two paragraphs of his *The Legend of the Nineties* sets the stage:

A romantic aura always hangs over the last days of a dying century for those who look back on it. It is as if the human mind was impelled to discover a special kind of life about the end of an era. And so there has grown up a legend of the Australian nineties as a period of intense artistic and political activity, in which the genius of this young country had a brief and brilliant first flowering. Something new, it is claimed, emerged into the light. A scattered people, with origins in all corners of the British Islands and in Europe, had a sudden vision of themselves as a nation, with a character of their own and a historic role to play, and this vision set fruitful creative forces in motion.

Literature, so the legend goes, showed this quickening. The dumb continent, silent for aeons, began to find voice. Balladists and storytellers appeared, taking their background for granted and addressing their audiences in the popular idiom instead of in the stilted language that had hitherto been thought appropriate for print. The painters looked at the landscape around them with fresh eyes and tried to capture its delicate colours and dazzling light. In politics there were impulses towards unionism, federation, and self-dependence, all shot through by a quivering awareness that these things were not ends in themselves, but steps towards the creation of a perfect commonwealth.

And later he wrote, "It would be too much to pretend that this dream affected the whole country, but it certainly affected its most conscious spirits, influencing art and politics." [3]

As Palmer points out there was not very much concrete evidence of this new spirit, particularly in literature, in the 1890's. Its seed was in the soil but it did not fruit until the 1900's. To change the metaphor one of those mysterious tides in human affairs turned in the 1890's and there were some that could feel it running like a strong undertow. It was like the troubling of the pool of Bethesda.

There were various portents. There was the move towards federation of the Australian States into the Commonwealth of Australia. It was a hesitant movement, gathering force and losing it again. It would never have been achieved in the face of the possessiveness and jealousies of the States if there had not been a growing demand for unity throughout the country. Womanhood suffrage was written into the new constitution, a reform to which the young Miles already attached great importance.

Trade unionism was growing amongst the workers. It had the down-to-earth policy of winning higher wages and better working conditions but there was an idealistic side too, carrying "mateship" and solidarity far beyond expediency. A series of disastrous strikes on the water-front and amongst the shearers were carried on in an almost crusading spirit.

Another ferment was supplied by the Utopians. They believed that, by one device or another, perfection could be attained in human affairs. This is the extreme of idealism and can only flourish in an atmosphere of hope—or despair. At first these Utopians were imported from America, Henry George of California with his single tax doctrine and Edward Bellamy of Boston with his book *Looking Backward*, in which he outlined the ideal commonwealth. Both had wide public support. The two were not mutually exclusive.

Then came the local Utopian William Lane. He saw merit in both George and Bellamy. "*Looking Backward*," he said, "is to industrialism what *Uncle Tom's Cabin* was to chattel slavery. It moves the world to thought because it moved the world to tears." [4] Lane himself advocated a clean sweep of all theories and institutions and a new beginning, under his leadership of course. His ideal was a socialist community without class distinction or privilege. It must cut adrift completely from the contamination of the old world. At first he hoped to form such a colony in Australia and sought a land grant for the purpose. But he realized that the old order was too firmly entrenched in Australia and led his little band to New Australia in Paraguay. He attracted people from all walks of life and the *Royal Tar* set sail freighted with almost as many pious aspirations as the *Mayflower*.

The settlement failed for very human reasons but Lane's ideal was not wholly lost. It lived on in the concept that Australia was and could remain a new country unsullied by the mistakes of the past and the old world. The poet Bernard O'Dowd expressed it:

> The cenotaphs of species dead elsewhere
> That in your limits leap and swim and fly,
> Or trail uncanny harp-strings from your trees,
> Mix omens with the auguries that dare
> To plant the Cross upon your forehead Sky,
> A virgin helpmate Ocean at your knees.[5]

Of Australia, he wrote:

> She is a temple that we are to build:
> For her the ages have been long preparing:
> She is a prophecy to be fulfilled! . . .

> She is the Eldorado of old dreamers,
> The Sleeping Beauty of the world's desire.
> She is the scroll on which we are to write
> Mythologies our own and epics new:
> She is the port of our propitious flight
> From Ur idolatrous and Pharaoh's crew.
> By dream, or god, or star we would not see:
> Her crystal beams all but the eagle dazzle
> Her wind-wide ways none but the strong-winged sail.
> She is Eutopian, she is Hy-Brasil
> The watchers on the tower of morning hail![6]

This view of the purity of the Australian earth, uncontaminated by the sins of the old world, lives on in Miles Franklin.

The world was their own and what a world! A thousand miles of unspoiled forest distilled an aromatic fragrance chaste as a puritan heaven with a character of loneliness and silence all its own, while near, above the queenly tree-tops the big white stars blazed like diamonds in the dome, and right across it spread the great white way where an old woman long ago had gone to heaven tipping her milk pail as she ascended.[7]

In both the militants and the idealists there was a revolutionary streak. This did not appeal to Miles. She belonged to the squattocracy. She was not politically minded. She was ready to campaign for Votes for Women because she felt that women were unfairly treated, that they were the equals of or superior to men. The more they exercised their power in public affairs the better the world was likely to be, or so she thought. She wanted justice, and plenty and kindness for all as a human right because she valued human beings and because her tender heart ached for sick babies, lonely old people and all who were deprived or handicapped. That did not make her a socialist. It sprang from emotion, not politics.

It was enough for Miles that there was a ferment, that minds were on the move. She hated stagnation and dumb acquiescence. Her forebears had battled to win a place in a difficult country. She was ready to do battle too and to align herself with the young and eager. It made her particularly happy that her beloved country was finding its voice. "The period was like a range of hills in our empty literary scene,"[8] she wrote—and how she loved the hills. Her favourite balladist seems to have been Barcroft Boake because he sang of the Monaro and "breathes of the reckless physical daring practised then and there, and his volume bristles with the names of the region of the Eucumbene and the Snowy—Jindabyne, Adaminaby, Tumut, Tumbarumba, Mount Bogong, Brookong."[9]

The girl in the bush, not having access to camp fires, would not have had much opportunity to hear or read these ballads but for one thing. There was a journal published weekly in Sydney called *The Bulletin*. It had begun its life in 1880 and after early vicissitudes was well in its stride in the 1890's. It has been called the bushman's Bible. It was in its essence Australian and it gave the man in the bush a voice. Something of a "sharpshooter," it commented freely on every subject, feared no vested interest, debunked florid writing and opened its columns to contributors. What is more it paid for everything it printed.

Miles commented: "Here was a forum for opinions, a focus, a school and market for writers, a club open to all who had the talent to join. John Feltham Archibald [10] pruned and ridiculed, he criticized and encouraged, he taught, he paid for everything he printed. A flock of writers was disciplined and given purpose and status." But she warned "the *Bulletin* was then considered vulgar, if not worse, and out of bounds for genteel females and clergymen." [11]

It is easy to see that this publication, whatever its merits or demerits, did a great deal to encourage writers and to assemble their product in one easily accessible organ. It is just as easy to see how Miles would be drawn to it by the fact that it was out of bounds for "genteel females." Cut off in the bush Miles might be, but eager, restless and rebellious, she still marched with the *avant garde* in those days of ferment.

II *The First Book*

To write was not amongst Miles's early ambitions. Her heart was set on music but in the bush and with little money behind her it was not possible to get the tuition she needed to develop her talent. She flailed about seeking a way out of her cage. She scribbled and scribbled. It was an outlet. If we can take the preface of her second book, *My Career Goes Bung*, as true this is the story of her literary beginnings:

Precocious effort in art is naturally imitative, but in localities remote from literary activity there is no one for the embryo writer to copy. Thus I was twelve before I wrote anything to draw attention to myself. I must have been nearly thirteen when the idea of writing novels flowered into romances which adhered to the design of the trashy novelettes reprinted in the supplement to the Goulburn Evening Penny Post. These stories, secretly devoured, presented a world enchanting to budding adolescence. They were prinked with castles with ivied towers and hooting owls, which were inhabited by the unaccommodating guardians, thrilling seducers and more thrilling rescuers of titled maidens, as pure as angels. I used to read my versions to two or three girls, who still gaily recall the entertainment we thus manufactured for ourselves.

An Englishman, to whom some of these lucubrations were shown, directed me to the Australian scene as the natural setting for my literary efforts. The idea sprouted. Huh, I'd show just how ridiculous the life around me would be as story material, and began in sardonically humorous mood on a full-fledged novel with the gibing title *My Brilliant (?) Career*.[12]

The Englishman referred to was T. J. Hebblewhite, to whom—among others important in her early literary development—*Laughter, Not for a Cage* is dedicated.

Miles was sixteen when she wrote *My Brilliant Career* and twenty-two when it was published by Blackwoods. Miles has given her own descriptions of its writing: "The girl's story was conceived and tossed off on impulse in a matter of weeks, spontaneously out of inexperience and consuming longings and discontents, and half humorously, as its author has stated in print, to show how impossible the Australian scene was for novel-making."[13] It was "an impatient animadversion" and "burns with the nationalism rampant at the time."

The novel, written in the first person, purports to be the story of Sybylla Penelope Melvyn, a spirited young girl. Her parents had fallen on hard times and had left their station property for a miserable dairy farm at 'Possum Gully. Life was hard and dreary. To make things worse Mr. Melvyn, unable to face up to adversity, became "a slave of drink, careless, even dirty and bedraggled in his personal appearance. He disregarded all manners and had become far more plebeian and common than the most miserable specimen of humanity around him."[14] Sybylla had to go to the public house at night to bring him home. There were nightmare journeys as he insisted on taking the reins and drove the horse in circles.

When not so engaged Sybylla had to walk miles to and from school, look after her younger brothers and sisters, endure her mother's nagging and work on the farm. Rearing poddies was one of her duties: "Poor little calves! Slaves to the greed of man. Bereft of the mothers with which nature has provided them, compelled to exist on milk from the separator, often thick, sour and very cold."[15]

The family could only make the barest living at the best of times. Then came drought. "The scorching furnace-breath winds shrivelled every blade of grass, dust and the moan of starving stock filled the air—vegetables became a thing of the past. The calves I had reared died one by one, and the cows followed in their footsteps."[16] Miles lays on her colours thickly. The plight of the farmers was desperate. "Not only was their living taken from them by the drought, but there is nothing more heart-rending than to have poor beasts, especially dairy cows, so familiar, valued and loved, pleading for food day after day in their piteous dumb way when one has it not to give."[17] The family spent most of its time "cow-lifting," getting beasts that had fallen through weakness on to their feet again in the hope of keeping them alive a little longer. The Melvyns' possessions were sold up by their landlord, the bishop, to pay their arrears—a good melodramatic touch —but neighbours, bidding very low, bought them in for a song and returned them.

Sybylla was intensely unhappy and could see no future for herself. "Marriage to me appeared the most terrible let down and unfair to women. It would be from fair to middling if there was love; but I laughed at the idea of love, and determined never, never to marry."[18] Worse still, Sybylla discovered her inferiority.

As I grew it dawned upon me that I was a girl—merely this and nothing more. It came home to me as a great blow that it was only men who could take the world by its ears and conquer their fate, while women, metaphorically speaking, were forced to sit with tied hands and patiently suffer as the waves of fate tossed them hither and thither, battering and bruising without mercy.[19]

Sybylla was rescued by her grandmother. A happy life began for the girl surrounded by every comfort and refinement. There were books and music and an admirer called Everard Grey with "two rows of magnificent teeth untainted by contamination with beer or tobacco."[20] This, however, was, as Miles might have said, only a preliminary canter. The real hero shortly appeared, handsome, wealthy, noble-minded Harold Beecham. Even Sybylla was a little tempted to break her vow of spinsterhood. She agreed to wear his ring secretly and consider the matter. There was a passionate scene in the orchard. Sybylla declared that she had only pretended to allow his attentions so that she could the more completely humiliate him. She threw away his ring and struck him in the face, cutting his cheek. Harold refused to give up hope.

Fate intervened. Harold suddenly lost all his money and his handsome station property as well. Touched, Sybylla offered to accept an engagement now that he needed her. She was "a perfect little brick." Harold was far too noble to take advantage of this. " 'Don't worry about me. There's many a poor devil, crippled and ill, though rolling in millions, who would give all his wealth to stand in my boots today' he said, drawing his splendid figure to its full height, while a look of stern pride settled on his strong features. Harold Beecham was not a whimpering cur." [21]

While Harold strode off to re-make his way in the world Sybylla received a fatal letter from her mother. She must leave her happy home with Grandma and help the family by going as governess to the M'Swat family. Mr. Melvyn had borrowed £500 from Peter M'Swat who now pressed for payment. If Sybylla taught his children he was willing to knock £20 a year off the debt. It was Sybylla's duty to go and go she did. The M'Swats lived in a state of unmitigated filth. They were kind enough but without a gleam of refinement and, of course, did not understand Sybylla's delicate nature. The strain was so great that she fell ill with brain fever and had to be sent home.

Her life had reached another full stop. She was disgraced, her mother was querulous, her grandmother, no longer interested in her, had taken a younger sister Gertie to live with her. Even the presents an uncle had brought back from his travels for Sybylla were given to Gertie because she was on the spot.

Harold Beecham, miraculously restored to fortune, came back to ask for Sybylla's hand. She could not bring herself to marry him. Sybylla had nothing to look forward to and, as it had at the beginning of the story, "Life jogged along tamely, and, as far as I could see, gave promise of going to the last slip-rails without a canter." [22]

There could be no doubt as to the authorship of this book. It is a genuine Miles Franklin. It is crude, inept, stiff, exaggerated, but it contains most of the ingredients of the later books. There is the mixture of romance and realism. Sybylla longs for love and scorns it. Her passionate feminism is recorded over and over again and Sybylla's "Unhand me, Sir" attitude is part of Miles. So is her love of and sympathy for animals. The music of rivers is already haunting her writing. Through all her activities, singing or reading or working about the house "came the solemn rush of the stream outside in its weird melancholy like a wind ceaselessly endeavouring to outstrip a wild vain regret which relentlessly pursued." [23] (This. I think, was Jounania Creek which ran past the homestead at Talbingo. Miles's ashes were scattered on it some sixty years later.) Even her highly individual vocabulary was sending out some curious sprouts, for example "realisticating" and "finnikin."

The question of how far *My Brilliant Career* was autobiographical has been asked over and over again. It was not autobiography, the author insisted. There was no drunken father in Miles's life, no M'Swats, no (as far as I know) Harold Beecham, no bishop foreclosed on the Franklins. Writing in the first person gave an illusion of personal confession. There were points of contact. Miles like Sybylla left a station homestead for a farm, she too loved music and reading, she found "paradise" with her grandmother and surely these lines describe Talbingo renamed Caddagat:

I suppose it is only a fancy born of the wild deep love I bore it, but to me the flowers seem to smell more sweetly there; and the shadows, how they creep and curl oh so softly and caressingly around the quaint old place, as the great sun sets amid the blue peaks; and the never-ceasing rush of the crystal fern-banked stream—I see and hear it now, and the sinking sun as it turns to a sheet of flame the mirror hanging in the back yard on the laundry verandah, before which the station hands were wont to comb and wash themselves.[24]

Everything that Miles was and was to be already showed itself in this first book, her loves, her militancy, her ability to observe and transcribe, her quirks of style and character.

It took ten weeks to write *My Brilliant Career*. It was offered to three Australian publishers, unnamed. They rejected it. Henry Lawson, poet and short-story writer, was sailing for England. Miles had not met him but admired his work and felt that since they were both writers there was a bond between them. She asked him to take her novel to England and find a publisher for it there. Lawson agreed and wrote a preface for her:

I hadn't read three pages when I saw what you will no doubt see at once—that the story had been written by a girl. And as I went on I saw that the work was Australian—born in the Bush. I don't know about the girlishly emotional parts of the book—I leave that to girl readers to judge; but the descriptions of Bush life and scenery came startlingly, painfully real to me, and I know that, as far as they are concerned, the book is true to Australia—the truest I ever read.

Whether this preface did the book any good is doubtful but it must have been very encouraging to the author. She was accepted as an author by an author.

Lawson, or perhaps one of his literary friends, found a publisher, Blackwoods of Edinburgh, for *My Brilliant Career*. The preface was dated 1899. The date on the published book was 1901. It was a long slow business for Miles, stretching from age sixteen to twenty-two, an eternity for one so young.

The question mark was dropped from the title. The author's name on the title page was Miles Franklin. The reason for this selection from amongst her baptismal names was her fixed idea that the world belonged to men and a book by a man, or that appeared to be by a man, had more chance of success than one written by Stella Franklin could hope for. By that act Stella became Miles and, except to members of her family, was Miles to everyone henceforth. She moved into the name and it suited her. She was a soldier rather than a star. The family name became her better than the one her young mother had fancied.

Miles had had faith in her book. She had persevered and had at long last achieved publication. That in itself was victory for a girl in the bush with no literary connections. The novel, moreover, was a success. It ran into several editions and only went out of print when Miles withdrew it from circulation. The financial reward was not great. Miles received £24, no more. I have her word for it.

There were other satisfactions. At her first attempt this unknown girl stormed the fortress of *The Bulletin*. A. G. Stephens of *The Bulletin* staff was a leading, I am tempted to say the greatest, critic of his day. He welcomed *My Brilliant Career* with enthusiasm:

It is the sunlight dancing through the veins of the author that makes *My Brilliant Career* interesting. "Miles Franklin" (of Goulburn, New South Wales) admits to being "a little bush girl;" and her book is memorable for this: that it is the very first Australian novel to be published. There is not one of the others that might not have been written by a stranger or a sojourner. But *My Brilliant Career* is Australian through and through; the author has the Australian mind, she speaks Australian language, utters Australian thoughts, and looks at things from an Australian point of view absolutely . . . Her book is a warm embodiment of Australian life, as tonic as bush air, as aromatic as bush trees, and as clear and honest as bush sunlight.[25]

This is hardly literary criticism. It was written while the impassioned nationalism of the 1890's still warmed the blood. It pleased Miles so much that she quoted the passage in part in 1950 when she was delivering the Commonwealth Literary Fund lectures on Australian literature in Perth, Western Australia. Stephens said other things in his review, which he called "A Bookful of Sunlight." For instance:

The book is not a notable literary performance; but it is fresh, natural, sincere—and consequently charming. All over this country, brooding on squatters' verandahs or mooning in selectors' huts, there are scattered here and there hundreds of lively, dreamy, Australian girls whose queer, uncomprehended ambitions are the despair of the household. They yearn, they aspire for what they know not; but it is essentially a yearning for fuller, stronger life—the cry of their absorbed, imprisoned sunlight for action, action, action! "Miles Franklin" is one of these "incomprehensible" ugly ducklings who has luckily escaped from the creek, and is delightedly taking her swan-swim in the river of literature.[26]

That is not truly literary criticism either. What was the book's value as literature? Today's critics are still undecided. Some consider it her best, her most original work. H. M. Green, the literary historian, found it dynamic. "It struck the Australian nineties with the force of a small bomb, taking readers and critics by storm." [27] That is an historical statement rather than a criticism. Havelock Ellis wrote of it:

It is a vivid and sincere book, certainly the true reflection of a passionate young nature, impatient of the inevitable limitations of the life around her. Such a book has psychological interest, the interest that belongs to the confessions of a Marie Basghkirtseff of the bush; but something more than emotion is needed to make fine literature; and here we miss any genuine instinct of art or any mature power of thought, and are left at the end with only a painful sense of crudity. Miles Franklin is ardently devoted to Australia, but to a remote ideal Australia, and in the eagerness of her own embittered and egotistical mood she tramples under foot the things that really make Australia.[28]

This is criticism from the angle of psychology, not literature.

Ray Mathew, Australian and poet, tells us what the book is about. In the process he makes some shrewd observations:

Its truth as a picture of reality springs from the way its narrator constantly snubs her own emotions and interpretations . . . Sybylla snubs herself constantly—her every success in argument or flirtation is cut to size by reminders of reality. All emotion is suspect (even occasionally, and guiltily, her very real feeling for parent, sister, ancestor) because no emotion will answer her need; all interpretation of event (be it nostalgic, romantic or otherwise literary) must fail her since it cannot encompass her conviction that she, herself, is important.

Her adolescent romanticism recovers from every snub, every attempt to repress it, and it is this which holds her book together and allows her to finish with a kind of optimism.[29]

Mathew sums up "on the certainty that *My Brilliant Career* is a classic (important in our literature, good in any), the case for Miles Franklin as 'established' could confidently rest." [30]

Cecil Hadgraft, the critic, is more specific and less impressed:

> It is a remarkable first book for a young woman. But it is foolish to praise it for what it is not. It is unlikely, for instance, that she should possess mastery. The book contains the artless outpourings of a youthful spirit dissatisfied with its material and spiritual lot. She wants companionship of kindred souls, the experience of art, and the love of her ideal man—though she cannot explain what this is to consist in. Odd, contrary, perverse, she seems doomed to find herself a misfit, and at the end of the book no solution is in sight. The youthful *cri du coeur* has been compared to the diary of Marie Basghkirtseff; but it is of slighter material. Inevitably it lacks depth. And it lacks sophistication of manner. The expression is immature, the devices of language not fully assimilated...
>
> There is the queerest mixture of the spontaneous and the affected in this book. Its liveliness, its verve, and its oddness of theme will preserve it. It is likely to be read for many years as a picture of an unusual Australian girl, with something of the pathetic priggishness of intellectual aspiration. But its literary value is not equal to its human interest. In a way it has the same claims as Daisy Ashford's *The Young Visiters*.[31]

This is fair enough except perhaps for the last sentence. *My Brilliant Career* has more in common with *Jane Eyre* than with the innocent and precocious "novel" of nine-year-old Daisy.

The trouble with a critical assessment of Miles's work is that while the memory of Miles herself still lives her writings are eclipsed by her personality. In the same way Sybylla steals *My Brilliant Career*. It rests on her and not on the manner of its writing. Sybylla is intriguing and aggravating and very young. As a character in a book she is an achievement, but of nature not of art. Without her, the book would be nothing. This, of course, is a foolish remark, and suggests the tag about Hamlet without the prince. Still, to achieve a detached judgement this elementary fact must be recognized.

My Brilliant Career is a first book by a very young author and it has the understandable faults of such. The story as a romance is incredible, but then it is not intended to be a romance. It is its very antithesis and pours scorn on ideas of romantic literature current in the 1890's. The heroine is plain and distinctly difficult, egotistical and hard to please. The hero, Harold Beecham, is set up as an ideal young man, handsome, well-mannered, honourable, wealthy. He measures up to the bush standards of manliness. Miles proceeds to show him up as a stuffed shirt, to complain that his courtship is too tame, that he is self-satisfied and worst of all that he treats her as a woman who might reasonably be expected to settle down as wife and mother.

Miles uses anti-climax with a heavy hand. Her reportage is brilliant but exaggerated as if she feared no one would understand or hear her unless she drew a heavy black line under everything she said. She is too young to dare depict any genuine emotion except rebellion. If she did try, not only her lack of artistry would be exposed but her very self. As usual she hides and piles on so much cover that the reader becomes suspicious. Later she was to let her romantic Irish nature have its say but at this stage she dared not. She gave back the image of realism and no nonsense impressed on her in her home.

Dialogue is very stiff and in the manner of the times. Take this snippet. The scene was the picnic races and the hero told his man to look to the horse, Boxer. Sybylla chipped in:

"Ladies before gentlemen" I interposed. "I want Mr Archer to take me to Grannie, then he can go and look after old Boxer."
"I'll escort you" said Beecham.
"Thank you, but I have requested Mr Archer to do so."
"In that case, I beg your pardon, and will attend to Boxer while Joe does as you request." [32]

Miles had not the strength to pull against the conventions of her time on all fronts. She rebelled against the "slavery" of marriage but accepted all the gentility that surrounded a young lady of the times even to the point of extreme prudishness. She is a rebel who holds on tightly to her respectability.

My Brilliant Career is very uneven both in its writing and in its general attitude. It is a book of great promise and little artistry. It lives on by dint of affection. A lot of sentiment and a little sentimentality go into its continuing vogue.

I have spent much space on *My Brilliant Career* because in the consideration of Miles as an artist it is a very important, if immature, book. As Ray Mathew puts it: "For Miles Franklin nothing—from a literary point of view—happened in her life after the publication of *My Brilliant Career* in 1901." [33] I agree with this. By the age of twenty-one Miles had assembled, in memory and experience, the background and characters and general stance of all her novels. When she occasionally, as in *Bring the Monkey* and *Prelude to Waking,* moved away from her quarry her work runs very thin.

III *Storm in a Tea Cup*

My Brilliant Career was published and widely read. Curiosity ran high in the Goulburn district where Miles lived and throughout the Miles Franklin country, the Monaro, where she was born and where many of her close relations still lived. Whatever strangers thought of it, her relatives were outraged. They must have known that the book was not autobiographical except in some unimportant points. Other people did not know this. Even A. G. Stephens in his critique seems to have taken it for granted that Sybylla and Miles were one and the same person. He wrote: "'Miles Franklin' has simply turned her girlish diary into a book; she has made literature out of the little things that lay around her—and this is what gives the book its value: she has had brains enough to make it true, and wit enough to leave it true." [34]

That was enough; Miles had sinned against the privacy of the family. She had libelled it. She had broken all her clan's rules of reserve and self-control. Or she appeared to have done so, which was nearly as bad. Her family, all those adored aunts and uncles, not to mention her beloved grandmother, was uncompromising. Its standards were fixed, and dear little Stella had broken every rule. The Franklins and the Lampes were not given to writing books. They were not even sure that it was "nice" to do so, especially for a young girl.

We do not know what was said behind closed doors. There is no record of reproaches. As far as I know, no letters on the subject have survived. But that something happened is obvious. Miles was hurt and humiliated in a way she could least bear. It was a turning point in her life, so bitterly did she feel the censure of those she loved most. The wound never healed. It was the more cruel because she had grown up with a sense of confidence within the family circle. She was loved and important and could do no wrong. Now she had done wrong and it was not a youthful peccadillo easily forgiven or wiped out by punishment, but a sin against the family so that she was hardly one of them any more.

It was not only the family that was outraged; neighbours round Thornford and in the Goulburn district generally, were incensed. They had been parodied, or, worse still, depicted with enough truth to make it sting. This, in turn, must have annoyed Miles's parents and moved her brothers and sisters to undue mirth at her expense. Her natural elation was quickly brought down to earth. Her faith in her first book was driven underground. It did not die but she dissembled it. In the preface to *My Career Goes Bung* Miles refers to the subject:

But INEXPERIENCE cannot possibly achieve any intended effect. Removed as I was from anyone equipped to understand or direct my literary attempts it was inevitable that I, of all my audience, should be the most flabbergasted. The literalness with which *My Brilliant Career* was taken was a shock to anyone of imagination.

> I set out to do the equivalent of taking two photographs on the one plate. I was to burlesque autobiography and create the girl of my admiration, and fill in with a lot of life-like people as a protest against over-virtuous lay figures . . . So my heroine was to be the antithesis of conventional heroines. All my people were to be created in the image of reality—none of them bad enough to be tarred and feathered, none good enough to be canonised.

But her characters got out of hand and were "as troublesome as Ma found me and I think in the end they made rather a pie of my theme." [35] So much for the apologia. To see the book in print was a shock.

> I wished now that I had written a ladylike book that I could be pleased with. If only I had known I would be printed I should have done so. Those poor lost girls who have a baby without being married must feel like I did. There would be the baby but all the wild deep joy of it would be disgrace and trouble . . . The bother raised by Sybylla Penelope in print so petrified me that I closed her book and have not reopened it. Could I bring myself to re-read it I could, perhaps, fabricate an essay to air the dubious guesses of psychoanalysis.[36]

The "dubious guesses" are puzzling. Can they refer to Havelock Ellis's review of it, already quoted? It seems improbable. I have found no likely answer. Miles always had a fine contempt for psychoanalysis and this may refer to an ill-judged remark which remained like a barb in her sensitive mind long after everyone else had forgotten it.

In the character of a literary critic, Miles gives *My Brilliant Career* short shrift in 1950. "It is a girl's story . . . conceived and tossed off on impulse in a matter of weeks, spontaneously out of inexperience and consuming longings and discontents . . ." It is "a girl . . . dashing off an impatient animadversion . . . a novel of sixteen." Yet she gives it space in her essay and stands it over against Joseph Furphy's *Such is Life*. She continues: "After a number of editions, the author firmly withdrew it because the stupid literalness with which it was taken to be her own autobiography startled and disillusioned then constrained her. It has long been out of print and therefore of no further concern herein." [37] This was not published until fifty years later. You would think that the matter no longer needed explanation but it must still have been rankling in Miles's mind.

Interviewed in the magazine *New Idea* on 6 May 1904 Miles made a public disclaimer of using live models:

I had no idea of hurting the feelings of anybody, but the book gave considerable offence in the district in which I lived, different people imagining that they represented certain types in the novel. That idea is a mistake, the story is certainly one of real life but there was no particular model for any one of the characters.

Miles was always prickly when asked about *My Brilliant Career*. Ray Mathew reported that when he told her he could not get a copy, she exclaimed: "Thank Heaven, for that." [38] He is also responsible for the anecdote that when someone brought her a copy and asked her to autograph it, she wrote, "The author has outgrown her adolescence, what a pity the owner has not!" [39] In her will Miles decreed that *My Brilliant Career* should not be republished for ten years after her death. But she did expect it to be published then and had no intention of burying it.

IV *A Time of Uncertainty*

So great was Miles's distress over the reception of her first book that she left home and came to the city. She was uncertain, at a loose end. She knew that she needed experience of life—but what experience?

She had some idea of being a free-lance journalist and wrote for *The Bulletin* under the name of Mary Anne, for once a woman's and not a man's name. Pen names were very fashionable in those days. It would hardly be an exaggeration to say that most writers used them. Joseph Furphy called himself Tom Collins, Arthur Hoey Davis wrote as Steele Rudd, Blocksidge became Baylebridge, Browne became Boldrewood, and so on.

She wrote for *The Bulletin,* not memorably, perhaps, and she was later to win a *Bulletin* prize for her novel *All That Swagger*. She was a familiar figure in the office for a time, yet she wrote, with, I think, a trace of bitterness: "Miles Franklin was outside *The Bulletin's* circle and is the only writer of comparable ability whose name is not in the weekly's seventieth anniversary roll call." [40]

Like Monica Dickens she worked as a maid servant for the experience. The report runs: "During the last twelve months she has been working as a servant girl in different swell houses in Melbourne and Sydney to get copy for a fresh volume and an account of her varied experiences as a smart and saucy Mary Anne may be expected before long." [41] She may have been writing for *The Bulletin* at the same time and chose as *nom de plume* the generic name for maid servants. I do not know and it does not matter.

Miles may also have begun to train as a nurse. She wrote a serial, of no particular literary value and long forgotten, called *A Ministering Angel*.[42] It is in the first person and tells the story of a bush girl training as a nurse. The detail suggests that she had practical experience or inside knowledge. It is dangerous, however, to take autobiography for granted in Miles's writing. Much later, during World War I, she worked as a voluntary orderly with the Scottish Women's Hospital unit in Serbia and Macedonia. The choice of this work suggests that she had some nursing knowledge. Miles still dreamt of a career in music but for one reason or another does not seem to have taken lessons or furthered her ambition in any other way.

The only positive value she found in this time of uncertainty lay in the friendships she made. One of these was Rose Scott whose influence coloured the next thirty years of Miles's life. Some thirty years older than Miles, Rose Scott had a similar background. She was bush born of a pioneering family in the Hunter River Valley. The Scotts were richer and more successful than the Franklins but they were of the same stuff. Rose was a beautiful girl; like Miles she was one of seven children and like her too "She was spiritually rooted in her native land . . . she knew the pioneer activities."[43] Stories of her youth read like pages out of some of Miles's books. There is this anecdote, for instance:

Her neighbourhood was visited by bushrangers. Her father and her uncle, Robert, organized a party and captured the Steel gang and handed them over to the Buffs, the regiment quartered in the district at the time. The Buffs allowed the men to escape. The Scotts, with superior bushmanship, recaptured them. The neighbouring settlers showed their appreciation by clubbing together and importing a silver service . . .[44]

At the age of seven Rose became a feminist. Miles quotes her own words:

When I was about seven years old my mother read to us *The Taming of the Shrew*. It was with suppressed indignation that I contemplated Katherine, at the bidding of her husband, taking off her cap and trampling on it! (I would have thrown it in his face!), and then her sermon (also at the bidding of her husband) to her sister Bianca and others upon the *duty of wives to their husbands* . . . When the reading was over I paced the garden, in a secluded spot, with clenched hands and fury in my heart! The craven wretch, to give in in that servile manner![45]

How like Miles! The idea thus implanted of life's injustice to women did not wither but took practical shape. Rose Scott continued: "Time rolled on, and the bush home was no more. As I grew up I found that Charity was certainly necessary and to be worked for, but to give others what you would not like to accept yourself seemed rather unsatisfactory. The weeds might be clipped but the roots were still in the ground, and again I felt Justice alone could pull up the roots." [46] She joined causes, like the move to win votes for women, and she inaugurated other movements. She was shocked by the working hours of shop assistants and campaigned for better conditions. Her efforts, and those of friends and public men she interested, resulted in the Early Closing Act of 1899. She worked for the rehabilitation of women prisoners when their gaol sentence was over and for more humane treatment while they were serving it.

Rose Scott had many interests and knew everyone of note. "A woman in a million," exclaimed Miles in admiration.

She was comfortable and happy in her home, and had zest in her housewifery . . . She brought the world to her home, which was said to be the most delightful place in Sydney. Her interests were so comprehensive that they were not above palmistry or telling character by hand-writing. Her drawing room was the only real salon that Sydney knew, and it alone would have made her famous. There public measures and social movements were encouraged or criticized, and public opinion clarified and shaped.

She was at home on Friday evenings, and on Saturday afternoons had an overflow meeting to give a chance to those who were getting on in years, or who had not enough years for late nights, or who lived at a distance. People went out to Edgecliff by tram, if not of the plutocrats who went by carriage or cab, and walked up the hill among the comfortable walled houses, which yielded glimpses of drive ways under grand Moreton Bay figs, to find Lynton, the famous two-storey cottage on Jersey Road, set in its thicket of bamboo, fuchsias, laurustinus, hibiscus, roses, camellias, and other shrubs and flowers. The cosy reception-rooms were often crowded. There came everyone of intellectual note or interest, residents or visitors to Sydney, regardless of clique, creed or political colour. There would be men in crumpled "slops" who did not believe in evening dress, rubbing shoulders with dandies, to whom tails in the evening were a rite; shy girls in high-necked frocks from the country or outer suburbs felt they were in high life as they chatted with some fashionable young person exhibiting every bare inch permissible in a gown that was the *dernier cri*. All were put at their ease, and found interest and companionship under the fusing influence of the hostess.[47]

Miles was obviously a frequent visitor to Lynton. She knew every flower in the garden. She would have been one of the shy girls in high-necked frocks. Rose Scott and Miles had much in common. They were both from the bush and loved it. By separate paths they had come to a militant but not ungainly feminism. Both hated war and its wastage. Both believed in and lived up to complete religious toleration. One of Rose Scott's *bon mots* as quoted by Miles was "that a curate should live in a palace and a bishop in a gunyah, on the principle that the deeper the man got into his calling the more humble and Christ-like his attitude and mode of living should be, and that the test for advancement should be the alacrity with which the curate would exchange the palace for the gunyah."[48] A gunyah, by the way, is a primitive shelter made from the branches of a tree. Rose Scott, despite her busy life, was also a writer of stories and verse. She had a saving sense of humour. She did not marry or wish to marry; "a pity there are not more like her," is said to have been Miles's comment on this.

Rose Scott opened a new world to Miles. Here amongst the many friends who gathered in the salon was the sort of companionship that Miles had always craved, intellectual, purposeful, witty. In Rose's drawing room women were equal and often superior to men. There was no sex bar. There was freedom of thought and expression and the equality that Miles had always thought essential to decent human relationships. Access to this society must have done much to mature the girl and also implanted in her mind an ideal of service which was to bear fruit.

Another friend, who came into Miles's life in 1904 and was to have a great influence on her as a writer, was Joseph Furphy. Over the pen name of Tom Collins he had written a vast discursive novel called *Such is Life*. Published under every possible difficulty, serialized, dismembered, abridged, this book has continued to live and influence Australian writing. It is a great panorama of the 1890's, the bush, and the curious and extensive scholarship of a self-made philosopher. Its publication was a major event which passed practically unnoticed. But Miles read it and admired it.

Furphy who had been born in 1843 was sixty-one in 1904 and a "mature philosopher" with a richly filled mind, a generous and upright character and a playful style in correspondence. On 27 March 1904 he wrote to Miles whom he had not yet met:

Your return to Melbourne on the 7th will merely afford me the best of reasons for extending my visit a day or two longer. And the meeting with you will be an epoch, an event to date from. There is no tincture of flattery in this. You are unconscious—amusingly unconscious—of how you have smitten the collective and individual Australian where he resides. Some months ago, I had a letter from Cecil Winter, a young N.S.W. sheep drover ("Riverina" of *The Bulletin*) in which he mentioned that, at a camp on the Billabong, a hawker (white) had shared their bivouac, and the local brat-walloper—seeing the fire—came across from his school. There ensued a feast of reason and flow of soul, for a bloke, a cove and a chap of literary tastes had met. But the point of the anecdote was that the hawker, in his travels, had been shown a letter written by Miles Franklin to some other girl. Yes, the hand that wrote M.B.C. had actually touched that paper; the hawker had seen the paper, and "Riverina" had talked to the hawker...[49]

Miles and Joseph Furphy met "in exquisite Easter weather" in the vestibule of the General Post Office and were joined by four other girls who had got wind of Miles's presence. Kate Baker was one of them. She was a school teacher who years before had boarded with members of the Furphy clan in the bush and so had come to know Joseph; a strong intellectual friendship had grown up between them. As Furphy was an incessant letter writer Kate accumulated a large pile of letters, and Miles was to have her share. The famous meeting was described by Furphy:

Drifting to the Art Gallery we went into committee in front of Longstaff's "Sirens" with the six chairs placed in a small circle. As the solitary he-feller of the synod, I fully expected to be given in charge every time Miles's merry laugh resounded through the galleries. But I came off safe—though something like 500 people appeared to take an interest in us. Then to Cole's where I gave her a copy of a certain publication which I am too modest to name...[50]

Furphy was disappointed by the meeting because he had no chance to talk to Miles. Girls swarmed round her all the time. He wrote to her: "Little thanks to me for sparking the ladies in Melbourne. It was *you* they were after; and I was merely the necessary link of connection."[51] This was Miles's only meeting with Furphy. He left his home in Shepparton, a country town in Victoria, for Western Australia at the end of 1904. He died there in 1912.

The core of the friendship was in letters Furphy continued to write to Miles even after she had left for America. She admired him as a writer and drew strength from his admiration of her book. It was balm to her to win the approval of this kindly, intelligent and well-read man. Sometimes he went too far in admiration.

Some of the letters to her in America Miles Franklin herself destroyed. Furphy expressed himself in terms of such enthusiasm for her gifts and had such high expectations of her that she was embarrassed. He considered her literary attainments unrivalled, and told her that she reminded him of himself, of Marcus Aurelius and also of Dean Swift and Daniel Defoe. The young woman struggling for self-support as well as for self-realization, with no encouragement for creative literary work, felt herself already too heavily handicapped by advanced political and other ideas, and to be likened to such heavy-weights frightened her into silence. One point she remembers is that Furphy insisted she would be a great man if she would only learn to hate.[52]

Furphy it would seem had a touch of the blarney and wrote in an exaggerated, humorous style that Miles at least half-believed. They were both children of their times, the 1890's; both loved and understood the bush and Furphy's discursive style did something to confirm Miles in the same habit.

V *The Second Book*

Miles wrote: "A writer cannot live for long on one book: it gives but temporary relief. Other work begins to fill his consciousness and push the completed thing from him. Also, the appreciation of a published book and the fellowship it brings flowers only for a season."[53] She was not thinking of herself but the words apply to her very well. Amid her many activities Miles was indeed writing another book. A certain bravado went into the enterprise. This book was, to use her own word, to be a "corrective" to *My Brilliant Career*. She called it *My Career Goes Bung*, and it purported to be the autobiography of Sybylla Penelope Melvyn.

To lay a false scent and perhaps to convince people that she wrote fiction and not autobiography Miles made some radical changes in Sybylla. She was now beautiful, an only child with a highly respectable father. She still lived in 'Possum Gully but the milieu was toned down. Most of the action took place outside 'Possum Gully. She was invited to stay with Mrs. Casterton, a social luminary, in Sydney. This was not kindness on Mrs. Casterton's part but a desire to possess the latest "lion" and show her off to society.

Sybylla, soon disillusioned, discovered that most of the grand folk were phony and that though she received a great deal of attention there was little friendship. "Few of the people I had met in Sydney had anything more in them basically than those around 'Possum Gully. The difference was in their having and doing, not in their being."[54] She had an affair of sorts, quite platonic, of course, with Goring Hardy, the man of the hour, and was delighted to find how easily she could manage him. She was sought after and had her choice of husbands including the catch of the season. As a final irony Henry Beauchamp appeared, declaring that he was the original of Harold Beecham in *My Brilliant Career* and claiming her hand. She would have none of them, being far too busy getting her own back.

Miles debunked the social scene, thoroughly and with zest. Did she learn how these people talked and behaved as she passed the vegetables or carried out the coffee cups? The final anti-climax came when she met "the really, truly GREATEST AUSTRALIAN Poet, Renfrew Haddington," was impressed for the moment and then saw through him too.

It is a novel of disillusionment but not of disillusionment accepted and taken lying down. Miles fights back. Sybylla goes home at last to help her family fight drought down on the farm. "The glorious escape from 'Possum Gully, or what was to have been a glorious escape, had ended in nothing but a wish to return to 'Possum Gully as an escape from the escape that was not glorious."[55] Gone is the wild innocence that informed *My Brilliant Career*. Cecil Hadgraft sums up the change:

The style, lively in the former novel, now becomes more colloquial, and develops in the process a chirpiness, a cockiness, that is not acid, possibly because the objects of it, "Society" and "birth" and the like, are more open to attack. They invite attack, true, but they allow the author to grow corners, to start to carry a chip on the shoulder. She underlines her dislike by using capital letters—SOCIETY—a device that relies on printing instead of on skill.[56]

The text bristles with strange words such as *drivellage, triffle-traffle, pillaloo, squashation* and *feraboraceous*. The meaning of these is generally plain enough but they are not an improvement on more conventional utterance. The book also bristles with rebellion. The main target is the position of women and the disabilities forced on them by the social system. This leads on naturally to men and their short-comings, whence it is but a step to the "slavery" of marriage.

Miles can explain her views to you better than I can paraphrase them. Listen to Miles:

I repudiate the crawl theory that we should be servile to our parents or to God for the bare fact of a mean existence. Most people are satisfied with a world run on a wasteful insanitary fashion. I am not. They are unashamed that seventy-five per cent of human beings are fit only for the scrap heap. I am not. They are thankful to thrive while others starve. I am not.
I rebel with all my living force against sitting down under life as it is, and as for a first child being an instrument of enslavement both for his own and his mother's sake, 'twere better he should never be.[57]

Of men and women:

I never can understand why men are so terrified of women having special talents. They have no consistency in argument. They are as sure as the Rock of Gibraltar that they have all the mental superiority and that women are weak-minded, feeble conies; then why do they get in such a mad-bull panic at any attempt on the part of women to express themselves? Men strut and blow about themselves all the time without shame. In the matter of women's brain power they organize conditions comparable to a foot race in which they have all the training and the proper shoes and little running pants, while women are taken out of the plough, so to speak, with harness and winkers still on them and are lucky if they are allowed to start at scratch.[58]

Of egotism:

All is egotism. The only people whose main-spring is not egotism are the dead and perhaps idiots—the one class having ceased to have a main-spring and it having been omitted from the works of the others.[59]

Men cannot help nearly always being duds from the lover angle. I suppose their delirium of egotism keeps them perpendicular.[60]

Of the ideal husband:

At least he would not be afraid of freedom and the light of understanding in women as well as men. His mind would not prescribe asinine limitations for women as part of God's will. He would not take rabies at the idea of a world where there would be no hungry children, no unprovided old age, and he would be ashamed to have harlots at street corners awaiting his patronage and then come to clean girls and blither about LOVE.[61]

On the superiority of women:

A woman has the advantage if she is equally matched in intelligence. To start, a man is an open book to her while she has depths that he does not suspect because some of them he will not concede to her. He insists that they are not natural for a woman, and it being impossible to fully cheat nature he only cheats himself.[62]

For herself: "The prospect of settling down to act tame hen in a tin pot circle and to acknowledge men as superior merely owing to the accident of gender revolted me."[63]

At last the childish cry that could have been for herself as much as for Sybylla: "To lean on FRIENDSHIP and find treacherous AMOUR in its sheep's wool. Old Grayling and Harry Beauchamp at 'Possum Gully, and Big Ears and Gaddy in Sydney. My career had certainly gone bung at both ends and in the middle. Kerplunk —Bang." [64] The hurt is visible though Miles was laughing too. She was still busy snubbing Sybylla and herself at the same time. She was lashing out furiously in all directions. The very idea of a suitor curdles her blood but at the same time she likes to count her scalps. As for any irregularity, "no man living could have tempted me outside a wedding ring. I had been so reared that any other suggestion was so deadly an insult that it iced any emotion I might have had." [65] However busily Miles covered her tracks she was still Miles and still very young.

The book ends, not in a quagmire as *My Brilliant Career* did, but on a quiet note, mature in contrast to the rest of it:

The seasons have smiled once more. The chief reminder of the drought which killed the stock and bared the paddock is that here and there a spot of richer green shows where in death some animal fertilized its pasture. The double value of remaining stock compensates for what was lost. Ridge and gully echo the cry of young things which replenish the earth.[66]

VI *Flight*

My Career Goes Bung waited forty years for publication. No publisher would accept it at the time it was written. It was too advanced; someone even said that Miles "wallowed in sex." How wrong they were, but the book frightened the publishers. Miles wanted to destroy the manuscript but did not. She kept at least two copies. It was written, as far as I can judge, in 1902 or 1903 and by 1905 it must have been clear that it would not find a publisher.

This may have been the last straw. In her disappointment Miles may well have decided that she was not cut out for a writer. Not only had her book been rejected, always a painful experience for a writer, but she was deprived of the chance publicly to refute the charge that she had used her own life and experiences in *My Brilliant Career,* and so perhaps put things right with her family.

Whatever the cause or causes Miles was unhappy and restless. She wanted to run away and hide. Her thoughts turned back to music. She would take it up again but not in Australia. She talked so much of going to America that, so the story goes, her father said he would like to see her "man enough" to do it. Her mother was still dubious. Miles was too young to step out into the world alone. There was no need to worry about the temptations of the world. Her daughter was of stout stuff. But she would have to keep herself. How was she to do it? She had not been very suc-

STELLA AND MILES

cessful as a free-lance journalist. It was one thing to pose as a housemaid in Sydney, for the sake of experience, quite another to do domestic work far from home in the States. Vida Goldstein, a public-spirited woman who had stood for Parliament, persuaded the family to let her go and gave her introductions which smoothed her path and reassured her mother.

So in 1905 Miles began what was to be a long, long exile. She took with her in her trunk the manuscript of *My Career Goes Bung* and her hopes. She herself was like one of the "exodists" she was to write about—young people full of hope and ambition who, seeing no opportunities in the bush, looked overseas for a career or at least for training. "They could not stay but it was grief to go." [67] They were romantics and so was Miles deep in her heart. Some of her "exodists" were to succeed like Mollye Brennan, the singer;[68] others fell by the way like Ignez, the girl who never came back.[69] Miles was nearer to Ignez than to any of her other characters but she did come home again to Australia and to writing.

CHAPTER 5

Thirty Years an Exile

I *Raising the Banner with Alice Henry*

DISAPPOINTMENT awaited Miles in the States. Her plan had been to work at anything that turned up, to support herself while she studied music. She found that her talent had been ruined by bad teaching and that the damage could not be undone.

There is no record of her despair except its shadowy image in the heroine of *Cockatoos*. Ignez too found that her voice had been spoilt by bad teaching. She had never been able to study properly because no one in her world took music seriously. Her practice was always being interrupted for house work, to wait on visitors, because some one had a headache, for any reason at all. She turned to writing as an outlet and published one book. Then, "She could not write; her heart was dead. She loathed her first attempt and the results. As a substitute for singing writing was a bin of dust."[1] Ignez fled to the United States.

When she found that two of her early outlets, family life and the arts, had been firmly cut off as by water-tight bulk-heads, she opened up other holds in her cargo of general capability and intelligence. She was soon in the dizzying rhythm of social service effort, with its stimulating contacts and colleagues of international renown. There was time only for snatches of strictly personal affairs and less for private letters.[2]

That is exactly what happened to Miles. She had lost her sense of direction, and for the moment she had no goal, no desire to go home defeated. Visiting friends in Chicago she met for the first time another Australian, Miss Alice Henry, a new arrival herself.

The two women had much in common. It was the story of Rose Scott over again. Rose, by example and by the stimulus of her personality and the interesting people she gathered about her, had fired Miles's imagination in the cause of justice for the underprivileged. Miles had an ingrained sense of the equality of men and a tenderness for all who suffered, whether human beings or animals. Rose Scott had channelled this trait in Miles and had shown her what could be done by selfless and intelligent campaigning.

Now in Alice Henry she met another such woman, who, in her turn, had lit her torch at the flame of yet another Australian, Catherine Helen Spence, writer, pamphleteer, social reformer and apostle for proportional representation in voting to assure a more effective franchise. Catherine Spence was born in Scotland in 1825; Rose Scott was born in the Hunter Valley, Australia, in 1847, Alice Henry in 1857, Miles Franklin in 1879. There was, you see, quite a dynasty of women, all unmarried, all practical philanthropists and reformers, all deeply interested in the cause of women, each in turn linked to another. Catherine Spence became one of Miles's heroines both as reformer and writer. I once heard her deliver a lecture on Australia's greatest woman novelist, none other than Catherine Spence.

Miles threw in her lot with Alice Henry. As practical as Rose Scott, Alice Henry had a different method of approach to the reforms for which she worked. While Rose Scott worked from the top down drawing prime ministers, premiers, judges and other prominent men with their wives into her brilliant social circle and convincing them by discussion and through sympathy of the need for legislation such as the Early Closing Act, Alice Henry worked from the bottom up. She saw the helpless and miserable condition of women in unprotected industries and she organized them into a trade union so that they could help themselves. Both methods gained their objectives but Rose's was by far the more glamorous.

Miles and Alice had something in common just as Miles and Rose had had. Alice too had grown up on a small property, out of Beaconsfield near Melbourne, raising cows and poultry. She knew the struggles and joys of such a life. She loved the bush and did what she could for bush children in advocating correspondence teaching for them. She had been a journalist in Melbourne not only writing articles under a pen name but also preparing speeches, anonymously of course, to be used on platforms where reform was being advocated. For family reasons she did not step out into the open in Melbourne though in the 1890's she had campaigned for Votes for Women. She had the courage to protest against the Boer War. She felt as Miles did about the horror and wastage of war and this one seemed to her utterly unjust. She went to America for greater freedom of action.

Her interests like Rose Scott's were far flung. She worked for the establishment of the Queen Victoria Hospital for Women in Melbourne. This hospital had the distinction of being staffed and administered by women. She also worked for the Flying Doctor Service which brings medical aid to the remote districts of the bush, saving many lives and taking much of the anxiety out of the lives of bush mothers. She was enthusiastic about music, an attitude that would count with Miles.

Miles now joined Alice Henry in organizing the Women's Trade Union League based in Chicago. Alice, Miles and the rest of the group of devoted women had a battle on their hands. They ran into opposition both from employers who would be forced to pay more for their former sweated labour and to provide better conditions of work, and from the trade unions run by men. They were suspicious of women entering their field. It was a long hard pull.

We know so little of Miles in those years. I have seen no letters; perhaps, like Ignez, she had no time to write them. We have to turn to Alice Henry to get a glimpse of her work. Towards the end of her life Miss Henry was persuaded to write a memoir. In it she says of Miles:

> A close friend, in more lands than one, has been Stella Miles Franklin . . . She came to America and landed in Chicago a few months later than I myself did. We met at the home of a mutual friend where she was warmly welcomed as another arrival from that distant and most interesting country, Australia. . .
> Her ready pen, her fresh interest in everything, her initiative and easy adaptability made her a valuable addition to the staff of the Women's Trade Union League . . . When in course of time the League established its magazine, she became co-editor with me on "Life and Labour." Here she was thoroughly at home. With the Labour men she was always popular and could be depended on to draw them out and obtain from them opinions and information, which they could never have put so attractively themselves.[3]

In *The Trade Union Woman* by A. Henry published in New York in 1915 Miles gets a bare mention. "Stella Franklin, the Australian, for long held the reins of the National Office in Chicago." That is all.

II *The Mystery Deepens*

The little we know of Miles during her stay in America includes practically nothing of her private life, only her work. I do not think she was very happy. She was homesick. That is an endemic disease with expatriate Australians and her health was not good. She suffered from insomnia, that most depressing of ailments. There was something else the matter too; perhaps already her heart was giving trouble, for in a fragment of a surviving letter she says she has to spend fifteen hours a day in bed. She speaks of herself "struggling for self-support as well as for self-realization, with no encouragement for creative literary work . . . heavily handicapped by advanced political and other ideas . . ."[4]

We have to look to Ignez again for a possible key to her state of mind:

The days in New York were, in so far as the development of her special talents were concerned, wasted. She had fallen among reformers, and that for an artist is more fatal than for a merchant to fall among bandits. Her heart was frozen by her secret tragedy. There were five heavy, sealed years when in the anguish of her own loss she could not bear the performances of other musicians, days when she eschewed concerts and was separated from music. She suffered no personal neglect but lovers were never permitted to become paramours or husbands, and perhaps she was no more unhappy while the fever of self-sacrifice lasted than she would have been on any other track. The days were a turmoil of high-geared living and hard work.[5]

There is another reference along the same lines, a scrap of dialogue:

Laleen: "I have Ignez Milford's book all about Oswald's Ridges where we all used to live. She must have had time to write."

"Ah," said Freda softly, "she was wonderful, for she had no one to help her . . . but she went away and never came back . . . and she never wrote another book."

"I wonder why."

"She once told me that she could not afford to. She had to earn her living, and she mistakenly took up causes that devoured her."[6]

It is quite possible that Miles while interested in her work and giving it her best energies had still in her heart the aching pain of a frustrated artist. Perhaps she was writing in her scanty leisure. A book came out of this time—*Some Everyday Folk and Dawn,* published in 1909—and there is the mystery of the trunk full of manuscripts. Miles tells of their fate in the very valuable preface to *My Career Goes Bung*. The manuscript of *My Career Goes Bung*

was deposited in a portmanteau of MSS and finally left with someone in Chicago U.S.A., while I went to the world war . . . When I returned the caretaker said Mr. X had needed a bag and, as my old grip was quite out of fashion and contained nothing but useless papers, she had known I would be glad to oblige him. I was assured that Mr. X had put all the papers in the furnace. I need have no fear that they had been left about. I made no complaint, being as sure as the caretaker that my MSS were of no consequence. Nevertheless I regretted the loss of stories and plays which glowed at the time and which will not come again. I thought *My Career Goes Bung* had gone with this collection, and had forgotten the copy of it which survived in an old trunk valiantly preserved all the years by my Mother.[7]

When did Miles write these stories and plays? Did she bring them from Australia with her along with *My Career Goes Bung* or did she find time to dash them off while working with Alice Henry? I think, though I cannot prove, that they were written in Australia and taken with her and that the same applies to *Some Everyday Folk and Dawn*. Ignez could not write and crusade at the same time and I doubt if Miles could either. Perhaps she was too disappointed to try.

Some Everyday Folk and Dawn shows no trace of foreign influence except its glossary of slang terms translated into their English and American equivalents. This could have been added later. Surely something would have crept in if it had been American born. (This is a weak argument, I know.) It is the last of Miles's immature books and the poorest of the three. The ungainly title and the long, clumsy and emphatic dedication set the tone:

> To the English *men* who believe in votes for
> *women* this story is affectionately inscribed
> because the women herein characterized were
> never forced to be
> > Suffragettes
> their countrymen having granted them their
> rights as
> > Suffragists
> in the year of our Lord 1902.

The story is told in the first person again, but this time the "I" who remains nameless is an onlooker, an actress with a "broken heart" who is hiding herself in the little river town of Noonan. Noonan has been identified with Penrith which Miles knew well because her family had gone to live there. The picture of Noonan is obviously drawn from life:

The journey through the town unearthed the fact that it resembled many of its compeers. The oven-hot iron roofs were coated with red dust; a few lackadaisical larrikins upheld occasional corner posts; dogs conducted municipal meetings here and there; the ugliness of the horses tied to the street posts where they baked in the sun while their riders guzzled in the prolific "pubs," bespoke a farming rather than a grazing district; and the streets had the distinction of being the most deplorably dirty and untended I have seen.[8]

This dreary picture is softened by the river, idyllic amongst its trees, and the abundant fruits of the earth—peaches, grapes, tomatoes, rock melons, water melons,—all of the finest quality and scenting the air with their fragrance. It was a place of careless plenty and easy-going life.

Against this background a simple romance unfolds. I suspect that Miles decided to write a book that would sell, after her defeat with *My Career Goes Bung*, and put plenty of sugar into it. But she could not erase her nature or views. They keep popping out through the meringue. It is not a novel of rebellion but a little tale with a happy ending.

Dawn is an insufferable girl, nineteen years old, orphaned in romantic circumstances and brought up by her grandmother, Mrs. Clay. The girl is praised *ad nauseam*. She is beautiful, wholesome, maidenly, spirited. We have a surfeit of her "fine-spun hair," "rose and lily complexion," her "tapering fingers," "high-arched foot," her "dainty toes." She is "a princess in her own right, by reason of her health, her beauty, her youth and her honest maidenhood." "Dawn's judgements were remorseless, as becoming clean-souled, fearless youth as yet unacquainted with the great gulf 'twixt the ideal and real, and untainted by that charity and complaisance which, like senility, come with advancing years." [9]

The narrator is utterly charmed by her and promptly takes charge of her life. She meets a young friend, a visitor to Noonan, Ernest Breslaw, and marks him down for Dawn. He too has everything. He is an athlete and athletes, Miles decides, make the best husbands:

When his brawn is coupled with a good disposition, he sees in woman a fragile flower that he longs to protect, and measuring her weakness by his beautiful strength, is easily imposed upon. His muscle is an engine a woman can unfailingly command for her own purposes, whereas brilliance of intellect, though it may command a great public position in the reflected glory of which some women love to bask, nevertheless, under pressure of the domestic arena, is liable to be too sharply turned against wives, mothers, and daughters to be a comfortable piece of household furniture. On the other hand, the athlete may have the muscles of a Samson and yet, being slow of thought and speech, be utterly defenceless in a woman's hands. No matter how aggravatingly wrong she may be, he cannot bring brute force to bear to vanquish a creature so delicate, and being possessed of no other weapon, he is compelled to cultivate patience and good temper.[10]

That is a fine pickled cucumber amongst the sugar plums!

Ernest is allowed to see Dawn asleep and is of course immediately smitten with love. Dawn is not easy to win. On one occasion she throws greasy washing-up water over her suitor, not out of malice towards him but because she is over-wrought by the thought of what some women have to suffer at the hands of men. This is passed off as the natural action of a sensitive maiden. All is well in the end. Ernest fortunately has an opportunity to save Dawn's life and he is emboldened to propose by letter. Dawn answers him:

Dear Mr. Ernest—Your letter received. I care for you, but cannot give you a definite answer at once. There may be obstacles in the way of accepting your kind offer; if you will give me a week to consider matters I will answer you definitely then.
Yours with love,
Dawn.[11]

There are sub-characters and sub-plots and slabs of propaganda. Mrs. Clay is a variant of the grandmother-figure so often to be found in Miles's later books, a character: "Her stiffness, like that of the echidna, was a spiky covering protecting the most gentle and estimable of dispositions."[12] A young boy, Dawn's cousin, also being brought up by the grandmother, supplies comic relief. A visit to the dentist allowed Miles to indulge her vein of comedy. It is curious that Miles's books always date most clearly when she is being comic or sententious or romantic. These three elements are over-represented in *Some Everyday Folk and Dawn*. There is a sub-plot in which a girl is seduced by the revolting Mr. Pornsch and, conventionally, drowns herself. Dawn takes her revenge by tarring and feathering the seducer.

Nothing is quite so musty as a long dead political issue. In this novel we are given a lengthy account of an old style Commonwealth election in which women voted for the first time. This event, with all the controversy it aroused and a long dissertation on the future benefits to be expected from women's influence at the polls, takes up a large part of the book. The narrator comes to the conclusion that votes for women are a good thing but that since the quality of politicians is so poor, there is not much progress so far.

Some Everyday Folk and Dawn is badly written with stiff dialogue and more split infinitives than seem humanly possible. If Miles thought she could write a best seller by conforming to the literary fashions of the day without relinquishing her soap box, she was sadly mistaken. This book is now little more than a museum piece, interesting only in the light of Miles's future work.

Miles did not mention it in *Laughter Not for a Cage* nor did she ever talk about it, even to defend it. Although she knew Penrith it was not with the deep understanding she felt for the country of her childhood and early girlhood. Her tale draws no nourishment from the earth and is like something stranded on an alien shore.

Some Everyday Folk and Dawn seemed to exhaust her creative energy for years. Or did she wilfully turn her back on writing out of disappointment? Possibly she turned on herself the same treatment as she did on Sybylla Penelope—the self-inflicted snub. Miles always did seem to enjoy, in an unhappy way, taking herself down a peg or two.

What private life did she have in all those years in America? She loved the country so she must have been reasonably happy there. Did she write and write and stow the manuscripts away in that old portmanteau? She must have had friends. Miles could not live without friends. There must have been some content to her days besides work. She travelled widely in the course of her work and met "all America." Did she marry? That is, I think, most improbable. But she did come back wearing a wedding ring. Perhaps it was to protect her from the advances of stray males. One day, by implication, I referred to this ring. Miles was talking about men, what conceited egotistical apes they were, they thought the world belonged to them—that sort of thing. I listened, put out my hand and touched the ring. Miles snatched her hand away, flushed and changed the subject.

Miles never to my knowledge talked about her time in America or the later years during the war and in England. She could not be drawn out. She put down one of her water-tight bulkheads. It was as if, when she began to write again, all the years when she did not write ceased to be.

CHAPTER 6

Miles Goes to War

I *Boiling an Egg in a Top Hat*

WHEN World War I broke out in August 1914 Miles became restless. Perhaps she had been restless for some time. The war made a difference. Suddenly she was a foreigner in America. She had never taken out American citizenship. It was impossible to think of giving up Australia. Now she discovered that if she wanted to stay on in the States in war-time she must become naturalized. She said no to that.

Alice Henry wrote of Miles: "In 1915, a year after the great war broke out, something called her and she felt drawn to the service of the British race, with which the Commonwealth was so actively co-operating. She left for London." [1] Behind this bare statement I sense an absence of warmth. There may have been a quarrel. The two women had worked together for ten years. Alice Henry may well have felt that Miles was deserting their common cause. Also Alice had a very low opinion of war as a method of settling disagreements in a civilized world. She had already expressed her abhorrence of the Boer War in 1900. She could not be blamed if she thought Miles had deserted a cause that served humanity for one that destroyed. There is an air of complete detachment in her statement and no expression of regret followed it. Miles, on her part, may have come to the end of her reforming zeal. A sentence in *Back to Bool Bool* suggests this: "When reform no longer is fruit to the soul of the reformer, the reformer cannot serve reform." [2]

Miles sailed for England and at first helped in slum nurseries for small children and as a voluntary worker at Deptford. Then she joined the Scottish Women's Hospital Unit for service overseas as an orderly. The Serbian army was then in exile in Macedonia and the hospital was set up close behind the lines to care for the wounded and fight an epidemic of typhus. The army was in retreat, and the hospital retreated with it.

Miles must have had many strange, terrifying and pitiful experiences but she would never talk of them. If pressed she would say that she learnt to boil an egg in a top hat. Alice Henry in her memoir says that Miles wrote "most interesting" letters from the front. If those letters had survived they would indeed be "most interesting." Nor did she use anything from this time in her novels except in one paragraph of *Prelude to Waking*, in which she told how the heroine, Merlin Giltinane, had served in the Balkans:

Merlin, being a bright young woman, had achieved the Balkan fronts during some of the first great battles and retreats, and had been persuaded to collect North American funds for the Women's War Hospitals. This, she explained, took much more courage than to cross the Plain of Kossovo in a blizzard, to gather up human fragments under shell-fire around Bitolf, or to go on retreat from Ushtsche to Podgoritza over a trail where the howl of the wolves sometimes blotted out the sound of the pursuing guns, where the lorries decorated the sides of precipices, and where the weak dropped out continuously...[3]

It would be rash to take this as a record of Miles's war experiences. But the ideas came to her from somewhere.

Miles was not physically strong; it argues a great spirit that she undertook and carried out this hard and dangerous service. She did not have a very high opinion of her own courage. Long after she recounted a small incident. She went to visit her Aunt Ignes, then a very old lady.

Miles: "Auntie, dear, I'm sorry. I always talk too much."
"No!" said she firmly. "You were always a brave and clever little girl and you haven't changed."
I thank her for her generous "brave"—it comforts me, who am *not* brave.[4]

Perhaps Miles was thinking of a different kind of courage. Some pride lingered in her heart, for long after she was to write: "To save common New Zealanders and Australians from reflected glory certified Anzacs wore a brass A on their sleeve, a badge rivalled in rarity and renown only by that of the Scottish Women's Hospital Unit that had been on retreat with the Serbs."[5]

II *Retreat from War*

The war ended and Miles returned to London, not to Chicago. She carried with her for the rest of her life poignant pictures of the wastage of war and of its futility. She called it "the great idiocy, the unforgettable betrayal" and that "recurring lunacy called war." She had also some enigmatic things to say about the peace. For example:

The cat for which the masters of finance and industry had really engaged in the grand war to end war was wriggling boldly out of the bag. It was clear to him that his masters never seriously intended him for the pond; there was no stone in the sack and its mouth was loosely tied. He shook the bells on his collar inscribed Status Quo. He sat up and began to clean his face in readiness for a saucer of milk. Cream would come later. His owners did not see him as a scarred old warrior whom another Armageddon would remove from his position as the world's Top Tom.[6]

This means, I think, that Miles had come to the conclusion that the war had been fought, not for ideals as advertised, but in the commercial interest, and peace brought no improvement. Further on she makes herself still clearer:

... England, my England ... must forsake the fleshpots of imperialism. She could afford no more wars. The great war to end all others for the present had winded dictators, profiteers, warriors and other belligerent duds, had blued England's investments and loaded her with debts. Another such debauch would make her a has-been and a beggar.[7]

Miles was not yet ready to return home to Australia. She took up another form of social work with the National Housing Council in London. For part of the time she shared a flat in Kensington with Mary E. Fullerton, her friend Mrs. Mabel Singleton and Mrs. Singleton's monkey. She had corresponded with Mary Fullerton while in America and used to show her witty letters to friends. The two women remained firm friends until Mary's death. Mary Fullerton, who was an Australian exile also, had written a book, *Bark House Days*, under her own name and several under the pen-names, "Gordon Manners," "Robert Grey" and "E." Miles and Mary, a gentle soul, had much in common and now, I strongly suspect, Miles was writing again with all the pent-up fervour of the lost years. In 1924 and again in 1930 she paid short visits to Australia and on the latter visit had in her trunk a novel she had just finished.[8]

CHAPTER 7

Brent of Bin Bin Steps out of the British Museum

I *Miles and Brent*

IN 1928 the publishing house of Blackwood, in Edinburgh, brought out a novel called *Up the Country*, a Tale of the Early Australian Squattocracy by Brent of Bin Bin. Who, everyone began to ask, is Brent of Bin Bin? No one had ever heard of him. His only address was the British Museum. There were all sorts of wild guesses. A famous Australian poet, Dame Mary Gilmore, assured me that Brent was her brother. He had not told her so but she knew it from internal evidence.

No one at first thought of Miles Franklin. She had not published a book since 1909; she had left Australia in 1905. Then gradually the evidence began to add up and suspicion fell on her. It could only be suspicion at first because Miles had only published two books, both by now out of print, but when Miles produced more books under her own name and the Brent books increased to six there was enough evidence to convict her.

As it would be most convenient to settle this matter now, I must go ahead of the story for proof. Evidence of authorship is internal, external and supporting. The internal evidence includes style, vocabulary, background, subject matter, general attitudes; and one of the Brent books, *Cockatoos*, is so close a reproduction of Miles's own history and known feelings as to be conclusive. There is a strong similarity of style between such books as *All That Swagger* by Miles Franklin and *Up the Country* by Brent of Bin Bin. Listen:

For supper Bert hurried on ahead to light a fire and prepare a treat of hot johnny cakes, cooked on the coals. The dogs regaled themselves on kangaroo rats, and at dusk Bert stole up the creek to a swamp and returned with a fine black duck. The satin-green wing feathers were soon decorating the hats of the party. Bert had recourse to the fire to get rid of the remainder. He took a look at the horses, tied up one or two of the kangaroo dogs, and made a number of fires to keep away possible dingoes. Then he surrounded himself with his pack saddles and stores,—rolled in a tent fly at the flap of Mrs. Mazere's tent. The bantam was set between himself and her to be safe from native cats.[1]

and

The silent traveller lay through the first night in Annie Fullwood's best room. The party rose by candlelight and departed at dawn. The rain had ceased for a brief interval and along the ridges the lyre-tails could be heard singing anthems in their arboreous transepts. The returning rain silenced the heavenly choristers who still accompanied the procession for some distance, and then fluttered across the track and disappeared down the precipices.[2]

It is difficult perhaps to hear it in short isolated passages but in page after page, volume after volume, the similarity mounts up. I chose passages with dissimilar subject matter in order not to cloud the issue. The likeness and the cadences are there.

Miles had a very individual vocabulary using a lot of strange words and phrases. Some of them were old-fashioned, traditional to the bush and rarely if ever heard today. Others she invented. They run through both series of books. Here are some examples from Miles's acknowledged work: *combobulated, chrysalism, drivellage, feraboraceous, squashation, dumpeddes, comflummixed, tormentatious, opuscule.* Other examples are from the Brent series: *temerarious exodists, circumioluted pioneeristically, impavidly, stultiloquence, flutterbudgets, obanbrant, mulierosity, ramfeezled, hornstooggled.* Then there are common to both those bush sayings—*good iron wingey, bottle of smoke, raised under a hen, to jump off his pannikin, bogey, poking borak.*

The shared backgrounds of the two series supply more evidence. Two areas in Australia were part of Miles's youth and left an indelible impression on her mind and heart. One was the high Monaro country of Brindabella, stronghold of the squattocracy and where horses and cattle were bred, the other was the area round Stillwater, Thornford, called the Goulburn district. Here on poorer less mountainous land small farmers made a hard living.

In her acknowledged novels Miles uses the Monaro as background in what is probably the most important of her books, *All That Swagger*, and the Goulburn district in *My Brilliant Career*, *My Career Goes Bung* (with excursions to Sydney) and *Old Blastus of Bandicoot*. Of two unimportant books *Some Everyday Folk and Dawn* is placed in Penrith and *Bring the Monkey* in England.

Of the Brent series *Up the Country, Ten Creeks Run, Gentlemen at Gyang Gyang* and *Back to Bool Bool* are set in the Monaro, the last named with part of the action in Sydney. *Cockatoos* is located in the Goulburn district with backward glances at the Monaro. The action in *Prelude to Waking*, a minor work, takes place in London with a few nostalgic dollops of Australian scenery thrown in. All this can hardly be coincidence.

To pick up one point amongst many the same rivers haunt both series. To the immigrant: "Day or night there was no relief from the Morumbidgee, so lone and dark and far, with the voice of a ravening wind—thousands of miles of it until it met an unknown sea."[3] To the Australian born:

... the song of the Yarrabongo floated in as cool and clear as a sigh from paradise. Pool, observing the ethereal loveliness of the bride— old Jack's young bride—was carried by that song of the river back to the funeral of his own bride-to-be nearly thirty-two years gone. He remembered that river song for ever. All this crowd and heat and perfume and undercurrent of strain brought a sense of unreality, only the faint cool music of the river remained.[4]

Both series are inhabited by the same sort of people—squatters, small farmers, bush characters in great variety. There is the same type of humour in incident and characterization, the same idealistic love of the Australian earth. There is the same diffuseness in treatment, the discursive, disorganized construction; similar lapses into stiff dialogue and obscure sentences; the same lift into poignant clarity in moments of tragedy, whether it be Brent's description of the drowning of Emily Mazere[5] or Franklin's picture of the utter loneliness of Johanna with her home burnt and her child dying.[6] The imprint of Miles is on them all.

It is clear to the perceptive reader that Brent is a woman, not a man. Her effort to write in the first person as Nigel Barraclough in *Prelude to Waking* is lamentable. The prevailing feminism is identical with Miles's brand of the same article; heroes and heroines all have the Milesian touch.

Names and events link the Brent books to the Franklin books. Incidents like Miles's mother's journey through the snow occur both in *Up the Country* as Charlotte's journey, and in *All That Swagger* as Della's journey. In *My Brilliant Career* we hear of family properties called Bin Bin East and Bin Bin West. Miles calls the Monaro town of Tumut Gool Gool. Brent calls it Bool Bool. And so it goes on.

The Brent book *Cockatoos* is as nearly autobiographical to Miles as her acknowledged book *All That Swagger* is to her Irish grandfather. As the Brent series progresses the cover of anonymity grows thinner and thinner. As for external evidence there is some of that too. Miles was annoyed when people asked her point-blank if she were Brent of Bin Bin but her canons of truthfulness did not allow her to deny it categorically. The handful of friends who were admittedly in the secret have never denied Miles's authorship outright either.

No one called Brent of Bin Bin has ever come forward to claim the books. No shred of private life has ever been pinned on him. No family has claimed him. It would be interesting to know into what account royalty cheques were paid. The publishers, Blackwood and Son of Edinburgh, kept the secret well. They also published *My Brilliant Career*.

Those who wrote to Brent at his table in the British Museum received answers. At least two reliable witnesses [7] corresponded with both Miles and Brent and they declare the letters from Brent were written on Miles's typewriter, a machine with various faults and tricks, and that both used the same type of flimsy paper.

An alternative to sole authorship is that Miles collaborated with someone else in at least three of the Brent of Bin Bin books. That is possible but no satisfactory person has ever been put forward as the collaborator. Mary Fullerton was the most likely. They were in touch at the time the books were written; Mary was an Australian writer of the bush school. Personally I do not think that there was a collaboration nor, if I am wrong about this, do Mary Fullerton's other novels suggest that she had anything to do with it. No, Miles wrote them all.

As early as *My Career Goes Bung* Miles was thinking of assuming a pen name: "In future I could have a *nom de plume* carefully guarded, so that my attempts could be taken on their own demerits without the impetus of scandal." [8] She had suffered acutely from the displeasure of her relations and the feeling of shame that this gave her. The wound was deep, the scar remained till the end of her life. Now after years of silence the compulsion to write was on her again and she planned a series of books set in the Monaro of her childhood and loaded with characters some of which may well be taken from life either directly or in composite form. She shrank from putting her name to such a chronicle. Even when she was seventy, and all the people she remembered in her childhood were dead, she could not bring herself in *Childhood at Brindabella* even to give place names correctly, much less to any of the people who thronged her pages.

This I think was the main motive for the subterfuge. There were others, whole layers of them. She had written three books; the first was successful and made a name for her but caused her so much pain that she never wanted to hear of it again. The second had been rejected by publishers and she thought the manuscript lost; the third was a poor effort. She never mentioned it, as far as I know. She may well have wanted to cut adrift her early literary history and start anew with a new name. Even success did not tempt her to reveal her secret.

Miles undoubtedly enjoyed mystifying people even when there was no reason to do so. I have already had something to say about this side of her character. You may well ask how the more than normally truthful, honest and forthright little girl developed this characteristic. I do not know, of course. But she did; it became part of her character to indulge in all sorts of minor evasions and deceptions. Her sense of humour was involved but it went deeper than a joke. It was Miles trying to hide even where there was no cover at all. She gained nothing by it and no dishonesty or any other sort of moral turpitude was involved.

There was nothing to suggest why she chose the pen name of Brent of Bin Bin. It had to be a man's name. It was a man's world and she was convinced that to pose as a man gave her a chance of success that would be automatically denied to a woman. "Bin Bin" was already in her mind. It may have been a code name for some place she knew. "Brent" has an American flavour and she may have picked it up there. The whole name suggests a squatter. It is quite usual to add the name of his property to a man's name; thus Miles herself writes of Mazere of Three Rivers. It always sounds like an aristocracy in the making, as one says Lord Montgomery of Alamein. That would appeal to Miles's romantic streak without offending her egalitarianism since it was ordinary practice. Finally, Miles is reported to have said that a mystery was a good advertisement and helped sales.

II *Saga*

Brent of Bin Bin published three books in quick succession. They were: *Up the Country: A Tale of the Early Australian Squattocracy* (1928); *Ten Creeks Run: A Tale of the Horse and Cattle Stations of the Murrumbidgee* (1930); and *Back to Bool Bool: A Ramiparous Novel with Several Prominent Characters and a Hantle of Others Disposed as the Atolls of Oceania's Archipelagoes* (1931). They represent the first, second and fourth parts of a saga. The missing books were *Cockatoos*, which was not published until 1954, the year of Miles's death, and *Gentlemen at Gyang Gyang*, published posthumously in 1956. They were deliberately held out of sequence because Miles felt her readers wanted to rest from the bush and the past. *Up the Country* covers the period 1830 to the end of the 1860's; *Ten Creeks Run*, 1870—

1895; *Cockatoos,* 1899—1906; *Gentlemen at Gyang Gyang,* 1926, *Back to Bool Bool,* 1927—1928.

It is a pity that Miles broke the flow of this great chronicle. She probably had reasons other than the one she divulged. *Cockatoos* does stand apart from the other books. It was written much earlier and later adapted to fit into the chronicle. *Gentlemen at Gyang Gyang* is also an old book brought up to date and in time it is almost a twin with *Back to Bool Bool*. I have thought it best to treat the books in chronological order—not necessarily the order in which they were written.

The five books of the saga form a whole as well as remain separate entities. Together they make a vast sprawling chronicle of life in the Monaro over nearly a century. It is, as the sub-title of *Up the Country* says, a tale of the squattocracy. When the saga begins, the first labour of pioneering is over, the station properties have taken shape, squattocracy is at its peak. Life is still hard and demanding; men must have courage and women must have more courage but a society has come into being. It is complete, touched with a bloom of idealism and memory. It has an appearance of timeless permanence but like dawn it cannot last and the chronicle traces the gradual destruction of the golden age. The pioneer families cannot keep their place, not even the Mazeres; they come down to being small farmers on poorer land and end up living petty lives in a suburb of Sydney. The descendants, the young, are scattered over the world, failures or successes, but all with haunting memories of the bush and deep-seated homesickness. Everything changes, everything passes, everything breaks. But life still goes on, following new patterns but unable to forget the old ones.

There are a great many characters linked together by marriage and neighbourliness, by needs and feuds. First there are the pioneer families: the Mazeres of Three Rivers; the Pools of Curradoobidgee; the M'Eacherns of Gowandale; the Brennans of The Gap; the Labosseers of Eueureunda; and the Stantons of Ten Creeks Run. About them cluster all the other characters—the men on the stations, the women in the kitchens, the townsfolk.

Nettie Palmer expressed the relation between author and characters with beautiful clarity: "Brent's angle of vision is that of some descendant of a pioneer family whose name is written all over the countryside he knows so well. Without having to read up genealogies or to fill notebooks in the manner of Zola, Brent can put up his hand and reach down any name like an apple from a low bough." [9]

There is no plot in the ordinary sense. The narrative winds and

Sarah Lampe, Miles's grandmother

Susannah Franklin, Miles's mother

Old Talbingo homestead where Miles was born

Miles, aged 4½ months

Brindabella homestead where Miles spent her childhood

Miles Franklin, aged 4 years

Miles with long hair, taken in Sydney

Miles Franklin, aged 17 years

Miles on horseback

Joseph Furphy who corresponded with Miles for several years

"Merry Maid Miles." Miles worked as a maid in Sydney and Melbourne

Miles in London with Percy, the monkey in her book *Bring the Monkey*

Miles (second from left) as a suffragette in Chicago

Miles Franklin in middle age

Miles at Grey Street, Carlton, holding sunflowers

Miles in later years in her "homestead" at Carlton, Sydney

Miles in old age

loops and circles about a thousand natural obstacles. The construction is, as Dr. Morris Miller puts it, "of the free sort." [10] Miles explained her own approach:

I find myself capturing a technique to retail the subtleties of Australian life and landscape. It seems to me that a story to be truer than reality (that mirage effected by grouping and selection) should follow natural contours and rhythms. A pulse artificially accelerated or extraneous outlines because of spurious conventions as to what is really "action" must be eschewed. The desultory style of pioneer settlements themselves should be suggested, growing up as they did to meet immediate need. An easy, unrazored, pipe-smoking-almost-casual method is needed. The old pioneer yarns "yarned" by the old bush grandads (with as like as not a grandma contemptuous of their inconsequences and deviations from original versions), rubbing their tobacco in their palms and holding up the climax (they mustn't have too much climax) to light and draw, have a charm as characteristic as their environment, but the assembling of a vehicle to carry that easily evaporated charm into print 13,000 miles away needs ingrained knowledge and patience.[11]

In the preface to *Ten Creeks Run* Miles offers an apology for her waywardness in construction:

I am faced by a patternless, trackless region out of which I must urgently beat my way like the early explorers, uncertain if I am merely going round and round, or right through or slipping out the side by a false route.

Her characters gathered around her. She reproached them: "You are not among those who have contributed ideas to human knowledge, nor have you taken the human race one flicker above the mud on that road to super-humanhood for which some of us grope." They protested "it's all a bottle of smoke in the end, and the end is before you can bally well get your pipe to draw decently..."

"'Hold hard!'" says an old philosopher, who has thought much in the solitudes:

"Is it real life here in this part of the world you're driven to make this blanky book about, or is it about some strange, unusual, far-away land, with kings and savages, or professors and millionaires, and other kinds of fantastic people?"

"It has to be set here in Australia, with none but you kicking up your heels and using bad language in the middle of the natural scenery."

"Well, then, it seems to me that all you have to do is yarn along and make us come alive just as we blooming well were. Let us drivel and meander like life itself. You have nothing to do with the way of our lives or the character of our performances ... If a funeral, or a marriage or a drought, or a flood, or a snake-bite, or a spree, or a broken leg was our greatest experience, that is not your responsibility ... You don't need to swell your head with shaping destiny or interpreting life according to those new-fangled blokes who never baked a damper, or felled a tree, or rode a buck-jumper, or killed a snake or a beast, or tanned a hide, or broke in a team of bullocks, or knocked up a coffin for a mate out of stringy bark, or drank water out of their hats. You just set us down on paper as we were without any of your own shenannakin." [12]

That is straight from the author's mouth. The organic discursiveness of the writing was then intentional. Miles modelled her style on her material; she gave it an authentic bush flavour by following the meanderings of a yarn. One critic adds:

To give significance to the yarning, and to add music, there is repetition of phrases, epithets (a trick from Homer?); the Mungee, for instance, flows always "like a sigh from Paradise," another river comes always "from the icy water where the eagles drink." The rivers run through the books like a chorus, indifferent and involved, witnesses that survive; they are time, are timelessness. Only human memory can try to hold against them. Talk, laughter, song—everything echoes and dies into silence, but the series ends with the Mungee singing its "immortal" song. [13]

But there is more to it than that. There is a dimly seen circular pattern. Event and memory repeat themselves. Fine threads of memory turn the circle into a cobweb. The death of beautiful Emily Mazere by drowning on the eve of her wedding echoes through the series: "as beautiful as Emily Mazere" the old hands say, Emily, the drowned forever enshrined in legend. The tragedy happens near the beginning of the trilogy, which ends in another drowning at the Mungee hole, but this time—in reverse—it is the fiancé of Laleen Mazere, who is the image of the lost Emily, who drowns.

Similarly at the beginning of *Up the Country* there is a description of how, on Philip's and Charlotte's wedding journey, Bert Pool sets up a camp and cooks a duck. It is the morning of the world. Long after, at her husband's funeral, old Mrs. Mazere remembers it. "I never forgot the duck you cooked in the earth, the little bantam hen in the cage you made, and riding in the rain with umbrellas. Ah, Bert, my boy, those days have gone forever." [14]

The effect is there, the reader accepts it because it is borne in on him, but unravelling all the devices by which that effect is achieved would fill volumes.

III *Up the Country*

Up the Country is often acclaimed as the best of the series. It is the richest and most complex. As Nettie Palmer puts it: "The fullness, the 'God's plenty' of that book, 'Up the Country,' was accompanied by a kind of bareness; there were many events, countless characters, and little development of these . . ."[15] There are so many events and incidents that there is not room in the book, long as it is, to develop any of them fully. Sometimes in a page or even in a line you have enough, if reasonably expanded, to furnish a whole novel. Miles found plenty of time for descriptions and for talk, the endless yarning and chattering of a vast miscellany of minor characters. The yarning and chattering forms a chorus reflecting on characters and happenings and throwing light on them from several angles at once. The descriptions are magnificent. For many people they are the best part of the book because they bring to life again a world that has gone forever.

There is the picture of a bush home, the homestead at Three Rivers, exact in every detail, and written with the clarity you always find in Miles's work when she conjures up a picture, perfectly remembered. It is not only that she tells you the plan of the house, the materials of which it is built and the use of every room but she conveys its orderliness, the near luxury even, that by good management and constant care has been created out of the simplest materials. Then there is the scene in the kitchen where the baking is in progress for Rachel's wedding. It is fully realized and lovingly detailed; you can see it and smell it.

Again it is Three Rivers being bedded down for the winter:

The crops had been gathered and sown again. The last of the apples and quinces had been picked and placed in fragrant hay in company with the pumpkins in the loft above the jam pantry. Vats of butter and a great row of cheeses kept house in the dairy with crocks of eggs pickled by Mrs. Mazere's own method, much esteemed around Bool Bool. Hillocks like burial mounds near the stables indicated the swede turnips and parsnips put down after the frosts had given them flavour. The potatoes had been sometime abed.[16]

Best of all, I think, is the arrival of the drays with a year's supply of provisions:

They reached Three Rivers and began to unload early in the morning, a time of bustling interest for the household. It was pleasurable to stow the cases of currants and raisins, the bags of white sugar and rice in the big ant- and mice-proof bins awaiting them in the store-room. There were chests of tea with queer Chinese characters on the strange paper wrappings, and a lining of lead, which later would be melted in a special crucible and poured into a mould to make bullets. There were straw mats in quantity of brown treacly sugar, delicious to the taste, that went to the rationing of the station hands week by week.

The women waited for the unloading of the cases of crockery, the men's slop clothing, the bolts of material, the medicines and seeds. Mrs. Mazere, particularly vigilant that small things like camphor, cloves, pepper, castor oil etc. should not get astray, while Mr. Mazere was eager for his negrohead and book. Even grey calico and needles and thread had a grand charm in such circumstances, and ladies' buttons were more beautiful and diverse than the beads of today. The children were gleeful when the tins of barley sugar candy arrived, and the crown of the spoils was the case of oranges which always came from Uncle Matthew and Aunt Jane at Parramatta...[17]

Many more words are expended on the descriptions than on events. When she comes to a crisis in her narrative all Miles's garrulity disappears. What has to be said is said simply and plainly and from this comes the sense of bareness.

It is not possible to summarize the story. It is, as someone has said, "like the billabongs of an inland river." It moves from episode to episode without much structure to support it, held in a far-flung net of personalities. It is as if this first book were a sort of quarry from which the blocks used in the following volumes are taken; it sets the tone for the whole, introduces the characters and provides the bouquet.

The action moves in loops. There are two main movements: the first comprises floods—Rachel's wedding—Mrs. Mazere's brave crossing of the river to help a neighbour; and in the second movement, Emily's coming-of-age ball—bushrangers—Emily's drowning. The wedding gets everyone onto the stage and the ball sorts them all out. From it springs most of the action in the rest of the book, the loves, the engagements, the heart-breaks. So little is drama considered that at one point Mrs. Mazere is left in a frail boat on the swirling, flooded river in imminent danger of her life, while the author breaks off to give a lengthy account of pioneering experiences.

Of all the characters, heroic and humorous, two stand out. Mrs. Mazere is the matriarch, the loyal wife of an irascible and unreasonable husband whom she nevertheless manages. "Men often thought they were master in their own houses when their wives were too motherly to undeceive them."[18] She was a superlative housewife and a tower of strength to all the women and children of the district. She was their doctor and their nurse. "They were probably correct in believing that she knew more and did more [than the doctor] and they were sure of finding her sober. She supplied them with linen and food and medicine from the provident store chests of Three Rivers homestead. Her liniments and ointments had wide fame, and in a later generation were the basis of commercial products."[19] She was the mother of beautiful daughters and rather unsatisfactory sons—they took after father, no doubt. She was tolerant and kind and above all courageous. Courage stood very high in Miles's calendar of virtues. "She had never croaked, but met each happening with faith and courage. She gave all who had known her a lot to live up to."[20] Her mantle eventually fell on her daughter Rachel Labosseer, who became the grand old woman of another generation. But Miles never loved her so well. She had a hard bright laugh.

The hero did not team up with the heroine as he usually does in romances. He was a man of another generation, Bert Pool, son of old Boko Pool, once a convict. He was handsome and brave, modest, even shy and a good bushman. All the maidens loved him. That this paragon was the descendant of convicts illustrates Miles's attitude towards these reluctant empire builders. Bert had always loved Mrs. Mazere's daughter Rachel who married Simon Labosseer. He had been engaged to Emily, her second daughter, and had lost her. Jessie M'Eachern and Mary Brennan had loved him to distraction. Jessie proposed to him at Leap Year. His gentle refusal mortified her so that she carried the scar all her life. With a glint of malice Miles took her hero down a peg or two. He is left a bachelor; Rachel, widowed, refused him, having had enough of married life. Jessie refused him out of pride. Mary had gone into a convent and died young. So Bert was left, for the time being at least, as the universal uncle.

The book ended with the death of old Mazere. Instead of "The End" Miles wrote "Interval."

IV *Ten Creeks Run*

The second book followed in 1930. It was called *Ten Creeks Run: A Tale of the Horse and Cattle Stations of the Upper Murrumbidgee*. If *Up the Country* was the richest, sunniest and most pleasing, *Ten Creeks Run* is the best constructed of the series. The narrative with its two main plots and one leading sub-plot is clear. It has to do with two marriages of May and December and the sub-plot is about a horse lost and found again. The setting is the same as in *Up the Country* and the characters are the same with a few new ones, like Ronald Dice, added and the Milfords brought closer into the picture. (They will be wanted later.) The action moves to Ten Creeks Run, the property of Jack Stanton, otherwise known as Skinny-Guts, or S P over J from his brand. From this it can be seen that he is not one of Miles's best-loved characters.

A great many characters mill about between the covers and each adds something to the narrative, a comment, a sidelong glance, a touch of humour. Nettie Palmer expresses this to perfection:

For this is clan life indeed. Nothing that affects one part of the group is without result upon countless others. Everything is known to people a hundred miles apart, and the complex story is told not only by the author's plain narrative but by repeated bursts of comment from two "choruses," one male—that of hangers-on, rouseabouts, horse breakers, and others round Ten Creeks Run; and the other female—that of Mrs. McHaffety, the mayoress who was also the hotel-keeper's wife in the town of the district, and her crony, Mrs. Jacob Isaacs. These two women make a piquant contrast . . . Usually, though, both the male and female choruses are chiefly valuable for their genuine elucidation of the matter in hand, whether some juicy, scandalous news, or some plan for a marriage or a mortgage.[21]

The book begins, as usual, with a social occasion, a horse muster; this brings everyone, human and equine, into the picture. The heroine Milly Stanton, S P over J's niece, is still a little girl not yet in her teens. Bert Pool is still the hero and Milly's adopted uncle.

One of two main plots concerns the marriage of Jack Stanton to Aileen Healey. He is middle-aged, she a beautiful but spineless young girl in love with the penniless Ronald Dice. Stanton wins his bride by the old old device of buying up her father's mortgage and putting pressure on him. She makes an apathetic wife and continues to see Ronald. One day while they are dallying together Aileen's baby boy wanders off into the bush. The country-side turns out to look for him. Aileen is crushed by grief and remorse. The child is found after hope has been abandoned and lives. That is the end of Aileen's philandering and Ronald looks elsewhere. Jack Stanton has discovered that the possession of a beautiful young wife has not brought him the happiness he expected. Their life settles into a humdrum rut.

As she grows up Milly watches this drama and is at first excited and then bitterly disillusioned by it. She is popular and Larry Healey is among her suitors. He has been involved in a scandal with Dot Saunders but Milly in her innocence looks on him as a good friend and turns to him in time of need. He goes too far in a bid to win her. They are riding in the lonely bush, Milly on Merrylegs leading another horse, Larry on Abracadabra.

But he was only a tiro Tarquin lacking the technique to play with his subject till the propitious moment. In his nervousness he blundered. As the girl descended upon his shoulder he crushed her to him, devouring her with kisses. Milly, stiff, a trifle weary, was angered and repelled and struggled from his grasp. She was not the least alarmed, only resentful that he should be guilty of such a breach of good taste and etiquette. In the course of moments it swept upon her that a demon had taken the place of her eager, pliant lover. This was no dream either but the reality of such a nightmare as occasionally tormented a girl of that period reared on the "complex" that most men were only kept from raids upon a maid's chastity by lack of opportunity. A spasm of horror shook her. Such a thing could not be.[22]

Larry tried to reassure her and proposed marriage then and there, on the next day.

His voice, proving that it was merely Larry and not some monster substituted by the night, had an electrifying result. Had she spoken she would have said, "You will, will you!" but no sound came from her. She could have screamed like seven among rocks and tree-trunks and nothing would have heard but the mopoke and curlews, the plovers and little wallabies. The kookaburras would have laughed and gone to sleep again. The marsupials, which had come out to feed in the dusk, sat up, arrested by the commotion and hopped away. The only light was the crescent moon, going early to rest, and for the moment placed like an ornament in the locks of a big gum tree. In an heroic moment fear and fatigue fell from Milly, and her being seemed to be transmuted into a white flame of rage that made the contest exhilarating.

They struggled. Milly bit Larry. Surprised he let her go. She mounted Merrylegs and fled. Larry rode after her crying: "Milly, don't panic, for no reason. I shan't hurt a hair of your head, I swear." Milly was now "out of herself with rage and revulsion, virginal frenzy against violation." She settled the matter by drawing out a hat pin and plunging it into Abracadabra's nose. "The introduction of that silver hat-pin altered the course of their lives."[23] Abracadabra threw Larry into a pit dug to trap animals and there he lay for days badly injured. Milly rode all through the night and the next day, headed for Curradoobidgee and Bert ninety miles away. Fortunately she had two "perfect horses."

Dawn found the girl and her trusty friends many miles on their way. At sunrise she toiled up the passage of the Wamgambril for two miles or so by a precipitous track to the famous Coolamon lying like a jewel at the base of the mighty rock, where the Wamgambril and the Coolgarbilli take their rise. Reaching the creek she changed saddles again and let her beasts have a mouthful of grass while she breakfasted on the fruit of a wild raspberry vine. Then on and on again by gully and spur with never sight nor sound of man, not even a wisp of smoke above a distant chimney, the solitude to her not at all distressing. The familiar birds fluttered and made music round her all the way; even during the night the little wagtails had never left her, tweetering all the time "Sweet pretty creature! Sweet pretty creature!" She knew too that Merrylegs was carrying her safely and directly homeward. It was the other thing that drove her unresting to Uncle Bert, the one of all who had sheltered her ever since she had been a passionate self-willed toddler. Uncle Bert, the great love of her infancy and girlhood, had never failed her spiritually, and would not cast her out now.[24]

Bert comforted her, soothed her, sent for a suitable chaperone and set to discover what had happened. He came back and Milly was waiting in quiet confidence. She knew now where peace and safety lay. She would marry Uncle Bert as she always said she would when she was a little girl. He comforts a child who falls asleep in his arms and when she wakes he finds he is holding his bride. The scene is well laid:

The old clock on the mantel ticked loudly. Queen Victoria in her girlish comeliness looked down upon them from above it, her consort by her side. A hen, feeling the moment auspicious, introduced her chicks to the flower-beds in the sunlight to be seen through the open doorway. She scratched like a hurricane, undisturbed. Cocky, dozing on a rail near the geranium-pots, screeched at the vandalism, and, waddling across the boards, hopped down the steps to investigate. No one came at his call, so he relinquished police duty and joined in the looting. Farther afield could be heard the cackling of hens, bad housekeepers these, late at their duties. Occasionally the moo of a cow, the neigh of a horse or the yap of a dog carried to the comfortable old room, arranged in bygone fashion, and a monument to the good taste of old Stepmother Pool. Such sounds embellished rather than disturbed the silence, and grew softer as the sparkling heat climbed towards 5 p.m.
Milly was sleeping easily, repose in every line.
Out through the open doorway was a wide rolling Monaro view, the road to Gowandale like an ivory ribbon running over a knoll, disappearing and reappearing and losing itself in the blue horizon of ranges far away. As the silence widened in the peak of the afternoon the lullaby of Pool's Creek drifted in like a far sweet wind faintly borne from paradise, and to Pool, this moment irrespective of all that had been in his more than sixty years, in spite of all that could be in the twenty or so more coming to him, was paradise unqualified.[25]

Bert was old enough to be Milly's grandfather. Her widowed

mother had hoped to marry him herself. Bert took his problem to old Mrs. Mazere, who thought the girl "over-young" but believed the marriage would work. Everyone came round to the same idea. It is part of Miles's skill that she could make such a union appear both natural and right. Milly was different and so was Bert. The unnatural and unhappy marriage of Jack and Aileen shows up by contrast the idyllic marriage of Bert and Milly. Jack was mean and Aileen spiritless, where Bert was generous and Milly spirited and brave. Larry in his slow convalescence had a change of heart. He remembered his responsibilities and married Dot Saunders.

The sub-plot ties the action together and runs through the whole book. At the horse muster we meet Milly's blue roan filly, Romp. Flash Billy, the horsebreaker, was furious when Bert Pool took her out of his hands to "gentle" instead of "break" her. He coveted the mare anyway. Some 120 pages further on, Milly, at boarding school, hears that Romp is lost and rushes home. The body of a blue roan horse was found at the foot of a precipice. Milly, not satisfied, got her proof when one of her admirers gave her an inkstand made from the hoof of the dead horse. "If this is so," wrote Milly, "the horse that was found dead is not Romp at all, and she is still alive somewhere. I am so excited. I could not be deceived in Romp's off-front hoof. It was small and double-banded and wide at the heel and smooth as a bottle. This bulges a bit like a cask that is going to burst the hoops." [26]

Romp was traced to a circus. Flash Billy had stolen her and Milly, believing in direct action, stole her back with the help of Larry. It was while taking Romp home by unfrequented tracks that the incident which changed all their lives happened.

The book ends with the funeral of old Mrs. Mazere: "There was something gallant in the last ride of the little old lady, of late stiff with rheumatism and age, swinging along thus bravely in accordance with her wish, something equally gallant and affectionate in her old friend officiating for her." [27]

The last word goes to Bert:

The song of the river was a symbol of continuity and of peace—with its memories of yesterday. For tomorrow, the immediate tomorrow—he looked down at the soft flower-like young face and tenderly pressed the little hand on his arm.
Milly. Thank God! [28]

INTERVAL

I have quoted freely from this book because it is, I think, in many ways the best that Miles wrote and only by quotation can I give you the true flavour of it or show you its quality of innocent romance. It is old-fashioned, even prim, but it has a spirit of gentleness and goodness, of something everlastingly valuable preserved with love.

V *Cockatoos*

Although not published until 1954 *Cockatoos* fits into the series at this point. Its first draft was written before Miles left Australia for America. Its original title was *The Outside Track*. When, in bush parlance, someone takes the outside track it means that he or she travels alone. For Miles it came to mean a hard and lonely journey through life. Why she changed the title I do not know; it is more attractive than *Cockatoos* and fits the subject very well. Possibly she thought that *Cockatoos* fitted better into the series as it focused attention on the whole group of characters instead of, as *The Outside Track* did, on one. Neither do I know how she went about adapting it into the Brent chronicle. Did she, for instance, introduce characters in the earlier books, the Milfords and others, in order to include them in *Cockatoos*? I think it more likely that she changed the names and some of the circumstances in *The Outside Track* and renamed it.

If *Cockatoos* does not quite reach the high standard of *Ten Creeks Run* in its genre, it is still one of the most sympathetic of Miles's novels. It is largely autobiographical and I dare Miles to contradict me. The scene is no longer the Monaro but Oswald's Ridges in the Goulburn district, poor country cut up into small dairy and other farms. The Mazeres and the Healeys had moved there from Bool Bool very much as the Franklins left Brindabella for Stillwater:

The Mazeres lived ... near the road that ran from Goulburn to Kaligda and Goumong. This family, as the Healeys, had come from up the country. Both had fallen to the rating of cockatoos, or farmer-selectors, through inability to keep on the higher ledge of squattocracy. The parents had known each other at Bool Bool, and their families were intertangled in the large clans thereaway. The Mazeres had tried to better themselves by shifting from the back regions of the parental holdings to the neighbourhood of Goulburn, where better opportunities could be expected for the young people. The Healeys had their own reasons, definite and private, for desiring to escape from Bool Bool and their relatives, and, having small capital, had landed on the poor property adjoining Mazere's.[29]

The Franklins too had hoped, and given as a reason for their removal, that the proximity of schools and a railway would benefit their children. For Miles and for the young people in this book the change was disastrous and bred frustration in their hearts. A bush school did not take the place of the rich life in which they had been embedded in the Monaro. Nor was a train a great advantage when they could rarely afford to use it. The loss of the grand scenery of the Monaro with its mountains and rivers was a factor in the young people's discontent.

When Miles wrote of the Monaro she was a romantic, when she wrote of Oswald's Ridges or 'Possum Gully she was a realist. Comic incidents in *Up the Country* and *Ten Creeks Run* only occurred in the lower ranks of society, simple fun like this:

Old Tom Saunders's prize dairy cow had been milked in the morning, and Diamond, son of Nanko, one of the aboriginal old hands, had requested a drink. He had been ordered to hold his hat. There was more than he could swallow; he passed some to his friend, Teddy O'Mara. It was also too much for him, and the silly creatures put on their hats, milk and all, with the result that their beards when dry were as if dipped in cold starch, and pursued by the flies like honey.[30]

Mrs. Mazere and her beautiful daughters were never never involved in incidents like this, even remotely. Neither were the Pools nor the M'Eacherns, nor the Saunders nor the Stantons. Mrs. Brennan being stout and Irish was exposed to a little fun when being hoisted onto a horse but it didn't blind the reader to her gallantry in going to the aid of a friend. Farce in Miles's novels is class-conscious.

When old Mrs. Mazere died Miles lost some of her interest in the Mazeres. They went down in the world, as is quickly illustrated in *Cockatoos* by the comic incidents that are allowed within the sacred precincts of the family.

While Mrs. Healey was lime-washing her fowl houses, Blanche, the eldest Mazere girl, was doing the same to the Mazere dairy, and her mother was carrying water from a dam some hundred and fifty yards distant in the effort to save her pot plants. Allan, the second boy, was feeding a miserable poddy on swill thickened with pollard, and allowed the handle of the bucket to slip over its ears. The calf bolted with a terrified bellow; Allan doubled with laughter to see it collide with a fellow sufferer; as it ran blindly in another direction Mulligan the dog and Billy the pet lamb joined in the chase. Dick, the eldest son, who was chopping wood, dropped the axe and ran after the trio.

As the calf passed Blanche with boys and beasts in pursuit she seized its tail and hung on till she brought it to a standstill.

"Poor little thing, it's a shame to run the flesh off it" she said as Dick released the shabby trembling creature.[31]

This is in the style of Steele Rudd who at the beginning of the century was exploiting every possible comic accident on just such a poverty-stricken farm.[32] It is also very much in the tone of *My Brilliant Career*, Miles's own rebellious reaction to life in 'Possum Gully, alias Stillwater. There is too the same pity for the calves. The background has beauty but no majesty:

The low rough hills southward ranged up with the miles from Healey's property to a view of Lake George, where all was blue, the water shading into the hills, the hills into the ether in soothing loveliness. From Bongonia to Jingera, from the Tidbinbillas and Coolgarbillies of the Murrumbidgee to the South Coast stretched an area warm and brilliant from prolonged drought, haunting, unique in the blue haze of distance, but acre by acre it was a piteous scene. The droning autumn winds lifted the dust in whorls, the little dam beds were dry and cracked, many water channels empty, paddocks as bare as roads, stock without condition to face the winter. Those animals still able to lift themselves staggered round the water-holes, famished and moaning.[33]

No rivers sing. In the Monaro, idealized by memory, no drought ever came. Oswald's Ridges also is country Miles remembered from youth. It takes on the colour of her frustration and rebellion just as the Monaro is drawn from pictures of happiness and affluence. The drought scenes are reminiscent of *My Career Goes Bung* but better done.

The Mazere daughters of the turn of the century are very different from Rachel, Emily, Fanny and Rhoda in the 1850's. With the exception of Sylvia, who after all does not live on Oswald's Ridges but with her grandmother in the Monaro, they have no glamour at all. Blanche is an "over-anxious girl" preoccupied with household duties and getting a husband. The latter activity never found favour with Miles, and Blanche suffers for it through two volumes. Phillipa is a kind, silly creature as unloved and unsought after as Blanche. Sylvia is the beautiful one, "like Emily Mazere, the drowned," and she is allowed to have her romance, but not for long.

The book is well supplied with heroines. Sylvia is in the glamorous tradition, and Freda Healey, "a little girl in kip boots splashed with whitewash and an apron of sacking over her frock,"[34] is being groomed as the heroine of another book. The real heroine is Ignez Milford. Her name, we are told, is pronounced Ee-nith. (Miles had an Aunt Ignes, whose real name was Agnes. It is doubtful if she pronounced it Ee-nith.) She bears a striking resemblance to Miles herself. "Oswald's Ridges was indebted to

Ignez Milford for adding spice to the daily round. Her lively and unconventional ideas caused commotion among tamer fowls." [35]

She wanted to study music, piano and singing, as Miles did. "Her parents, as a great concession, sent her to Oswald's Ridges to learn the piano from Mrs. Healey. She sat beside Ignez for some weeks, but Ignez speedily discovered that her teacher had not the musical knowledge to see or even the ear to know when her pupil was playing other works than those placed on the piano rack." [36] Her parents considered two guineas a quarter for music lessons in Goulburn was too expensive. A teacher with cut rates was found. The question of a chaperone was raised.

The only dangers to which Ignez was open in her attempted musical training were artistic. These were so grave that she was foredoomed to defeat, but she and those around her were all so abysmally innocent of what any muse demands of those who would follow her that tragedy did not yet cast its shadow. Now sixteen the girl had a singing voice of extraordinary depth and resonance that filled her adolescent head with dreams.[37]

Like Miles her talent was ruined by bad teaching and the complete incomprehension of its worth of all around her. Her throat was injured by faulty training and the only possibility of cure was an operation in Paris.

Ignez had other gifts. With Dick, the sensitive member of the Mazere family, and little Norah Alfreda she started a school of writing in a bush hideout. They wrote and criticized one another's writings. This innocent pastime was discovered and the worst interpretation put upon it by Blanche. Out of her abundant energy and to ease her unrest Ignez wrote a book, just as Miles had done.

Life in the Ridges eddied in semi-circles and relapsed into stagnation until another stone was flung into it. Ignez one day received a parcel by post. When she opened it she was startled as though a figure had stepped out of a dream and confronted her in broad daylight. Before her were six books all the same. She turned them over and read on the cover:

NITA

That had a dizzying effect.
Inside the cover was:

NITA
The Story of a Real Girl
by
Bryan Milford

Astonishment shook her. Fear sickened her. It could not be yet it must be her own book! She opened the cover.

Chapter I
No Make-believe.

Horrors! It *was* her book!

Ignez shivered and went cold with shock. She had long since lost consciousness of the story. It had been shed far down the track like a chrysalis.

Trembling she peeped into the pages. All the notions she had scribbled down, half in fun, half in protest, to read to Dick and Norah Alfreda were here petrified in print. Real, and yet so unbelievable. She had imagined that a book would be transformed into conformity with other books and was dumbfounded because all the things she had striven to make different remained so, strikingly. Writing that book had been a kind of shouting at the top of her lungs into an uninhabited silence. Seeing the shouts in cold print was like discovering that the silence had all the time been full of listeners. This was confounding. She was helpless under the ordeal. If she had been informed that *Nita* was to attain print she would have withdrawn her. There was no one who would really understand her fresh disaster. She had learnt to dissimulate her feelings and to take all her terrors inwardly and alone.[38]

The book was a nine days wonder, almost a scandal. Ignez felt her privacy torn away.

In all her troubles Ignez had a faithful friend in Arthur Masters, one of the very few successful farmers in the district. He loved her but without hope. He knew that she was not for him but in the meantime he was glad to be her protector, loyal and true. Ignez liked him but she never thought of marriage with him, or with anyone else. Hers was a free, aspiring spirit:

Suppose by some horrible mischance she should find herself married to a man of Oswald's Ridges, and clamped down to this for ever. It frightened her as a bad dream; as a bad dream it fled. These people's minds had no wings—hers could range far like an albatross. Day-dreams, sprouting from inwardly sprouting potentialities, counteracted the short-comings of Oswald's Ridges.[39]

Ignez, like Sybylla, went to Sydney and she too fell among the "right people," particularly Moray Delarue, a name which should have given an innocent girl pause. He played with her affections.

"Could you love a man so much older?" He knelt on the hearth rug and drew her to him. "Come, tell me." She was serious and spoke without coquetry. "I shall never marry anyone."

"Little sleep-walker, don't you like kisses?"

"That would be wicked, wouldn't it?" He could not be sure whether it was the firelight or a smile on her lips. "Who said that kisses are wicked?"

"I thought everything entertaining might be." The humorous ripple was clear this time, and the long, curling eyelashes lifted.

"I want to keep you always" he murmured, as a thousand lovers were declaring, even the shopworn. Could he have seen into her heart, she was more defenceless than he could have grasped. The knowledge derived from first kisses and Milly's information was but a morsel in the jungles she had to travel alone because of her hyper-fastidiousness, her abnormal sensitivity.[40]

News of a financial disaster wiped Ignez from Moray's thoughts; he was like any other man.

These passages of love do not ring true; they are a novelist's stock-in-trade. It was matters other than *amour* that reduced Ignez to despair. Compare the paragraphs just quoted with those describing Ignez's feelings on receiving the first copies of her book and you will see which are sincere and which are phony.

Ignez went home; her visit to Sydney had been as unprofitable as Sybylla's. It was all over. "But robbed of the emotional release of her voice life was as dull as beggary to Ignez though she was too young and healthy to be hopeless. Over the seas and far away glamour still shone."[41] She tried to write again. "There followed much disappointing effort. What she wrote was not what editors or publishers expected. She diligently tried to please these mentors and her work lost life and originality."[42]

Ignez at last, like Miles, set out not to conquer the world, but to see what could be saved from the wreck of her careers. At her departure she extracted a promise from Freda that she would bring her her troubles first as she had gone to Milly, Bert Pool's Milly, with hers. Ignez was the girl who never came back. Dick too longed to be gone and finally escaped. The Boer War lured away other young men of the district: Wynd Norton to his death; Archie Munro to marriage far from home. Isabel Mazere died, Sylvia married. The pattern was broken, the characters scattered.

Cockatoos is a sad book. Everyone is frustrated and comes to grief. Ignez is irreparably hurt by life and with all her promise achieves nothing. Arthur loses Ignez and has to make do with second best. He is haunted by the memory of her. Freda, or Norah Alfreda as she is called in childhood, is unhappy in her home life. It shatters her to find that Norah and Alf, on whom she had looked as her "real parents," had only adopted her to avert a scandal and that Dot and Larry with whom she feels no kinship are her father and mother. She too escapes overseas. Blanche, who had hoped to marry Arthur, becomes each year more bitter and warped. Sylvia dies young. Poor clumsy Bridget Finnigan breaks her heart when Wynd is killed and no one even notices. Larry Healey trudges on through his hard dull life with his nagging wife; he too once had promise. If anyone comes out of it well perhaps it is Richard Mazere, who when his wife dies, marries a bouncing school teacher.

Cockatoos has much in common with *My Brilliant Career* and *My Career Goes Bung* but is more mature. There is the scenery, the drought, the spirited and rebellious young girl who writes a book and is horrified by the shock of seeing it in print. There are the visits to Sydney, the satire on society, the machinations of the sophisticated man about town. In *My Brilliant Career* Sybylla has to go to the pub to bring her drunken father home. In *Cockatoos* Ignez must do the same service for Larry, but here our sympathy is enlisted for the sensitive badgered man who takes refuge in drink when he can no longer bear the conditions of his life. Ignez, however, is a more lovable character than Sybylla. Sensitive, spontaneously affectionate, always willing to help, she has little in common with the spirited egotistical girl whose career went bung. *Cockatoos* is dedicated to Sybylla: "Salutations to Sybylla Melvyn the legendary and temerarious."

The book is circular in construction. This was a favourite device with Miles; apparently she found it satisfying. The action is securely tied in. The novel begins:

Larry Healey was ploughing. His horses were hidebound and weak, and the earth was caked like cement. Broken it took the thirsty winds so that the ploughman moved in a suffocating cloud which filled his ears and nostrils and at times obscured the beasts from sight. Some of that virgin dust did not resettle, but floated high into the air to waste far and wide on the Pacific. For several seasons past the seed had been decoyed above the ground by occasional showers, only to wither before reaching the ear, and Healey had pondered for a fortnight whether it would not be wiser to feed the grain to the starving stock than again to waste it in the earth.[43]

It ends on the same note:

All day long Larry Healey followed the plough and the birds followed him for the grubs that were dislodged from the caked earth. Birds were with him continually—magpies, butchers, and an occasional kookaburra. He was soothed by their pleasant companionship, though he was noting the immutable cruelty of life in the weaker falling prey to the stronger. The season was lean again. He guided the plough up and down the arid lands hoping that there would be rain with the new moon. At the top of the slope he spelled his attenuated hidebound animals and, taking a view of the clear cold sky, wished to God it would rain.[44]

The author should have the last word. She wrote in an explanatory note:

The young author wrote this story contemporaneously with the happenings involved . . . Here are people really young. Time stops still around them for a moment as for figures seen through a stereoscope. They frolic in the spotlight of their own egos in the centre of the floor while their elders are relegated to the side seats. They are surrounded by the idiom of their day and a background of current events and opinions. Caught in the net of adolescence untarnished or unfurbished by Time's perspective they struggle in a maze of inexperience against defeats, hopes, dreams and despairs, normal but so poignant and tragic at their time of life. . .[45]

VI *Gentlemen at Gyang Gyang*

With *Gentlemen at Gyang Gyang: A Tale of the Jumbuck Pads on the Summer Runs* Miles has moved out of the past into the present. It is set in 1926 or thereabout. But the scene is still laid in the Monaro; the summer runs are the mountain pastures to which sheep, the Jumbucks, and cattle are taken in summer for the superior feed that they offer. Gyang Gyang is the name of a bird, and in this book the summer run leased by Sylvester Labosseer, son of Rachel and Simon, is named after it.

Miles is never really happy writing of the present day, or that is my impression. Nineteen twenty-six was the present for her although it is fast becoming our past. As she moved into the present she felt more and more impelled to take a satirical view of life and happenings. This will become clearer in the last book of the series, *Back to Bool Bool*. In *Gentlemen at Gyang Gyang* she puts a brake on time. Amongst the immemorial mountains time stands still. Everything or nearly everything, is the same as it used to be in the golden age of the squatters. Men do not have a chance to grow soft. Miles may be said to have retreated to the mountains to make her last stand for idealism.

This is not one of her important books. There is something makeshift about it, something unreal and manufactured. Compared to *Up the Country* it runs very thin indeed. It is not well written, apart from some highly quotable descriptive passages. The dialogue is stiff, the tale is novelettish.

The story, in brief, is this: Bernice Gaylord, an artist of great promise, left Paris where she had had a harrowing love affair, to stay with her godfather, Sylvester Labosseer, in Australia and recover as best she could. Gradually in the peace of the mountains she came to life and saw everywhere about her a new world to paint. She was re-born as an artist. The men about the place sat for their portraits and she recorded the life and work of the bush as it had never been done before.

There was a hero and a villain. The hero was Black Peter Pool, related to that hero of heroes, Bert Pool. He was not, by the way, black-skinned, only black-haired and bearded. The villain was Ced Spires, and a thorough Victorian rascal he was too. Both men fell in love with Bernice, with her strange beauty and withdrawn air. Peter was himself an unconscious artist, a woodcarver. He had a past, a very innocent one, and it made him shy with women. His "spontaneous male delicacy"[46] was so great that he modestly fled from the sight of Bernice drying her hair.

Ced Spires was of different metal. When he found Peter was his rival he blackmailed him with his past. He pressed his suit on Bernice:

His face paled with the stress of passion, but it did not touch Bernice. She had her scorching in that fire. No matter how touching its pretensions or ravages might seem she knew it for the wolf it was; when stripped of its false glow, as cruel, as selfish, as relentless as the breath of the Arctic.
She spoke harshly to him: "If you are discussing irregularity, it does not interest me. I am as old-fashioned as Eve there, and subscribe to the doctrine of monogamy." She even said on one occasion: "You presume, Mr. Spires."[47]

He tried to blackmail Bernice with a reproduction he unearthed in Sydney of a nude she had painted of herself, as Lady Godiva, when under the influence of her sophisticated lover. This was too much for the chivalrous Peter who fought and almost killed Spires. He survived to be trapped into marriage with a girl of bad antecedents and worse character. Bernice had practically to propose to Peter. They married but her career was not affected. Peter gave up the bush to live her life. The reader feels that sooner or later she will devour him.

This book may well have been an early one which Miles adapted for her Brent of Bin Bin series. If so, she did not do as good a job as she did in *Cockatoos*. She did not have the same personal stake in *Gentlemen at Gyang Gyang*. The main reason for disappointment is that the characters are not sympathetic. They lack warmth and reality. Bernice is not a typical Franklin heroine; Miles does not love her. Even if she is as "old-fashioned as Eve" she lacks the embattled purity of the genuine heroine. There is nothing of Miles herself in her. She is little more than a peg on

BRENT OF BIN BIN STEPS OUT OF THE BRITISH MUSEUM

which the story is hung and to which Miles hitches some of her favourite hobby-horses. Peter Pool, for all his excellent "press" and Miles's adulation, does not come alive. He is quite impossibly noble and the reader is apt to tire of him. The minor characters, Beardy Tom, the Dude, Mona, Doll and the rest are better done and certainly talk more naturally.

The value of the book is in its background and its Australian rhythms of life. The mountains are pure, untouched. It is a landscape of hope. Here was the new beginning and the men who inhabited the country. Ced Spires excepted, took on its virtues. Bernice reflected:

> The place was apart from the centres of art, from the ateliers of Europe and their gossip, their scandals, their conventions of unconventionality—and their men! Ugh! She was filled with sudden nausea to remember the soft-handed, sex-sated *flaneurs* fond of a bed and of . . . Of course, some of them had panned out well in the war, but the men at Gyang Gyang underwent a war training twelve hours a day, six and a half days a week—seven in emergencies. She compared the man who had rent her existence with Peter of the piratical beard and terrifically blue eyes.[48]

There is local colour enough, a plague of caterpillars, fly-strike, a sudden mountain storm, and the tale of the snowed-in sheep. The cattle were mobilized under Bluey, a bullock, to trample a path through the snow so that the sheep could be rescued and brought out. There is genuine bush lore here but there is not enough of it to save the book from its pervading triteness.

VII *Back to Bool Bool*

In *Gentlemen at Gyang Gyang* war was declared between the bush and the city. One of the characters, a squatter named Oliver Burberry, thought he would retire to the city and take his ease but it did not work:

> Good lord! I was like a cockatoo in a cage . . . There isn't a blasted thing to do in those beastly suburbs. Nothing but that infernal idleness that rots a man and among a crowd of bally imbeciles who don't know a gummy ewe from a two-tooth wether, or a heifer from a cow, or a store beast from a fat, when they see it. . .
> Dull is no name for it. It is hell and damnation. It's no use, a man who is used to handling sheep all his life, the gambling with them and the pleasure of seeing them all white and clean from the shears—even the worry about drought or flood or flies and strikes—he can't do without it, that's all, or if he tries to he won't live long, I reckon.[49]

This is the theme, or one of the themes, of *Back to Bool Bool*. The worst has happened and the cavalry has been unhorsed; the remnant of the Mazeres has left the bush and gone to live in the suburbs among the "bally imbeciles." *Back to Bool Bool* is set in Sydney but with (about two-thirds of the way through the book) a pilgrimage of all the characters back to Bool Bool and their origins. The Mazeres have come via Oswald's Ridges to the suburbs. As I have already pointed out, Miles grows progessively tarter and less idealistic the further she gets from the High Monaro. The sub-title and dedications by their obscurity should warn readers that in this book she is a long way from the sweet romance of *Up the Country* and *Ten Creeks Run*.

Back to Bool Bool is described on the title page as "A Ramiparous Novel with Several Prominent Characters and a Hantle of Others Disposed as Atolls of Oceania's Archipelagoes." The meaning of "ramiparous" escapes me. It has nothing, I should say, to do with the breeding of rams. It may be a discursive way of saying discursive. Dictionaries have not helped me to elucidate it. The reference to the "Atolls of Oceania's Archipelagoes" may be Miles's way of saying that all men and women are lonely, cut off from one another by the salt sea. Miles was indulging in a little mystification and no doubt enjoying it. In moments of high tragedy, as the drowning of Emily Mazere,[50] or tender romance as those describing the love of Bert and Milly,[51] Miles's prose has a pure and simple line. When she descends from these heights and writes satirically it becomes coy and encumbered. The *enfant terrible* in Miles comes to the surface.

The dedication of *Back to Bool Bool* is intentionally provocative and is intended to throw some more darkness on the authorship of the Brent of Bin Bin books. It is dedicated:

> To M.F., but for whose loyalty and support this
> effort could not have thriven.
> To rare MSS. who nourished its inception.
> To D.C. who can keep a secret.
> To others to be mentioned later or excused as they
> stay or betray the course.

M.F. is generally accepted as Mary Fullerton, the Australian friend with whom she stayed in England. Some people believe that Miss Fullerton collaborated in the Brent of Bin Bin books, or at least in the first two. She was certainly in the secret. Those who think she shared in the writing take this dedication as a veiled acknowledgement.

A rare MSS. at first glance suggests an old manuscript, possibly belonging to the Franklin family, on which Miles drew for incident and atmosphere. This manuscript, if it exists, has never come to light, or, as far as I know, been referred to elsewhere. Miss R. F. Bridle, a relative of Miles, declares—and no doubt she is right—that M.S.S. stands for Molly Scott Shaw, a relative of Rose Scott, and adds that Miss Shaw knew the secret of Brent of Bin Bin but would not be drawn into expressing even an opinion.[52]

D.C. is identified by Miss Bridle as Dan Clyne, once in partnership with Miles's father on the Hawkesbury, later a Member of Parliament and Speaker in the New South Wales Legislative Assembly. His connection with Brent of Bin Bin is not at all clear. Others have thought D.C. stood for Dymphna Cusack with whom Miles was to collaborate later, but dates are against this. The friendship with Dymphna did not ripen until 1938 and *Back to Bool Bool* was written in 1929, published in 1931.

The last clause of the dedication contains a quasithreat along the lines of those connected with her secret diary, from the revelations of which friends and fellow-authors were to receive their deserts after Miles's death.

The period covered is 1928—1929 or right up to the moment of writing. Miles who was sentimental about the past was caustic about her present. For example take *My Brilliant Career, My Career Goes Bung*, the political parts of *Some Everyday Folk and Dawn*, and, to some extent, *Cockatoos*, though here her attitude softens to disappointment and youthful frustration.

To return to the contents of the book, the story it tells is a large and sprawling one. The "exodists" of *Cockatoos* come home again and with them several other expatriates not described in detail before: Molly Brennan, who first changed her name to Mollye and then became Madame Austra the famous singer; and George, who has returned from America and can do nothing but sing its praises. The only surviving Pool or Poole, as they became, is Sir Oswald Mazere-Poole, M.P., and he is not a tin-pot Australian Member of Parliament either but holds a seat in the mother of Parliaments, the House of Commons. Only Ignez does not come back.

The story begins at sea. The "exodists," those who fled in their youth to find a better world and more opportunity overseas or who simply ran away from the scene of their despair, are returning on two different ships. Madam Austra and Sir Oswald return in luxury as befits their success. Dick Mazere and Freda Healey, the little Norah Alfreda of *Cockatoos* who has now disguised herself as Miss Timson, the name of her foster parents, come back more cheaply in a small ship. Dick, now a poet and a sick, disillusioned man, does not recognize her but they strike up a friendship and feel that there is something special about each other. Freda's reserve, however, sets up an impalpable barrier between them.

On arrival Dick is claimed by his sisters Blanche and Philippa and half-sister Laleen living at Nanda, an unimpressive house at Ashville, a southern suburb of Sydney. Dick is suffocated by the household at Nanda, and so is the reader. Blanche was a tiresome girl in *Cockatoos* with her fussy housewifery and her aggravating air of self-sacrifice. Time has not improved her: she is still sorry for herself, still a martyr to domestic duties with only one answer to any social occasion—food. Miles, the little girl who hated crochet, belabours Blanche mercilessly. She is everything that old Mrs. Mazere was not, just as Sir Oswald is everything that Bert Pool was not. Philippa, who oozes loving kindness, is also a domestic tyrant. "Philippa literally battened on the housework . . . She shredded the beans to tatters, polished and unpolished the floors whether they were trodden on or not, immolating herself on the altar of restlessness with an unselfishness to try the nerves of a hippopotamus."[53] Together the sisters make an invincible team. "She and Philippa would have interrupted Bacon and Shakespeare clearing up the great controversy to press second helpings."[54]

The reader is treated to a great deal of inane conversation which builds up the picture of life at Nanda with Blanche in command, the stepmother taking the line of least resistance. Laleen, her daughter, rebels and longs for a fuller life, just as all the Franklin heroines have rebelled and as Miles herself did. The conversation may be true to life, bristling with prejudices and clichés, but that is no advertisement for it. It is a hair shirt on the sensitive Dick. Laleen is the one bright figure in these trite surroundings.

Over against Blanche is Mollye Brennan the prima donna who is her antithesis. She is built on the heroic plan. She has "strength and glory and godliness of person and song."[55] Miles asks, "Was Mollye's organ supertrained to be too big and dramatic, Mollye herself too heroic in build and personality?" We see her in action:

She passed out like an empress to execution in her fabulous gown and glittering tiara. She was so big and able she could toss off Brunhilde's battle cry as a recall number, as an average singer dispenses "Comin' thro' the Rye," but that evening she made it such a magnificently breath-taking yell that her audience was astonished by her dramatic ability.[56]

In a moment of relaxation: "Her strumming was such as an archangel might indulge in on a Saturday morning in some private celestial cubby while St. Peter was superintending the spring cleaning of the public music room." [57]

Perhaps Miles was laughing just a little at Mollye. But she was not laughing when she wrote:

Nothing in all human experience can be so intoxicating as the welcome to a great prima-donna returning to lay her wreath before her own people of her own far land after triumphs in the centres of art. Not that of a prince of a reigning house politically engineered; not that of a warrior over a road of the dead between an avenue of the bereaved; not even a sports idol can be so inebriating. It is for the ecstasy the singer gives and takes and withal a disarming fame far from legitimate opposition.[58]

Was Miles thinking of her own lost ambition to be a great musician at last to bring her triumphs home? When Mollye meets Bernice, that other great artist, their hands touch and "That fleeting manual caress was enough to fill every interstice of the day with babbling radiance." [59] That, however, is not one of Miles's happier sentences.

Mollye is there larger than life; Freda is more elusive. We do not know what she looks like. She is the intellectual; on her lips Miles hangs a number of her own opinions. She is intelligent, quiet, firm of purpose and pure of heart. Under the assault of love she is like a little girl. Her innocence has nothing to do with age or with experience of life. It is part of her. She had an "incurable disgust for marriage." [60] Freda is born to be lonely and recognizes it.

She was too self-contained and inhibited. Her heart might break with love and longing, but she would dissemble it to the death, never confess her love unless it was sought; thus with many lovers, and she supremely desirable, love passed her by. She wanted too perfect an adjustment of circumstances and personalities and eligibility. Love was a blossom to bloom for love more than to be plucked by the lover. Only thus could love be shriven, only thus deserve love's fulfilment.[61]

Miles does not use the word lover in a technical sense but as a synonym for admirer or suitor. Freda is a typical Miles Franklin heroine and a variant of Miles herself.

Laleen Mazere is the young girl eager for life and for love. She asks: "Isn't there any real and lasting love—not ever?" and Freda answers her: "One kind of love is only a delusion of animal magnetism, a *fata morgana*. Sometimes when its glow has dimmed, two people miraculously find themselves enjoying a sweet friendship and continue in companionship—they are blessed."[62] That is not what Laleen wants; she still believes in the star of romantic love. Also, like Ignez and Sybylla and Freda, she longs to escape from the petty life that hedges her in. Even Dawn[63] and Dora[64] had hankered after a larger, freer life.

Mollye, Freda, Laleen are all Franklin heroines. Mollye and Freda had escaped to the big world. Mollye had returned with laurels thick upon her, Freda with empty hands. Laleen broods on escape but is willing to settle for the golden apple of love. All in one way or another are frustrated and brought low.

Miles is never as successful with her male characters unless they are oddities whose peculiarities can be caught in a lightning sketch. Then, as we have seen, she can be very witty as their expense. In *Back to Bool Bool* there are three main male characters. Sir Oswald Mazere-Poole is a figure of fun. He is a man of the world, unfaithful to his wife, pretentious, a stuffed shirt. His fortune is built on sweated labour.

His father had had enterprise to invest in what in its day was the greatest cheap-jack business in Sydney. Social workers had condemned it as a feminine sweat shop, but royal fortunes have been built by sweating women. The Grilling Bros. strategy had been to employ girls under sixteen for half a crown a week, keeping a few harried permanent seniors to train them. As soon as the girls were of an age to command higher wages, they were dismissed and a fresh crop took their place.[65]

This must have come straight out of Miles's American case book.

Dick is a poet, delicate, sensitive, wounded in the battle of life. His marriage in America has fallen apart in a humiliating manner. His hands are empty too. He has come home because he longed for the sight and smell of his native land.

Nat Horan the pianist, Madam Austra's accompanist, or as they say today associate artist, had come up from the Melbourne slums. He was ambitious and music came first in his life. He has fitted himself with a polished and sophisticated mask.

These six characters are caught in a net of emotion, mocked by life and brought to naught. Mollye falls in love with Dick. He is horrified. She proposes to him. He faints. At last he finds escape into the responsibility he owes his young daughter in America. Mollye beneath her scintillating triumph is cut to the heart. Freda loves Dick too, and Dick, Freda, but they know that marriage is not for them. Sir Oswald Mazere-Poole tries to seduce Freda, the poised, the clever, but he comes up against the young girl still hidden in her heart and beyond taking her to dinner makes no progress.

> What a vulgar situation! She did not want to surrender. *She did not know how!* She was as reluctant as a girl of eighteen, but at her time of life, and supposedly veneered in sophistication, she could not assume vestal airs.
> She did not desire Sir Oswald, with his prominent eyes and teeth and fat neck and middle aged spread. And the ugly little old pub! Ugh! Is this what was prized as the greatest adventure in life?[66]

Sir Oswald's attempts at seduction flop badly. Freda reproves him in a manner that Queen Victoria would have approved. "Such doubtful exploits are not for us. I should be ashamed if any gentlemen with whom I had a friendship should ever be less a gentleman because of friendship with me. Drugged hours grow stale and poisonous." [67]

Laleen falls in love with Nat Horan and he, finding that a paralysis in his hands will soon extinguish his career as a concert pianist, proposes marriage to her. She is radiantly happy but not for long. Nat is drowned is the Mungee water-hole as Emily Mazere had been so long ago.

The other characters are largely stage properties or thumb-nail sketches of people to fill the canvas. Here is Judith Lawrillard, the actress: "She was pathetic and willowy and shrinking, with her great eyes and twisty sensitive mouth. She looked a cauldron of society emotions and the composite heroine of smart novels of Mayfair life." [68] This is an example of the sort of character Miles could not draw. She is more successful with James, a familiar of the Nanda household:

> James was a tall lean man with a consequential bellow, an uneven stare, and a name for large eating and much talking. He enjoyed a reputation for business acumen in the Nanda household, where they had none themselves, or they should have been wealthy . . . He was a York Street farmer of some sort. He was trying to impress Freda, but she had outgrown his type of arrested mental development years since.[69]

This is life-like and acid. In Sydney dealers in agricultural products have their offices in York and Sussex Streets, hence the phrase "York Street farmer." It is a term of contempt here; they are the middle-men who make profit out of wheat, butter and the like, without knowing anything about their production or understanding the farmer's outlook or hard work.

The action in *Back to Bool Bool,* as in most of Miles's novels, moves in jerks from one occasion to another. There is the family reunion with a great deal of trivial talk faithfully reported, and much food (Miles, abstemious herself, had little sympathy with heavy eating); Madam Austra's concert; Bernice's studio party; the opening of a memorial park; and so on. These occasions bring all the characters together. Two-thirds of the way through the book the mass-return to Bool Bool acts as a catalyst. They all go back to their pioneer origins and the beauty and reality of the bush purges the artificiality of the city.

Sydney is that "sheltered blood-sucking city." It is riddled by human greed. The bush is uncontaminated. It cared nothing for man and so he could not spoil it. Even the pioneers left only small traces on its vastness. "Coming again, the wanderer found nought of that effort but mayhap a few alien trees among the stately scrub, a post, a mound that once had been a hearth, and the great wilderness was still unconquered, still undefiled."[70] Man could sink into its vastness and its silence and be comforted. It is even reassuring to know you don't matter.

Dick, as the most sensitive character, realizes poignantly the eternal quality of the bush:

All that was permanent here was the river and its song to the brooding ranges. The unutterable, immutable beauty of that swiftly flowing river! The breath of it rose at the approach of sunset, celestially cool and inviting, its song a sigh from paradise.[71]

He was circuitously nearing Coolooluk, where all the waters sang and where the Mungee river leant on the hills, the hills leant on the sky, the sky leant on eternity.[72]

Dick's return was balm to him. "To sleep to that river song, like wind if wind could be motionless; to sleep with its lullaby running through his dreams, his dreams to be dreams of peace; to wake and know it was the river, was heaven to him."[73] Here, I think, speaks Miles the insomniac. Did she invoke ". . . the river rushing past for ever in wordless song like an untamed wind of triumphant, unearthly beauty?"[74]

In this, the last book of her saga, Miles shows all her faces; she is in turn the idealist, the sad disillusioned onlooker, the satirist, the romantic, the little girl who never missed anything, the *enfant terrible,* the campaigner, and Miles. The book suffers from having too much of everything. There is certainly too much soap-box oratory. By the time she wrote *Back to Bool Bool* Miles was no longer an active feminist. There was no need to be. Women in

Australia at least had full civil rights, the vote, the right to work and to exercise their talents in the professions. The unions had recognized them as workers and the law protected them. The large families of the Victorian era with the consequent strain on the mother were almost a thing of the past. Her cry here is fewer people and a better life:

Take the bilge about the sacredness of human life. The race would be better if most children and their parents were dropped overboard. It would be a greater thing if the last far continent could be preserved till man has some plan of regulating numbers. He is on the plane of deer or kangaroos, a nuisance when he becomes too prolific. The motor car has superseded horses and camels. On some of the out-stations they are shooting hundreds of horses, as well as camels that were once £60 per head, to save grass for more profitable sheep. The world can only healthily use so many men . . . A man has to secure a licence to keep a dog but any moron can have half-a-dozen children as his right though society has no opening for them. This fuss about the virtue of hordes to devour products so that a few manipulators can make vast profits selling to them is an ante-diluvian notion and works like a snake swallowing its tail. Neither Big Business efficiency nor combines nor war can much longer retard the evolution of a better system, so I don't want Australia filled with a repetition of Europe or Asia. There are very few people for whom I'd displace the gentle kangaroo or the regal gum tree.[75]

There is something facile about all this. The will to shock is there, but where now is Miles's egalitarianism? Politically Miles still stands in this book very much where she is in *Some Everyday Folk and Dawn*. The theory of democracy is good but the politicians who implement it are poor stuff. "The political debate exposed the absence of statesmen, the limitations of local politics, all politicians."[76] Perhaps if you could only read one book by Miles Franklin *Back to Bool Bool* would be the best to choose. It is characteristic in so many ways. All her virtues and all her faults are there, but you would not be bored.

CHAPTER 8

Miles Takes up her Other Pen

I *Episode with a Monkey*

IN LONDON Miles had the pleasure of a monkey's acquaintance, in fact she lived in the same house with him. In 1931 she published in London a book called *Bring the Monkey*. It is witty, gay, amusing, original, slight and unimportant. It is a satire of a satire of a satire, a thriller to end all thrillers. Jewels are stolen and a man is murdered. To add piquancy to this the murdered man is a policeman.

In the manner of many good detective stories the action takes place at a house party in the country, in England of course. The house belongs to Lord Tattingwood, Swithwulf George Cecld St. Erconwald Spillbeans, the sixteenth baron. Michael Arlen would have been hard put to it to think up a better name. His seat is called Super Snoring. This noble lord won a Victoria Cross in the Boer War "by standing at the head of a pass and pitchforking the enemy over his head with a bayonet, or some equally highly esteemed military feat."[1] Shades of Childe Roland and Leonidas!

The guests included Ercildoun Carrington, the narrator; Ydonea Zultuffrie the film star (who had "the hardiness and simplicity of an aspidistra in her freedom from any need for privacy. She was of a school to whom privacy is concealment and what should any decent person have to conceal?");[2] Jimmy Wengham an aviator; an elephant hunter; a film magnate with a big nose—"an imposing thing carried altogether too far" and bearded inside which thickened his accent;[3] Captain Stopworth, the handsome policeman who was keeping an eye on Ydonea's jewels and Lady Tattingwood's heart; Zarl Osterly, a beautiful and witty woman much sought after by the gentlemen. She was the scourge of the menfolk; many were called but none were chosen.

The monkey belonged to Zarl.

I beheld a creature the size of a half-grown kitten, only more slender, an appealing, shrinking mite that tried to creep out of sight under Zarl's furs. He shuddered and showed his teeth in a piteous grin, as if I were a big baboon that would demolish him. I can never resist any animal, even the so-called human ones, if they appear distressful, and I took this poor little soul in my arms and attempted to stroke his fur, but he shivered through every fibre at the slightest touch, and looked so woebegone that I was instantaneously and permanently enslaved.[4]

His name was Percy Macacus Rhesus Y Osterley and he stole the show. Ercildoun was a "coolie on the end of his string."[5] She wrote, "When the cruel, self-indulgent character of human association with animals is considered, it is profoundly touching that any beast or bird can be so generous and brave as to treat one as an equal and a friend."[6] Percy is, in truth, the only real character in the book. To Zarl go the epigrams "Only a bad publicity merchant fouls his own limelight"[7] and "Marriage is the colossal example of carrying love too far."[8]

The story has many twists and turns, red herrings and false scents. It reeks with suspense and comes to a dramatic end. But no one would mistake it for a true-born thriller. Miles has a heavy hand with burlesque and here she is burlesquing a theme quite foreign to her genius. She herself called *Bring the Monkey* "a light novel." It was published in Australia in 1931 by the Endeavour Press, a subsidiary of *The Bulletin*.

II *Old Blastus*

Old Blastus of Bandicoot, first published in London in 1931, with the sub-title "Opuscule on a Pioneer Tufted with Ragged Rhymes" is the perfect type book, displaying in compact form, if not at their highest, Miles Franklin's qualities as a novelist. It began life as a play but was later rewritten as a novel. It is romance with a big R and humorous trimmings. Local colour is abundant and the setting is in "the blue and timeless splendours of the *Murrumbidgee* Ranges"[9] in the days when beards called "hirsute adornments" were funny because they were going out of fashion and motor cars were comic because they were just coming in. *Old Blastus of Bandicoot* is situated at the junction of the beard and the motor car.

The main story is of the feud between the rival pioneer families in Lindsay and Barry. Lindsay had climbed socially, aspired to Parliament, changed the name of his property from Dead Horse Creek to Chesham Park, sported an overdraft and neglected his fire breaks. William Barry—called Old Blastus, from the favourite word in his vocabulary, and Bandicoot after his property—remained a plain man, prospered and was meticulous about his fire breaks.

Their enmity dated from a time when Lindsay, in desperate

need of money, showed the city-bred bank manager a paddock full of Barry's prize merinos and raised a loan on the strength of them. Barry failed to see the humour of the situation and resented other people's mirth. The quarrel was fomented by Barry's suspicion that Lindsay was mustering his clean skins and became irrevocable when Sid Lindsay seduced Mabel Barry and abandoned her in favour of her maid.

When the book begins these events are well in the past but Mabel is still expiating her guilt. She was thirty-seven, looked older and had become the household drudge. Sid had been disinherited by his father. Barry's sons had migrated to Queensland to hide their embittered heads and the Barry family had banished itself from society. The scandal was a welter. Mabel herself "was the one person forgotten whilst the others fought it out." Dora Barry, born after the scandal, was the only person in the neighbourhood who knew nothing of it. She thought Mabel's son, Arthur, was her brother. Nevertheless it blighted her young life because her father never let her out of his sight and the whole household was marshalled to protect her virtue.

The inevitable happened. Romeo met Juliet. The dashing young Ross Lindsay was thrown by his horse almost on the doorstep of Bandicoot. The hospitable conventions of the bush forced Old Blastus to take him in. It was weeks before he could be moved and by that time, despite all parental precautions, Ross and Dora were indissolubly in love. They continued to meet secretly. The Lindsays gave a ball to which the whole neighbourhood, except the Barrys, came. Ross persuaded Dora to slip out of the house after her parents were asleep and ride away to the ball with him. Her youth and beauty took the occasion by storm. Ross entreated her to marry him. Her brother Bob arrived unexpectedly from Queensland, having come to his senses after twenty years and decided that Mabel's lapse was no longer a valid reason why he should do without his true love, Kate Lindsay.

All was going merrily when Old Blastus arrived. Mabel had discovered Dora's absence and roused her father. He brought his stockwhip. " 'Hussy!' he cried, 'is this where I find you? I'd sooner see you in your coffin',"[10] and he threw Dora violently to the floor. In the mêlée Dora learnt for the first time of her sister's shame and her whole world fell crashing to the earth. All she could think of was fleeing to Queensland. But there was no time for lamentation. While the whole district had been revelling, a bush fire had broken out and everything was forgotten in the battle to save Chesham Park. Old Blastus, hero of the occasion, organized the final victory. The description of the fire is very spirited and dramatic. The common cause cleared up the old feud; Old Blastus received the reward of his heroism when the grateful neighbours presented him with a motor car. A visiting notable, in search of local colour was brought to call on him by Lindsay. Old Blastus decided that his family could now re-enter society. Bob married Kate; the families were reconciled. Only Dora remained bowed down with shame and it looked as if she would go into a decline. But even her difficulty was solved. It occurred to Mabel that there was still something to be saved from life. She decided to marry her steady but unromantic suitor, Concertina Mick (who knew that she had a nice little hoard of egg money) and, with him, leave the district for ever. That concluded the matter as far as everyone was concerned and Dora was able to marry her Romeo. Like Dawn and Milly, Dora marries for love. (This is a concession, from Miles.)

That is the plot; it is a typical one. However, it is much better in practice than in theory. Dora is a figure of pure romance, cherished and adored by her author just as Dawn had been. We see her first: "An arresting figure of young womanhood . . . Galloping in the breeze and blazing sunlight had made her delicate cheeks fiery red. She pulled off her neat felt hat and white veil showing a mass of red-gold hair, restrained in a heavy plait but escaping in shining tendrils around her snow white brow and ears."[11] Dora is spirited and innocent—a dainty rebel. She is a fetish and Ross is her golden boy. He is a little—just harmlessly and romantically, of course—the reformed rake, the lady killer caught in sincerity at last. These two occupy the centre of the picture and are the least important people on it.

In proportion as she moves out towards the periphery of her design Miles sheds convention and the book takes on individuality and wit. She swallows the camels of romanticism and strains out the gnats. She has a naughty wit, more than a trace of the *enfant terrible*. She delights to prick minor pomposities in her characters, sacrificing her story time and again to lay traps for her own people. She cannot resist a joke even if it is aesthetically inopportune, and yet apparently fails to see the comedy in situations she takes seriously, even portentously. To specify one touch of delightful, but perhaps unconscious, humour: when Old Blastus hears that Lindsay intends standing for Parliament he is incensed and exclaims: "I will not stand for a scoundrel like that being made a god of."

Characterization proceeds by a series of *bons mots* and sometimes they run away with the character they are meant to illuminate. It is patchy, owing apparently to changes in the author's intention. The juvenile leads are put on a pedestal out of harm's way and remain consistent, but Old Blastus himself suffers a gradual change from figure of fun into hero. He is not dramatically conceived but is used by the author alternately as butt and hammer. He is the butt of her wit and her militant feminism, a comic figure: "His head was naked as an ostrich egg in a slight nest of bleached grass."[12] He was so mean that he sat on the verandah of Bandicoot homestead with a telescope spying on his hands. To that end Bandicoot had been completely deforested: "Never a blackberry, briar nor castor oil plant remained to hide from view sheep, horse or man."[13] He was as rough as bags but modest as a violet where Dora was concerned. On one occasion Dora "sat down and crossed her knees exposing slim ankles which looked a picture amid her flounces. Father became pontifical: 'My girl, I don't want to talk about these things but never let me see you sitting in that loud way. It is the first symptom of a girl going to the dogs, like a fast woman, if she's immodest about showing her lower limbs.'"[14] Miles Franklin is, of course, taking a rise out of Old Blastus but there is just a suggestion that she is rather advanced and daring to do so, and that Dora is a "new woman" because she behaves naturally.

Old Blastus is the scapegoat of many male sins. His self-satisfaction is monstrous.

It never occurred to him that he was mean to accept so much work from Mabel and Arthur without wages. On the contrary he prided himself as an unsurpassed husband and father. He had not struck Mabel nor kicked her out upon the dreadful discovery. He kept both her and the boy ... They were free at the table to eat their fill without comment save Dora's animadversions upon the youth's astounding gastric capacity. They were clothed. In making out the list for his own dungarees, boots etc. he always provided a good supply for Arthur, and his wife purchased Mabel's dress requisites with her own. After the first outbreak he had never directly attacked nor abused Mabel. His roarings were no more directed at her than at Dora, the darling, only in Mabel's case they fell on a wound that never healed, on her own count and her boy's.[15]

Mabel's situation would be pathetic were it not grossly overemphasized to belabour the thick-skinned male. Old Blastus oppressed Dora also in a different way and from a different motive. He treated her like a doll and so almost deprived her of the hope of normal life and happiness.

If the luckless man is exhibited as bully, he is also shown up as coward. "Father rumbled like a Hereford bull but acted as obediently as a trained dog."[16] His quiet, rather colourless wife was more than a match for him. "Mrs. Barry had an unerring facility in deflation."[17] Their marriage was a success because although she could manage him expertly, she was a thoroughly commonplace woman. "As a rule men prefer inferior wives. The superior can be so uncomfortably super-toploftical." Dora too was quite a match for her father and given the context of a good family disagreement could rake him fore and aft with her raillery. Mrs. Barry, in her leathery way, quite enjoyed family rows: "Mother went to tickle her plants to be within hearing. The disturbance was going quite entertainingly. There were no radio sets in those days to bemuse the empty minds of the half-occupied housewives and rouseabouts. They were dependent on other pabulum."[18]

That is Old Blastus from the domestic angle. As a social character he is used for another purpose, to belabour his neighbours and show up their faults. Here he shines as the honest man, the good neighbour, the expert flock-master, the sturdy democrat—who nevertheless could be flattered silly by the visit of a titled gentleman. Old Blastus ends up as the sturdy pioneer, hero after all.

The book is at its best in its portraits of minor characters and in the picture it draws of the day to day life in the bush thirty years ago. There's the taste of the bush about it and it captures and holds some of the old ways and old words. It has a sort of intentional yet natural old-fashionedness that is not without its charm.

Old Blastus of Bandicoot then is a romance on which a tract has been imposed. It is sweetness garnished with tartness. It reveals a certain irresponsibility in character drawing, a poverty of invention which drives the author to fall back on stock situations, and a pleasant ability to portray the features of a world now almost lost. I have dwelt so long on it because it shows all the trends and ingredients of the other novels. It is, as it were, the palette from which they were painted.

III *All That Swagger*

Many people think that *All That Swagger* is Miles's greatest book. It is massive, running to 500 pages and covering four generations of men, from the 1830's to the 1930's. It was written in Australia in 1933, her first Australian-born book since *Some Everyday Folk and Dawn,* published in 1909. It is true that *Cockatoos,* in its earliest form, was lying somewhere in a trunk, but it was not to see the light of print until 1954. *Old Blastus of Bandicoot,* for all its strong Australian flavour, was written in England and so were all the Brent of Bin Bin books: memory sometimes shines more clearly from a distance. *All That Swagger* was offered as amends to her family. The dedication reads: "To the memory of my paternal grandparents whose philosophical wit and wisdom and high integrity are a living legend of the Murrumbidgee."

This book won the Prior Memorial award in 1936, a cash prize offered in successive years by *The Bulletin* in memory of S. H. Prior, a former editor. The successful book might be a novel or a biography or a piece of reportage. It must be Australian. Entries were sent in, as for a competition, under *noms de plume*. *The Bulletin* claimed the right to publish the winning entry as a serial or otherwise. *All That Swagger* was published in book form by *The Bulletin* in the same year that it won the prize.

The story opens in Ennis, County Clare, Ireland, when Daniel Brian Robert M. Delacy was eighteen years old. His father was a school teacher, poor but claiming gentility. There was little prospect for the boy in Ireland and he was land hungry. He was also in love with Johanna Cooley of Cooley Hall. Her family did not approve of a penniless, Protestant suitor, so the young pair eloped, married and sailed for Australia. Here is the first picture of Danny:

He stood before her, not yet eighteen, and the meagre stature of five-feet-seven-and-a-half inches wherewith to attack the wilds of the antipodes in bravura days of convicts and aborigines, before the explorers had finished their surveys. Neither had he the features of the classic heroes; a small pointed nose, a stubborn mouth, now full of ugly teeth, and later to be ambushed in an unmolested beard. But Johanna doted on his eyes, as blue as the heavens on the days when the salmon wait to go up; his hair with the raven sheen and as soft as floss silk; his forehead broad and full; his voice as deep and brave as a stag hound's.[19]

On the ship Danny met Mr. Moore, a well-to-do man going out to Australia to settle. He took a fancy to the boy and offered him a job on his property, Bandalong. Danny took it to gain experience. Then he obtained "a sliver of land on the Murrumbidgee" once granted to a convict who had deserted it after the drowning of his wife and child.

Johanna soon moved to her home, with her belongings on a slide. The early settler's heart sank as she struggled down the declivity to the rough spot without a road, and far from neighbours. Terror invaded her when she saw the wild river rushing past so near her door. She clasped her toddler against the mesmeric danger. The river had a long

MILES TAKES UP HER OTHER PEN

harsh name and was lined with uncanny trees, strangely called oaks, and clothed in green hair that was tormented by the breeze to the melancholy cadence of the banshee.

The new home was a wooden shell. The cracks let in the sun. Johanna found no bar on the door, and when Danny went out of her sight in the gathering dusk, she wailed that the bunyip would devour her and the child.[20]

They called the place by its aboriginal name, Bewuck. That was pioneering for Johanna, fear, loneliness, the struggle to bring up her children and to maintain some of the "elegancies" dear to her heart, even if it were only a linen sheet spotted by rain off a bark roof. This was only the beginning. The Delacys pushed out into the lonelier mountains, to Burrabinga. By comparison Bewuck had been civilized. And then tragedy:

No baying of dogs. No whuffing of Rover—part bloodhound—who guarded the children and their mother. Not a yelp from a cattle cur. Only the click of the disturbed plovers, and the vesper chortles of the master ironists tossed from point to point, taken up and repeated softly from afar, as in an orchestra—crescendo—diminuendo—da capo—coda.

No smoke above the chimney. The nearing homestead looked strange and small. Delacy's senses had to accept the impossible. The main portion of his home had vanished as completely as the fences and lakes that melt upon approach from the vast levels of mirage land. No woman nor children, nor black retainer, nor cow; only the voice of the wild river which deepened a lornness, ghostly and dismaying.[21]

The house was burnt down, their eldest child lost with it, and Johanna had made a desperate journey to neighbours carrying her dead child with only two aborigines, a dumb boy and a young girl to help her. Never could she forgive the bush for those days of anguish. For fearless Danny pioneering meant adventure. "Danny's courage was as inexhaustible as his energy. Johanna therefore merits extra consideration, as her fortitude was cold and stricken." [22]

Johanna suffered keenly during his absence . . . When the jackasses ceased, the dark fitted over the tree-tops like a night-cap and the boo-books hooted, or the native dogs howled, or the little booraby bears wailed like tortured children . . . Sometimes she wept, but Empires are not wrought, nor won, without the tears of the weak, ay, and of the strong. "Tears wash the eye," as the young Delacys later wrote in their copy books; and Johanna had fine, flashing eyes, independent of spectacles, to the end.[23]

The story is condensed, event hurries after event: the elopement, the voyage, the interlude at Bandalong, pioneering the wilderness at Bewuck and then at Burrabinga, a high valley in the mountains, two fights with neighbours who coveted his land, the adoption of the piccaninny Maeve, the rescue of a dumb aboriginal boy Doogoolook, the death of a baby, the salvaging of the horse Nullad-Mundoey to be the sire of a long line, Danny's accident and loss of a leg, the burning down of the house and the death of Kathleen Moyna; all this happens in the first seventy-two pages. This speed is kept up throughout the book. *All That Swagger* is not so much a novel as a quarry from which a hundred novels could be taken. To vary the simile, the story is like an avalanche gathering more and more characters and incidents in its impetuous flow.

The children grow up and their characters diverge. Gold is discovered and Danny goes to the diggings. There is cattle duffing and Danny bides his time. There is the comic interlude of Hennessy and the designing widow, and the bizarre one of the carriage that Danny buys for Johanna, to fulfil an old promise, and a hundred other incidents winding in and out of one another. There is a perfect maze of marriages. The grandchildren are born, grow up, marry and take over the stage. Johanna dies and Danny dies and the spotlight moves to Clare Margaret, the daughter of Danny's eldest son, Robert. She carries the rest of the book and her son Brian closes it. Where Danny and Johanna pioneered the earth he pioneers the skies. He flies back to Danny's country, the Miles Franklin country, and sees it with new eyes.

It was glorious weather in the heart of spring, warm and soft, the winds asleep. Up like a god, from the drome carpeted with dew-sopped grasses, which had come when plentiful rains followed the winter drought. The works of men shrank as the machine climbed into the rosy dawn. The receding dwellings resembled verminous incrustations flat upon the soil, the movement of traffic that of insects. Only the Pacific, blue abeam, and the roads stretching across and beyond the wide horizons retained their dignity. Along the best of the roads, old Danny and his Johanna had crept for weeks like ants under the mighty timber. Today in an hour or so, their greatgrandson sped the distance in the eagles' domain, a spot upon the sun. Below him a million acres cleared and paddocked danced in waves of light where scarcely enough trees remained to lend graciousness.[24]

All the action revolved about Danny so long as he lived. When he died some of the light went out of the book. It might have ended there, but the indomitable Miles went on for more than another 130 pages. She wanted to end on a note of triumph.

Danny's spirit lived on in his children and grandchildren and Miles wished to give him his immortality. Danny was the pioneer of pioneers. He not only had endless courage and drive but he had vision too. For him Burrabinga, a variant of Brindabella, was always the dream, and to possess it the highest attainment of his life. People would say today that this mountain valley was his Shangrila. It was a possession of the spirit in its peace and beauty, its solitude and purity. Danny was fortunate because he attained his dream; it never disappointed him. His son reigned there after him and the granddaughter, Clare Margaret, in whom his spirit shone most brightly, was born and grew up there. In an ever-changing life that was a fair share of immortality. The bush and its creatures were always ready and waiting to take back the land won with so much hard work. When Danny turned his back on Burrabinga for a moment of time "saplings sprang up in the orchard, holes were worked in the fence of the garden, and marsupials destroyed everything. The possums were always first to harvest the fruit." [25]

Danny paid a high price for Burrabinga; it lost him Johanna. She not only did not share his dream but she hated the place because of her sufferings there and because the new country never really became hers. She had given up Ireland and her religion, her father had cursed her and no member of her family had even written to her again. For what had she made these sacrifices? For a wilderness without any of the graces of life and for a man who asked too much of her courage and did not put her first in his life. She could say, "Och, if marriage were gone into knowing what thirty years would bring, most women, I'm thinking, would be nuns in preference." [26] Disappointed in Danny and his famous pioneering she set her heart on her son Robert. In her eyes he was perfect but his father saw his faults. This further opened the rift between them. She banished Danny to the "end room," the one that was, in homesteads, traditionally kept for visitors.

Miles's sympathy was with Danny not Johanna, though in a general way her loyalty was to women in the hardships of pioneering life. She drew the character of Danny in depth. "He triumphed by force of mind over body. With an 'Arrah, by damn!' he dismissed obstacles. 'The moind, the moind, it's all in the moind!'" [27] He was physically frail but by reason of his unconquerable spirit he surmounted all difficulties. His disposition contained the innocence of a pure heart, "as all through-going decency demands." He never even looked at any other woman than his "brave Johanna." He was fearless and no respecter of persons. "I'm free myself and would wish every jack-man, black and white, to be the same

—aquil before his Maker."[28] Pretensions never took him in, not even Johanna's.

He gathered lame dogs around him—Maeve, the child abandoned by her tribe; Doogoolook, the dumb boy; Nullad-Mundoey, the injured horse; Wong Foo rescued from the snow—and that at a time when Chinese were looked upon as a menace. Doogoolook and Foo were his constant companions "and the inimitable trio was long a decoration to the district."[29]

"'Sure, he's as big a swell as the best, and honester than all the others put together, only he's never concerned with houldin' on to schnobbery,' said the publican, one Hennessy, a big fat man of Danny's age."[30] As well as being a sterling and honest man Danny was a character. "Danny in his loose slops, clumping on his peg, was a leprechaun figure. He settled his hat full of leaves, with the chin strap jostling his pipe."[31] He went to meet his new daughter-in-law, sprig of a genteel home.

Josephine rose to meet a small figure in a soiled linen duster. His weather-beaten cabbage tree was buckled about his formidable pipe. Under one arm he had a peacock and under the other that gentleman's wife.

"Take the faymale, I'll be obleeged," he said to Margaret. He was then free to display the tail of the cock to Josephine. "Sure, me dear, I'm proud to welcome you as a member of me family. I've brought this beast as a fitting creature to celebrate such an event. Sure, I could lepp over your head this moment with pride."[32]

There is a picture of Danny in his old age:

Danny was becoming a worn-out pioneer. Empires rise on the unrewarded efforts of such indomitable individualists. Only a few of the many emerge to the ken of recorders to give new lease to tales of daring and fortitude. They pour out their strength and courage in taking new territory. They are givers. They provide lashings and leavings of raw material, or father the exploitable rank and file for the shrewder investers—the takers.

Danny, the ineffectual old pioneer, was to have his reward—if any—in a zest in life which did not stale until he was past seventy, and which sheltered him from all the ghosts and devils that invade the pillow of the complex and introspective. And he rarely had an ear-ache or stomach-ache; when a tooth ached he prized it out with a pen-knife. Rheumatism passed him without toll, indigestion was a stranger to him, though his most constant food was a cut from a salt round enlivened by mustard applied like treacle, a diet which had become a habit while he batched. The fiends of physical torture, finding his courage invincible under their first attack, were won henceforth to leave him unmolested.[33]

Danny is not without faults. In his loneliness he drank too much. He had little understanding of women. He alienated Johanna and in the end let her die without a priest. When he took his sons into partnership he gave nothing to his daughter Della. She was passed over. "Della had slipped into drudgery without anyone being aware of it. She was growing scraggy and her thin little hands were as rough as Harry's. She dressed in drab winseys or something equally cheap and depressing, was firmly embedded in spinsterhood, seldom mentioned, never discussed, unnoticed by anyone but her mother . . ." [34] "Della was of unbroachable maidenliness" [35] and "It looked as if Della might be an old maid—a failure and a disgrace." [36] But she, hard with anger and in the face of her family's opposition, married a man much younger than herself.

Danny too like the other pioneers of his generation had not yet come to an understanding of "a sensitive continent, gently fierce." [37] As a result:

No one thought of conserving anything. Men worked to the limit, grunting with effort. Women bore children without restraint and thought it God's will. When jellied, fly-blown backs had the sanction of society, there was no tenderness towards animals, no artistic and scientific realization that in Australia's living unique flora, fauna and avifauna were masterpieces beyond anything she can ever contribute to museums and galleries. Here was a wonder continent, a vast garden of Eden free from sin and disease, left intact by the aborigines. The aim was to rifle it, exploit it in greedy haste. People unable to project themselves beyond the ancient soul-case wrought for them by the inspired members of their race through a hundred generations in Europe were driven by their immediate needs to uproot Australia, to tame it into a semblance of familiar fields and towns. And there was abundance for all. Fire the forests, destroy them, man was merely an ant against them. Millions of square miles of the stateliest trees in creation remained. Exterminate Menura[38] for his tail regardless of his magic powers of mimicry. Snare and trap the possums, the kangaroos and all the marsupial tribes, droves of them still appeared. Nemesis was not in that generation, nor the next.

That generation earned by sweat, endurance and deprivation the right to a harvest of some kind, salted with a little swagger. It lies forgotten now, while a less-inspired host of exploiteers, without hard toil, reaps where the old hands blazed the track in sturdy if ignorant hardihood.[39]

The story of Danny Delacy merged in the story of Australian pioneering. The title of the novel is half ironical. In the 1930's when it was written, pioneering was very much the vogue. It was surrounded by an aura of bravura. Miles set out to show a true picture of what all that swagger meant in terms of life and effort.

We see what it meant to Danny who after all got most out of his pioneering because he was a dreamer. His son Robert came nearest to the figure of popular romance with his taste in smart horses and with his wife whose pretensions as a great lady of unlimited hospitality ruined him. William was the shrewd one, calm and cool; Harry, the almost transparent image of his father, doomed to failure. Harry's son, Darcy, who married his cousin Clare Margaret, brought that spirit to the vanishing point and died young. Danny's virtues are scattered through his many descendants and sink back anonymously into the soil.

When Danny died one novel ended and another began within the same covers. The first generation of pioneers was laid away, their sons and daughters were already middle-aged; the grandchildren were stepping out. The wilderness was thinned out and they had to face the Boer War and the 1914—1918 war. The Delacys were in eclipse:

"Big streak of fool in all the Delacys—riding horses no sane man would back."

"Yes, and spouting poetry without being drunk either."

"They were eaten out by loafers—worse than rabbits."[40] The new hero in this smaller world was Clare Margaret Delacy of Burrabinga "the lilting girl on the blood filly."[41] She had many suitors but she went gaily on her way. The only one she cared about was John Darcy Delacy who had nothing but two horses, a dog and a pound note. He went droving and came back a man with a moustache but no richer. He would have disappeared again this time for ever but Clare "took her life in her hands and voted for love and poverty."[42]

When all the linen was folded they sat together on the ironing table and swung their feet and talked to the lullaby of the river till the lantern went out for want of oil, and all the household was in bed. They had caught a gleam of the light of life and were exalted by its radiance. In it they ripened and laid plans within the fortress of their preference for each other for a partnership against the world at large.[43]

None of the family came to the wedding. Darcy and Clare battled for a livelihood on their small selection. Darcy literally worked himself to death, and Clare Margaret was a widow at thirty-three "in a battered hat and shabby coat . . . the quince blossom girlish beauty had left something of gypsy defiance in her unheeding despair as she stood by the filling grave, a sorely smitten woman, but clearly of fighting mind."[44] The link between these two stories of Danny and of Clare Margaret, apart from their relationship, is persistence. Danny held to his own road through every hardship, demand and catastrophe. So did Clare Margaret, and through her and her son the ultimate victory of the Delacys is achieved: the fine thread of courage held and could not be broken.

It is not easy to make a critical estimate of *All That Swagger,* nor is it necessary. It is a rich book and we should be thankful for that. To write it was a *tour de force*. It repeats the triumphs and the faults of the Brent of Bin Bin saga. It is another saga, a family chronicle, a chapter of national development. It is well sprinkled with wit and those period touches so dear to Miles. "Victorian draperies called for prestidigitation in handling but the need produced the virtuosi" [45] or "Masculinity leant heavily on beards. All the bushmen had beards. Some of the older imported men had theirs trimmed in hedges around the chin, or lawns under the ears. Others cleared a putting space around one or both lips, or the chin appeared as a bald hill in a jungle—diverting patterns to modify the affliction of a frowsty mane on the face." [46]

In its pages you will find pictures of an age that has gone treasured in the amber of Miles's imagination—old attitudes, old phrases, tangy talk in the idiom of the bush, the rich Irishry of Hennessy and his like, patches of bad writing, snatches of bathos, some scenes like Darcy's funeral movingly and beautifully written. This book has so much of life in it that it would be heartless to carp at its faults, like spoiling a friendship because of some small imperfections.

All That Swagger had a good reception from the critics. With the passage of time they have become more analytical and less enthusiastic. Cecil Hadgraft, a man one must listen to, wrote in 1960:

> The novel has been frequently claimed—and acclaimed—as Miles Franklin's best work. But many will prefer her first fresh and breathless effusion.
> The middle section of the novel is best: here she deals with persons. The last section is sociological and economic, as the first was historical. The danger in dealing with large conceptions, with visions of a national future, with idealistic panoramas, is the collapse into the bathetic on one side or an inflation into the pretentious on the other...
> Her work has been over-praised. One may dismiss comments... affirming that she is "one of the greatest of Australian novelists," as benevolent farewells: in writing obituaries, said Dr. Johnson, a man is not upon oath.[47]

To Miles herself it was an important book. Just as she put much of herself into *Cockatoos*, she put the story of her family into *All*

That Swagger. Her grandfather, her father's father, was the model for Danny. It would be a mistake to think that this novel was his biography. It is nothing of the sort. He was the tuning fork; Miles picked up the note from him.

There are many points of resemblance in facts as well. Joseph Franklin came from Ireland. He was the son of a school teacher. He worked first in Australia as the overseer for a man he met in the ship coming out. He took up land on the Murrumbidgee River. Burrabinga is another name for Brindabella, the valley amongst the mountains which Joseph pioneered and was to share between his three sons. Joseph too was lame.

Grandpa Franklin appears in *Childhood at Brindabella*.[48] It is a child's eye view but even there is a recognizable likeness to Danny.

Spring was near. Grandpa arrived to divert my attention. The horse muster was imminent and Grandpa still liked to be in it, if only thereby. His two elder sons said he was getting childish but his ageless wisdom was increasing and my father had great reverence for him. He was respected by all youths and outsiders as "the old gentleman." He had a resounding voice and an Irish brogue. It was claimed that he could be heard for miles out on the runs as he reproved the dogs or exhorted the ignorant colonials. He deplored their lack of conversational powers...

Grandpa was audible otherwise. He inhabited the end room and his pitiful limp resounded on the boards of the verandah. He had too a definite odour of strong plug tobacco, which he smoked all the time and sometimes enhanced by a toddy of rum.[49]

It is useless to ask which of the three sons Robert, William and Harry was Miles Franklin's father. The answer would be that none of them fitted the role. John Maurice Franklin may have had Robert's physique, handsome and tall, but Harry's gentle spirit. It was Harry who left Burrabinga for a poor farm in the south. He was the unsuccessful one, and his wife Josephine, competent and a lady, bears some resemblance to Susannah Franklin. She too had a piano. "Every man was proud of the chief article imported, Josephine Delacy's piano. It established Burrabinga's social standing . . . Even the bullocks had gained prestige through hauling the piano."[50]

Reading *Childhood at Brindabella* you pick up as facts many incidents used later in *All That Swagger*. Do you remember how Susannah rode to her old home through the snow for Miles's birth? Here we see Della, Danny's eldest living daughter, perform the same feat:

She took care of her home and husband until within six weeks of her time. Then she set out on a side-saddle, and her horse heaved and struggled under her all day like a canoe in rapids through snow which lay as deep as the girths, as far as Birrabee. She was bruised and fatigued but cheerful, as people are when making a grand gesture.[51]

So it goes on. Miles was on her home ground using family lore and vindicating all that she was and had been. It was, at several removes and well mixed with fiction, her family chronicle.

CHAPTER 9

A Mixed Bag

I *Adventures in Collaboration*

THE LAST big book Miles wrote was *All That Swagger*. She was not to do anything on this heroic scale again. It rounded off a period of intense creative activity. *Up the Country* was published in 1927; when it was written and how long it took to write I cannot exactly say, but between 1927 and 1933 when (according to the date at the end of the text) *All That Swagger* was finished, Miles produced or re-wrote the whole Brent of Bin Bin chronicles, *Old Blastus of Bandicoot* and *Bring the Monkey*. That is no mean achievement. Eight more books were to be published, four of them posthumously, but of them at least three, *My Career Goes Bung*, *Cockatoos* and *Gentlemen at Gyang Gyang* were written earlier and held back from publication. *Prelude to Waking* may well have been of an earlier vintage too and very likely was written at the same time or just before *Up the Country*.

The strain of writing so many long books in so short a time was considerable. Between 1927 and 1933 Miles wrote herself out; she was physically, mentally and spiritually depleted after such a great effort. The books actually known to have been written after 1933 are two collaborations, a book of criticism based on a series of lectures, and the reminiscences of her first ten years. They are not in the fullest sense creative.

Had the trunk full of manuscripts survived the furnace[1] we would probably have had more books from Miles's pen. She did not waste much. A rough draft of a book, a sketch, a play could always be expanded and re-written into a novel. Miles preferred working on old material to breaking new ground. She changed very little after writing *My Brilliant Career*. She matured but she did not alter. The same sort of raw material continued to appeal to her: she already knew her characters, her plots, her backgrounds, her periods of history. "It becomes clear," writes Ray Mathew, "that nothing since 1900, her adolescence, is real to her or can be accepted by her as reality."[2]

Miles had an early highly productive period in writing from, as she tells us, the age of thirteen until she sailed for America in 1905 at the age of twenty-six. Some of this time was ineffectively used because of immaturity but from an even earlier age she was using her eyes and storing her memory. She was sensitive and perceptive; the life around her made a sharp impact on her mind and emotions. She wrote from what she knew, not as young girls often do, from what she dreamt and imagined.

The early creative period was followed by a long fallowing. When Miles began to write again she was forty-eight and she had material for a spate of books dammed up in her mind. They all had their spring in her youth. The two periods of creative productivity were separated by more than twenty years, but as soon as she began writing again they joined as if there had been no hiatus.

After 1933 Miles was spent. She had no programme of reform to fill her time. She had more leisure to write than she had ever had. She was home in the country she loved. She continued to write but the books she produced were disappointing to herself and to everyone else.

Surprisingly, she turned to collaboration. Miles, I should have said, was one of the last people to make a success of such a venture. She was an individualist. She was into her fifties and set in her ways, both literary and personal. She had an idiomatic prose style that she could not, with the best will in the world, adjust to anyone else's writing, nor could anyone else successfully imitate it. It takes a life-time to develop a highly individual style, while the writing of correct prose can be learnt like other things by anyone with the advantage of education.

In 1938 Australia celebrated the Sesqui-centenary of white occupation. On 26 January 1938 it was 150 years since Arthur Phillip, the Captain-General of the first contingent to land and settle, raised the flag on the waterfront of what was to become the city of Sydney. There were extensive celebrations—processions in the streets, garden parties at Government House, memorial gardens opened, prizes offered. Every section of the community was drawn in and had its appropriate celebration whether it was thanksgiving services in the cathedrals or special race meetings. Interest in history and pioneering flared up.

A panel of writers was enlisted to bring out a volume in praise of pioneer women, called *The Peaceful Army*. Miles was on the sub-committee for this book and wrote an article on Rose Scott, as a pioneer in social service. In the same book there was an account of Mary Reiby, one of Australia's first business women, by Dymphna Cusack. Members of sub-committees were invited to many official occasions and parties and were constantly meeting one another. One of the other projects in which the women of Australia were interested was a memorial garden and statue in the Sydney Botanic Gardens dedicated to the wives of pioneers. The statue is an Eros with the words "Love led them." Miles, as a distinguished writer and a descendant of pioneers, was present at this and on many other occasions.

Through the celebrations Dymphna Cusack, herself a prominent writer, and Miles Franklin became friends. Dymphna has pinpointed the moment of contact:

My friendship with Miles Franklin began one blistering day in February 1938 when we sat on the edge of the lily pond at Government House (it was a Sesqui-centenary Celebration for "distinguished women!"), ate soggy sandwiches, sipped luke-warm lemonade and exchanged views in keeping with the weather, on what Miles called the survivals of the "garrison-mind" in a young country. We'd met before certainly but this was the first time we "knocked sparks off each other" —again Miles speaking.[3]

From this meeting sprang a collaboration. Both women had a racy sense of humour and they saw plenty to laugh at in the celebrations—the little pomposities, the jockeying for place, the petticoat of ignorance showing beneath the draperies of admiration, the false position into which pioneers were being forced as national idols, the snobbery, most particularly the snobbery which took advantage of the occasion.

They laughed. They planned to perpetuate the joke in a novel called *Pioneers on Parade* which was published in Sydney in 1939 while the joke was still topical. It is labelled "For Australians Only." As it is impossible to say what contributions to the whole each author made, it is in order to treat this as one of Miles's books without detracting from Dymphna's share. Similarly, if I were writing a book about Dymphna I should treat it as part of her literary output. Collaborators should not publicly claim their contributions to a shared book; it is not fair to the book. Miles certainly left some very clear finger-prints on *Pioneers on Parade* but I must admit that it is rather more militantly political than her usual style. It is a very amusing book and I hope that it will continue to be read for its humour if not for its wisdom.

Pioneers on Parade is satire bordering on farce. The scene is in Sydney during the Sesqui-centenary celebrations with, as in *Back to Bool Bool*, an excursion into the bush. The characters are straight out of the comedy of manners. The leading ones are George du Mont-Brankston, a business man; his wife Audrey, a crashing snob whose main object in life is not only to keep up with the Joneses, but to leave them standing; their only child Primrose who has possibilities of being a real person; her unfashionable boy friend Dr. Greg. Moore who is useful as mouth-piece for the authors' opinions. Then there is Aunt Lucy Brankston, a pioneer, previously neglected but now seen as a social asset, and her grandson Little Willie, who is quite unspoilt by sophistication. Audrey works hard to get Aunt Lucy and Little Willie invited to the celebrations as official guests. The overseas guests of honour are Lord Cravenburn, his daughter Lady Lucy Horsehurst, a nymphomaniac, and the Honourable Ninnian Skimpole-Blaise. The authorities had had great difficulty in persuading anyone to come and these rather poor specimens represented the bag.

It is, you see, a promising cast—all snobs or effete aristocrats except sterling old Aunt Lucy and Little Willie, who is a big sunburnt bush man. Primrose and Greg. are of the younger generation who may still be saved. Plenty of fun is poked at the Sesqui-centenary and its offspring, the Society for Purer Australian History and the Women's Conference on the Status of Women in International Affairs. A meeting of the latter is parodied at length:

There was such a large cast to be disposed of that the meeting had eight openers, and by the time the opening was over, it was time to go home. Two leading politicians lauded their Excellencies and themselves and let drop a hint—in view of the coming elections—that Australia's 150 years of achievement was due solely to men of their own kidney. Three Lady Excellencies, of doubtful excellence as speakers, praised the politicians and exchanged courtesies with each other, mentioning Australia in passing. Then a lady delegate from London—the wife of a politician—flattered their Excellencies, the politicians, the celebrations and her husband. Mrs. Meddlington extolled everybody till all loyal Australians wished she would drop dead—they did not want to hear any local-grown product.

The two big speeches came on, one (imp.) the other a product of local manufacture. Between them, after talking for over an hour, this pair of speakers left some harmless advice in the minds of the populace. When the chaff whirled away from the bellows of motherhood, on which they blew a soporific hurricane, one of them had advocated better use of the Sabbath, self-control and the management of hubby by the art of blandishment with the relief of very limited divorce in case he was entirely a liability. The other advocated families unlimited— especially for poor women. The poor, she said, always managed very well, and she loved to see a line of baby's washing in the working class districts. This was heartily applauded by the elderly from the high class suburbs.[4]

There is a lot of this type of humour but the authors sometimes unsheath real claws:

This Sesqui display was a repetition of the old bread-and-circus rackets to distract the masses because there was no one big enough for a constructive policy against the insanity of Europe, the resurgence of Asia. In that far-flung mess Australia was a cork on the currents—a child with a big prize that might be wrested from it if it did not cling to Grannie's skirts. If Australia could be freed from the nightmare conjured up by the warring tribes of Europe and the fecundity of Asia— but oh, no, peace would not be there. Man so loved war that he would never abandon it. The kookaburras laughing all round him cheered him.[5]

All the characters are disagreeable, degenerate, stupid or just plain ridiculous. They are not real people; the authors use them as if they were puppets. The book is an avowed farce so that this lack of reality in characterization cannot justly be held against it: it is a pastiche and should be judged as such. If you laugh as you read you have had your value from it.

The story winds its way through obstacles. Aunt Lucy and her Willie are brought to Sydney as exhibits—real live pioneers. They are a great success. Their novelty charms the overseas visitors. Lady Lucy, a very tiresome girl given to tantrums, thoroughly spoilt and worse, falls in love with Willie and he, having no idea of her real character, with her. The whole party, Lord Cravenburn, Lady Lucy, the du-Mont-Brankstons, Ninnian and Greg., accompany Aunt Lucy and Willie back to the bush.

Lord Cravenburn watched fascinated as they plunged down the road to Picton. The straggling town lay baking in its hollow. The very distance here was moving—the near silent fawn hills, the far lupin blue ranges—austere and demanding. Aunt Lucy seemed to fit here. He could imagine those deep-set eyes searching such hills. The raking nose, the serious mouth reminded him of some old portrait he could not place. She looked like the country itself—and that was intrinsic greatness, he reflected, in the illumination of this landscape, flooded by yellow light—illimitable.[6]

The bush put the visitors to an acid test, showing up their shallowness. Willie and Ninnian get on very badly together. When Willie finds Ninnian in his Lucy's bedroom he knocks him down. Then to Lucy: " 'Get into bed and cover yourself,' ordered William, 'at once, when I tell you. From this out I take care of this sort of thing. It may go in your world, where men are too decayed to handle it the right way, but it is cut out of our world now. Any fellow who as much as looks at you the wrong way has to deal with me.' "[7] Lucy is quite enchanted by this robust attitude. It appeals to her much more than the Willie who said: "I would never offer the only girl I ever loved the slightest shade of disrespect—anything that I could not tell my mother, if she had lived ... Better our hearts to break than to dirty the most wonderful thing that ever happened to two people."[8]

Lucy and Willie are to marry. Lord Cravenburn is only too pleased to have her off his hands and settled even if only temporarily. Then a hitch occurs. Willie discovers that he has convict blood. An ancestress was transported for stealing a currant bun. This infuriates Aunt Lucy:

People who could starve a young girl so that she stole a currant bun, for no one will take food unless they are hungry, and all God's creatures have a right to eat. I've always fed everyone about me as much as they could swallow. To send a man out branded as a felon for life because he took a ride on a draught-horse—no one would get on a draught-horse unless he had to—I could never forgive people for that. Bringing life-long disgrace on them and on their descendants for trifles like that! They had no right to such power. And to use it like that! Worse than Hitler, they are![9]

Lord Cravenburn could only marvel at the Australians' craving for respectability.

There are further revelations: the bun-stealing Lucy had come from the village of Horsehurst and the Horsehursts had had her transported. No wonder the noble earl found Aunt Lucy's face familiar. There was now no impediment to the marriage and, happy to relate, Lucy reformed as a result of the pure Australian air and a strong man's love. Primrose too put away frivolity and decided to study medicine so that she could be a useful member of society:

"Anyway I don't want to marry for a profession. If it came along naturally and seemed worth while—well and good, but I don't want to be chasing around doing nothing any more. These silly Sesqui performances have opened my eyes. Those idiotic parties in honour of this one and that one; we sat around kowtowing to some woman with a title."[10]

George du Mont Brankston renews himself in the bush he had known in his youth. The knighthood he had been angling for no longer appeals to him. "If we have titles here, and I'm not sure I approve of them at all, they should be Commonwealth rewards for genuine service to the country. At present they are merely political plums—sops to social snobbery."[11]

Greg. Moore points the final moral:

"It's the old story over again" he continued more quietly. "The bondage to foreign ideas. Are we to be nothing but a milch cow and a dumping ground for Europe? Can't we develop something new, something that has never been seen in the world before? Break free from the ideas foisted on to us in the name of loyalty by a war-mad civilization, smash the financial bondage into which we've been plunged by financial shysters ... build a civilization." [12]

The authors are tilting at windmills that do not even exist, but perhaps that is just part of the farce and Dr. Moore is just another crackpot like all the rest. There is a flavour of *My Career Goes Bung* in *Pioneers on Parade*. Both are adolescent in outlook. Miles showed herself as still an *enfant terrible* capable of such things as the hostess's plaint: "Birds were all right in cages, and she'd like to tell those who advocated sanctuaries just what happened last time she erected a marquee in the grounds for a garden party. The savouries ruined; so extraordinarily like anchovies; she would never get over the humiliation." [13] It is pleasing to know that the collaborators remained friends but they wrote no more books together.

Miles's second collaboration was of a very different nature. She had always a deep admiration for Joseph Furphy and for his large discursive novel *Such is Life*, which he published under the pen name of Tom Collins. They met only once but they corresponded for years until Furphy's death. When Miles admired a book she campaigned early and late to win it public recognition. *Such is Life* had not had the success it deserved. In the 1930's it had been long out of print. Miles wanted to see it reprinted and she wanted also to preserve the memory of the kindly, studious, humorous man who had written it. She conceived the idea of writing his biography. It was not to be an ordinary biography; it would not invade his privacy. Miles makes that clear in the Prefatory Note:

The Australian attitude towards biography opens the case for Mateship versus Modernity, and so far Mateship holds the pass. No frankly searching study of the lives of our prominent personages would be tolerated by their relatives or descendants, nor indeed by the public, because of the still lingering conventions of modesty and reticence by which British middle-class behaviour was regulated until inhibitions loosened in the preliminary war of 1914—1918...
Joseph Furphy's life in the bush or the small urban community, where the affairs of each member are exposed to observation, was open for all to see: examination of the obtainable data discloses no action unbecoming to an honest man, but, out of consideration for others still living, certain facts cannot for the present be given the publicity of print.[14]

A MIXED BAG

Miles's plan was to reveal Furphy through his letters, of which he wrote an inordinate number. She had, as a beginning, the letters he wrote her, most of which she had kept, only destroying the ones that embarrassed her with too much praise. Since they were not enough for her purpose, she sought the help of Miss Kate Baker, for long a close friend of the Furphy family. It was to Kate Baker that Furphy's mother entrusted all his letters and papers after his death.

On the title page the author is given as Miles Franklin in association with Kate Baker. In a note of acknowledgement Miles carefully defines Kate Baker's share in the book: "Without Miss Baker's valuable collection of original matter and recollections this memoir would not have been attempted. The first draft of it was compiled in consultation with Miss Baker and with the aid of her collected Furphiana. Chapter II is built on her notes and care has been taken to preserve where possible Miss Baker's actual words so as not to impair the charm of her reminiscence." [15] Sad to say the collaboration between Miles and Kate ended in a bitter quarrel. Kate was awarded an O.B.E. for her services to literature, notably this one. Miles did not receive any public acknowledgement, other than two S. H. Prior Memorial Prizes for hers.

The full title of the Joseph Furphy book is *Joseph Furphy: the Legend of a Man and His book*, and the dedication is "For Australia." "For Australia" was Furphy's battle cry. He would end letters with it instead of the more formal "yours sincerely." It is for this reason a very suitable dedication. "Legend" is a curious word for Miles to use here, as her aim was to present the truth about her subject, to show him as he was in his day-to-day life.

The book is a conglomerate of letters with explanatory text in between. As Miles herself said: "There is irony in Furphy's story being taken from his letters, for he held that a letter belonged to the writer, and that the person to whom it was addressed should destroy it as soon as he mastered the contents. This was not affectation; he did not bother to date many of his own letters nor to keep those from his friends." [16] Some of his myriad letters were, of course, destroyed because friends took his words seriously or because they were just not the types who kept letters. Some to Miles were burnt with other papers she left in a trunk under the care of a friend when she went off to the 1914 war. Enough remain.

It must be admitted that Furphy's letters are dated. He had a rather coy style in writing to his friends and indulged in a lot of what I think used to be called "funning." One sample will show what I mean. He was writing to A. G. Stephens of *The Bulletin* after reading some unfavourable reviews of *Such is Life*.

> Beyond doubt the popularity of *S'Life* would have been enhanced by illustrations. Heaven *may* forgive Vincent [17] but the writer never will. Bismillah.
> When will you be ready to take on *Rigby's Romance*—if ever? Gordelpus...
> But I don't wish to take up your time just now, so
> Pax (adj.) vobiscum.[18]

Or he can be ponderous and obscure. There is an example of this on the same page:

> So Phil May[19] and Victor J Daley[20] are gone the way of Neanderthal Man and him that died o'Wednesday. I wish I had known Daley better. I recognized in him—or fancied I did—the almost pure type of a race which my own crude and imperfect studies in ethnology have led me, forced me to postulate. Ethnology shows a worse hiatus in treatment of the Irish race than of any other.

But the man does shine through the letters in his kindliness, courage and sincerity.

This is a dull book, there is no question of that, but it has preserved material that would otherwise have been forgotten and lost. It will be of great use to future biographers of Joseph Furphy. For Miles the writing or compiling of this volume was a labour of admiration. She wrote this epitaph for Furphy: "Here lies a man good because he was great, and great because he was good. Joseph Furphy's integrity remains as a comforting and valiant reminder that human character is the one stable element amid turbulent and menacing revolutions in the terms of human existence." [21]

The object of this book is not entirely Joseph Furphy, it is Miles Franklin as well. Miles manages to slip something of herself into it. For example she claims that Furphy

> could not fail as he matured to observe what every woman knows, but what few men have moral courage to admit; that men's creative work needs to be nurtured by women somewhat as horticultural cuttings are fostered in potatoes. Examination of data suggests that Furphy had hardly any support or inspiration from women: but he was extravagantly grateful to Kate Baker as a stimulating tuber.[22]

Miles is also able to air another of her deeply held beliefs—that literature must come from the soil and that Australian literature must be national in character. For her the hardy Australian "prized originality and vigour above conformity, consciously repudiated mental vassalage, and demanded an independent state of literature as a factor in national self-respect." [23] The "distinctive quality" of a literature "relates it to the soil of its origin." [24] Furphy "whose emotions and outlook were never disrupted and reorientated by residence abroad, was admitted to be intrinsically native in atmosphere and thought." [25] (This sounds as if Miles regretted her early escape and years spent abroad.) She continued: "Furphy's book has come to serve as the touchstone for the Australian literary intelligentsia because, by his feeling for it, any literary Australian betrays whether he lives in a state of Australian grace or in one of mental colonialism." [26] This is clever of Miles. She insures that if you disagree with her on the merits of *Such is Life* you are no true Australian!

It took Miles from 1939 to 1943 to prepare this book for publication. Kate Baker collaborated only in the first draft; it was Miles who did the checking and co-ordinating. The first draft was submitted for the S. H. Prior Memorial Prize and won it. The two women divided the prize money of £100. It was not until 1944 that the book was published in Sydney. It is illustrated by a number of photographs and facsimiles. It has not, so far, gone into a second edition.

II *Excursions in Criticism*

By stretching terms *Joseph Furphy* might rank as a work of literary criticism. It is full of admiration mixed with some explanations and observations, but there is little analysis. Miles was not of a critical turn of mind, nor was she of the stuff from which reviewers are made. She admired or disliked books and their authors very heartily. Her reactions were generally emotional. In *Joseph Furphy* for instance, Miles's attitude is largely influenced by her knowledge of the man and her high opinion of his character, by what he himself called his "offensively Australian" bias and his book's "insultingly Australian character." All these things weigh heavily with her. Of the literary value of *Such is Life* very little is said. There is no analysis of its story or approach. (This is an observation on my part, not a criticism; Miles did not set out to reveal Furphy as a writer but as a man writing.)

It was not until later that Miles entered the field as a critic or, as she might have phrased it herself, a torch carrier for Australian literature. In 1950 she was invited to give a series of lectures on Australian literature at the University of Western Australia. The

Fellowship of Australian Writers, Sydney, of which Miles was a faithful member, had earlier approached the Commonwealth Government with a plan for the fostering of literature in Australia. A scheme was adopted by the Government and its administration was put into the hands of the newly set up Commonwealth Literary Fund. Its aim was to encourage interest in Australian literature by promoting lectures in all the Australian universities; to help writers by giving grants of money to support a few authors each year while they wrote; and to guarantee publishers against loss when a book of merit was not likely to be a financial success.

As for the lectures in Australian literature, an interesting aspect of the plan was that writers and not members of the academic staff of the universities were asked to give them and were paid for the series. In this way writers could have contact with students and students with writers. An author is not necessarily a good lecturer but the arrangement has worked well and many people have felt that a fresh breeze blew through the academic corridors. The lectures in Australian literature became part of the degree course in English and attendance at them is compulsory. They are also open to the public if the public cares to attend. Each university could choose the writer they wished to lecture to its students. Miles accepted the invitation to go to Perth and gave a very successful course of lectures there. Her wit, her charming smile and her friendliness made her popular with the students.

During the next four years she amended, polished and enlarged her lectures into a book which she called *Laughter, Not for a Cage*. It was published locally in 1956 after her death. The title is explained in the last paragraph of the book; summing up her views on Australian literature, she wrote: "Truly there are no nightingales to enchant the night, but the mellow carillon of the magpies enlarges the spacious sunlit days and the mocking laughter of the kookaburras is not for a cage."[27] In the dedication Miles paid a debt of gratitude to four men who had encouraged her writing: T. J. Hebblewhite who read her early writings and advised her to look homeward, Henry Lawson who wrote a preface for *My Brilliant Career*, A. G. Stephens who acclaimed it, and Joseph Furphy who thought well of it.

Miles began at the beginning. The first chapter is called "Invasion of Aboriginal Australia: The Convict Brand." She rooted her argument firmly in the soil. The Australian nation began in the bush; all that is uniquely ours had its origin there. In it germinated the first seeds of a national literature. There was loneliness and it was a challenge to the creative in man. It had to be filled.

The loneliness equalled an occupational risk with its "back-block lunacy" of the "hatters" added to dengue and Barcoo rot, but the land was liberating in its extent and had such abundance and treasure for the reaping as were enjoyed in old-world communities only by potentates and the privileged castes.[28]

And "The exiles in their necessity to fashion anew not only fields and habitations, but the intangibles such as literature, were like James Ruse[29] with his alien corn and no humus." [30]

Miles stated her credo:

Without an indigenous literature people can remain aliens in their own soil. An unsung country does not fully exist or enjoy adequate international exchange in the inner life. Further, a country must be portrayed by those who hate or love it as their dwelling place, familiarly, or remain dumb among its contemporaries. The fuller its libraries, the louder its radios, the more crowded its periodicals with imported stories and songs, the more clearly such dependence exposes innate poverty.[31]

In considering Miles as a critic it must be fully understood that she never saw literature as detached from life, as a special skill or something for experts. It was for her a part of living, a necessity, not a luxury. It came up out of the earth, flowered and fell back into the earth enriching it. Literature, she told us over and over again, was something natural and necessary. It had little or nothing to do with scholarship and was essentially democratic in origin. Miles laid no claim to an academic attitude; her education, by her own showing, was patchy but she was well read in a number of literatures as well as her own.

In *Laughter, Not for a Cage* her personal likes and dislikes, her prejudices and enthusiasms are given full play. She makes no attempt to be impartial. She describes the book as "a simple excursional survey" [32] and later, as "parochial." She brought zest to the writing of it because she enjoyed what was obviously a sort of literary picnic. Because she liked people, particularly people she did not know, she probably liked lecturing to students. If she had not given this course she would never have embarked on a book of literary criticism. Miles was never stuffy, often challenging, frequently unexpected in her judgements.

Miles's criticism had three prongs. She told the story of the novel. (The accent, by the way, falls strongly on novels throughout the book.) She compared it and its writer to some well-known author or book and she related the literary product to the social scene. Thus Catherine Helen Spence whom she admired is compared to Jane Austen and her book *Clara Morrison* to *Madame Bovary*. Is then Jane Austen comparable to Flaubert?

In a passage that is surely a *tour de force*[33] she compares and contrasts Joseph Furphy and Henry James. Who else would ever have thought of this? It begins: "This slow and subtle process of transplanting the inner life of a people from ancient cultures to raw soils is illustrated by divergences and parallels in the case of Joseph Furphy and Henry James." The comparisons are often provocative and piquant, sometimes plainly wrong-headed.

Miles shows herself shrewder and less capricious when she relates writing to time, place and society. In considering Australian novels written in the second half of last century Miles pointed out that in the field of English literature they had to compete with giants like Dickens and Thackeray, Sir Walter Scott and Jane Austen. That they did not measure up to them was understandable but that did not rob them of value:

Consequently no claims are here made for the Australian examples, save that they were nourishing in their day and remain historically important to us. Thus: envisage the need for chairs to be made from indigenous green hardwoods. The results would be treasured for their aid to dignity and comfort, for rescuing the settler from balancing on the hunkers or squatting on the earthen floors; there would be no fingering of these useful products to judge how nearly they approached Hepplewhites or Sheratons, no demanding from the available materials the fairy lines of a Louis XV that yet could support sixteen stone. And with that idea in mind these and other novels are presented.[34]

Personal prejudices, favourable and unfavourable, are rife in this book. Joseph Furphy marches through its pages; he is the paragon and the touchstone by which other writers are judged. About Henry Handel Richardson,[35] who is probably Australia's most famous novelist to date, although Patrick White is running her close, Miles was exceedingly bitter. She even carried her warfare into H. H. Richardson's private life. Her sin was that she had left Australia and was a permanent expatriate; the pose of an Australian writer was a barefaced piece of poaching. The best she can say is H. H. Richardson had a "dark, costive talent."[36] D. H. Lawrence also, in his two Australian books, came in for the rough side of Miles's tongue, and other "garrison-minded" writers get short shrift. It would almost seem that success prejudiced Miles against a fellow author. She was all for under-dogs and misunderstood, neglected writers. On the first count she flourishes, as usual, her brief for convicts:

Aristocrats sent convicts to New South Wales, not because convicts were more immoral than aristocrats, but because convicts were men who in various ways disturbed the comfort of aristocrats . . . In the eyes of the aristocracy of those days,[37] crime and poverty were synonymous; but since Jesus held a brief for the poor, Christians should accept our convicts as martyrs, and revere their memory with due humility.[38]

Miles may have been laughing up her sleeve but she meant it too. Miles also uses the book to exercise her various hobby-horses. An apparently harmless sentence "Oh what is there more valuable to Man than Woman whom he mostly values little" inflames Miles's feminism.

Such an apostrophe places women in the mouldy category of "wine, women and song"—women as toys or drudges, as toothsome loot in trade and war. In such unwholesome dominance men value women as instruments of delight, comfort, usefulness or debauchery, not as human equals—half the race, the saner as well as the less dispensable half biologically.[39]

Miles also insists over and over again on her own brand of patriotism which is an unpolitical devotion to the earth. "A land beloved is the foundation of national harmony and international sanity."[40] Or: ". . . the writer, of all artists, is most indissolubly of his native soil and is liable to emotional impoverishment by exile from it later than infancy."[41] And: Henry James "provides a notable example of the irrecoverable wounds suffered by the writer in divorce from his own soil."[42]

You will have gathered that as a piece of literary criticism *Laughter, Not for a Cage* is biased, emotional and sometimes ill-informed. As reading matter it has much to recommend it. Miles had wit. She described Jane Austen as "the full-rigged ship in a narrow-necked bottle."[43] There are dozens of flashes like this. Only in the last chapter, where Miles looks towards the future of Australian writing, does she become turgid and often difficult to understand. It is overwritten, a bonnet full of bees. She attacks the phoniness of psychology, the false dawn of science, the decadence of Europe, and thanks God that Australia has no tradition. "Let laughter return."[44]

The blurb on the jacket of *Laughter, Not for a Cage* sums it up very aptly:

The assessment of a literature by a determinedly unacademic person is both a curiosity and a challenge to those who claim it as their province. All Miles Franklin's judgements are made on human-moral-aesthetic grounds; she belongs to no school; she follows no precedent; she is merely herself; and this is her triumph in entering a field to which she professedly did not belong.

III *Tail of a Kite*

Every kite, no matter how high it flies, has a tail. There are three works—a one-act play, a story for children, and a novel—which can be said to form the tail of Miles's kite. They do not fit in with the rest of her work and are not of the same calibre.

The play, *No Family,* was published in *Best Australian One-Act Plays,* edited by W. Moore and T. I. Moore, in 1937.[45] Unless some turn up in manuscript this is Miles's only surviving play. She mentioned plays amongst the manuscripts destroyed by a friend in America. She never had the desire or the energy to re-write them. *No Family* was probably written much earlier than the date of its publication. It is not in any way remarkable. The scene is a domestic interior in Sydney shortly after World War I. Mrs. Morton is celebrating, if that is the right word, the anniversary of her son's death, a pilot in the Air Force, when, all unheralded, a beautiful girl with a baby in her arms arrives and claims that she is their dead son's wife. She sees a photograph and cries "That is my husband." The family realizes that their son's mate, Gordon Randolph, a foundling ashamed of having no family, had taken his name after he was killed and had married under it. The Mortons decided not to disillusion the girl but to accept her as their daughter-in-law and bring up the child as their grandson. The plot can hardly be said to hold water and the treatment in a very short one-act gives it no space to develop or acquire credibility. The characters, except Minnie, the maid-servant, are stock figures. The outspoken Minnie is a Milesian creation and the best thing in the play.

Ten years later Miles published locally[46] *Sydney Royal, a Divertisement*, a story for young people under sixteen. The title needs some explanation. An important event in the Sydney calendar is the *Royal Easter Show*. It is a world-famous Agricultural Show at which the State of New South Wales displays its wealth in pedigree animals—sheep, cattle, pigs, goats, dogs, even cats—and the pride of its harvests and primary products. There are also Halls of Industry, of Horticulture, and of Handicrafts. Tacked on to this great display is the lighter side of fairs, side-shows, merry-go-rounds and the like. The show takes place at Easter time and draws huge crowds.

The story which unfolds against this authentic background is sweet and pawky, as Scots would say. It is about a group of children who gather at the side-shows and about Rosalie, the Governor's beautiful daughter who finds her true love again among the riders. He had disappeared without a word on the eve of their wedding.

He had, as a matter of fact, lost his memory in an accident. Another accident restores it and he is reunited with Rosalie and his sorrowing parents.

The children are a little hard to take. They might have stepped off a picture postcard. They are Tootles and Toddles, the irrepressible twins from Government House; Hoppy, a crippled boy from the 'loo;[47] and Junior from America. Democracy is so rampant that it looks like snobbery. Even Governors and Premiers appear at the Slippery Slide. Descriptions of the Show and the animals are the best part of the book and give it quality. For instance:

It was a comparatively peaceful day for the equestrians while sheep-dog trials occupied the ring. Dogs had long been called upon to provide cheap labour in the wool industry, which was not available from submerged masses. Carefully bred, ruthlessly trained and controlled, a good dog could do more with sheep in the open than possibly two or three men. Little kelpies and barbs, hypersensitive and uncannily intelligent, had taken the places of the assigned convict shepherds . . . The ordeal of the dogs with a few stupid, frightened, displaced woollies was very popular with the crowd and gave the horses the opportunity to doze in their stalls.[48]

Sydney Royal has all the marks of a juvenile work touched up later for publication.

Prelude to Waking is very different. It purports to be the first of the Brent of Bin Bin books but has nothing in common with the long chronicle. It was written in 1925, published in 1950; it comes, then, at the beginning of Miles's second great spurt of writing. The title could well refer to the awakening of her muse. Miles was trying her wings, and this was a preliminary flutter.

The setting is England just after World War I. Miles was never happy when she laid her action outside Australia. She knew Australia as she was never to know England or America; it was home and she had a great store of memories and folklore to draw on. When she wrote of other places her ink ran thin and pale.

In *Prelude to Waking* she also attempted something that she was not equipped mentally or emotionally to carry through successfully. It is, or aims to be, a discussion novel. The action is slight, the characters talk and talk and talk. The result is poor. Critics have been unkind to *Prelude to Waking*. Ray Mathew wrote, justly I must say, it "is so involved, conceited and facetious that only courageous readers beginning with it will persevere through its Michael Arlen Mayfair world of would-be Shavian talk. The characters are all artifice . . ."[49]

Prelude to Waking is written in the first person. Miles had not outgrown that device. The narrator is Nigel Barraclough, an Englishman. The heroine is Merlin Giltinane, an expatriate Australian, and a genuine Miles Franklin heroine—spirited, intelligent, virginal. It is her intelligence that is her undoing: she loves Nigel but will show nothing; he is so delighted by her mind and conversation that he forgets to fall in love with her until too late. He has entered the "purgatory of marriage" and must behave honourably. This is how he puts it:

"Well then, I must take up the married man's burden. I shall not fall behind you, la ffollette; as you say, if a man has a soul above beasts, he must demonstrate it. Let's lay a clean oblation on the altar of love and see what happens. It will be better to transmute *l'amour* into pure affection than to degrade it in lust. The perfume of old lavender may be epicene, but it is preferable to the odour of the kennel." [50]

Merlin marries Sir Hugh la ffollette who asks nothing of her but gives her the protection of his name and wealth. For her "it's all over, but the long, slow pull from now till eighty, and that's implacable as God, inexorable as Time." [51] That, surely, is Miles speaking. It is a homesick book too, expressing Miles's longing for Australia, its pictures forever floating before her mind:

Mile by mile we caressed that wide, strange country whose silence has a voice, and whose eerie beauty, before man defaced it, captures the senses as does no other land I have seen. Out on the ridges I could still see the leaves of the bimby box gleaming like silver; the soft grey waters of the Bogan and Namoi gliding noiselessly past coolibah, yarram and belar, in the perfume of the native mignonette; the flower carpeted plains quivering in the sunlight, undulating to the mirage that ever retreated before the traveller. Already my heart gnawed to be there again.[52]

Again Miles expresses "The anguish of having two countries, one by birth, blood and affection, the other by affection and congeniality." [53] Guy Giltinane, Merlin's brother, is the embodiment of this country, a thoroughbred on a blood horse, without fear and without reproach. But he dies, and unmarried, of course.

Miles is at her most rampantly feminist in this book. Hers is a very special and illogical sort of feminism, not a reasoned case for the equality of men and women. It expresses itself in an attack on men, a denial of love and a plaint that the possession of intelligence puts women at a disadvantage in this man's world.

... for a woman must let slip the glamour of intelligence, and let the light of the coquette, or the noodle (which sentimentality will exalt into that of a dove), rather than that of Minerva or Saint Joan, glint in her eyes ere *amour* will experience a coming-on disposition. What I mean is illustrated by this thing in its lower reaches, when a beautiful girl of eighteen, if intelligent, can roam the world alone unmolested, while her moron sister of any age, and lacking beauty, is not in her own bailiwick safe among so-called gentlemen.[54]

Or she mentions "That delirium which, among the chief of mammals, is called love . . . this thing that demolishes reason and honour." [55] On this subject I could quote indefinitely from this book alone.

Prelude to Waking is a sad, perplexed book in which happiness is missed by a narrow margin: Nigel marries the wrong woman when he could have married the right one; Merlin is frustrated, Guy dies untimely and Sir Hugh makes a selfless bargain. Miles shows her hand too clearly for art. She hammers in her points deafeningly. Perhaps this book had to be written to get Miles into the habit of writing again. It did not have to be published.

CHAPTER 10

A Homestead in the Suburbs

I *The Return*

IN 1915 Miles Franklin's parents bought a house at Carlton, a suburb on the south side of Sydney. It was a modest home, built of weatherboard in an uninteresting neighbourhood, but it had a garden and that made all the difference to John Maurice Franklin. His daughter has left a picture of him enjoying this garden:

When he grew old and had leisure, gardening became a passion with him. He had the industry and patience of a Chinese gardener and such tenderness that no care irked him. Were there a garden hereafter, all the little plants therein would troop towards the entry to welcome him. When he was very old to see him set a fruit-tree or a rose-bush was a privilege. No haste, no skimping, no failures.[1]

It was on one of her visits home in 1924 or 1930 that Miles saw this picture. Her father died at Carlton on 31 October 1931. His death finally decided Miles to come home to live with her mother. This was her duty but she wanted to return for other reasons. There was nothing to keep her in England, and she longed for her native land.

It was not the beloved bush she came back to but the city. The Mazeres in *Back to Bool Bool* lived on the south side and the setting described in it is much the same as Miles lived in during the later years of her life:

Spread beneath were half a dozen suburbs, ranging from scattered red roofs amid the trees of the nearer ranges to agglomerations such as Erskineville and Newtown. Botany Bay in the distance was the old Madonna blue; Cronulla's sands gold-tinted snow; the white fountains that are never still on the quietest Southern Pacific day played about the feet of Cape Banks and Bare Island. The dark and unique native scrub was still to be seen in that direction. Nearer around were miles of bungalows as if designed with cake cutters, six or eight to the acre, bespeaking open air, sunshine and private garden space such as can hardly be matched in proletarian areas in other continents.[2]

Mother and daughter lived together until June 1938 when old Mrs.

Franklin died at the age of eighty-three. Miles was stricken with remorse as well as grief. Her mother was "clever at all things" and Miles always admired her, but they were very different in disposition. The years that Miles spent abroad living an independent life did not make it easier for them to live together. There was no serious rift—just little things that got on Miles's nerves. I never heard her mother's side of the story. When the old woman died Miles was sad because she had not been able to love her more.

From 1938 until the time of her own death Miles lived alone in what she sometimes called "my shabby old humpy." It was a frugal existence and sometimes lonely, but she had many friends. Miles always declared that she was not interested in the domestic arts, though she praised them in her books when they were exercised on the grand scale in a homestead up the country. Nevertheless she knew all about them and kept her small house very neat. The living room was lined with bookshelves. She had a large collection, mostly Australian, and many signed editions.

Twenty-six Grey Street, Carlton was as nearly a bush homestead as Miles could make it, everything authentic but on a reduced scale. In winter a big wood fire burnt on her hearth. There was a joke about her stealing the wood from Government land, of which she was as proud as a schoolboy who had successfully raided an orchard. She fed visitors as much as possible from the produce of her garden —eggs from her bantams, jam made from the fruit of her fig tree, bread and honey. If you were a writer or someone important Miles gave you tea in her waratah cup. This was of very fine china, six-sided, with a waratah painted on each panel. After this Miles produced her visitors' book and one was expected to write something in it in the style of an old-fashioned autograph book. It is characteristic of Miles that this was an old exercise book she had had since a child. Like the figs, she could not bear to waste it. Everything was carefully conserved—manuscripts, clothes, lares and penates. She lived so thriftily that some of her friends feared she did not have enough money and might even be quietly starving. They began agitating to get her a literary pension from the Commonwealth Government until relatives of hers asked them to stop and assured them that she had an adequate income from property. Nothing came to her from Brindabella; that had passed out of the family in the 1920's.

Miles's interests were almost entirely literary. She was generally to be found at the meetings and functions of the Fellowship of Australian Writers in its bare upstairs club room in York Street,

Sydney. She served as a writers' representative on the Commonwealth Literary Fund Advisory Committee which met regularly in Canberra. It is said that here, as elsewhere, she showed herself an *enfant terrible*. She was nominated, as we have seen already, to give the Fund's lectures in Western Australia in 1950. She visited Melbourne occasionally and was warmly welcomed by Vance and Nettie Palmer and other senior writers.

Miles felt that writers, particularly in Australia, had a raw deal. Not only did they receive a poor financial reward from their books but there was practically no constructive or stimulating criticism. They were lapped round by a vast public indifference. She aired their wrongs in public and private at every possible opportunity. Books that were, she claimed, of national importance were allowed to go and to stay out of print. She campaigned for the re-publication of many of them, most particularly of Furphy's *Such is Life* and of Catherine Helen Spence's *Clara Morrison*. She wrote: "The Australian nation, despite talkies and football and tin hares and horse races in pandemoniac plenitude, is filthily poor mentally and spiritually while it cannot afford to print and buy and read *Such is Life* in its entirety."[3] *Such is Life* was re-published both in abridged and complete editions, but how much Miles's influence counted for in this I do not know. *Clara Morrison* is still out-of-print and likely to remain so.

As part of her campaign for the recognition of Joseph Furphy, Miles organized a competition. She told the story of it to Nettie Palmer and it illustrates her entwined militancy and despair. She wrote that she

> threw a competition into a little circle of junior writers: the best critical analysis of Furphy's *Four Half-Crowns*.[4] There was a lively response. Not one trivial entry in the lot of about a dozen—the diversity of opinion was bewildering. Among the entries was an exhaustive analysis, NON-COMPETITIVE. This happened to be from a scientist, so I co-opted him as a co-judge. The result of this was that the three that I placed as 1, 2 and 3 were completely dismissed to the bottom of the list. So I pondered. I discovered that he knew nothing of Furphy but this story and, though his critique started in condemnation, in the end he had given the story much attention, which I pointed out to him was a tribute to the power and potentiality of Furphy. I did not call in a third judge. I let him have his head. He gave the first award to an unsympathetic review and the next to two other young things. The maturer writers earned nothing but contempt from him.[5]

To other writers, particularly the young ones, Miles always held out a welcoming hand. One of them, the South Australian poet,

A HOMESTEAD IN THE SUBURBS

Ian Mudie, gives this account of a visit to her home. It is a most delightful picture of her and her inseparable

> dilly-bag . . . of which she once said "When I begin to scrabble round in this thing like an old hen I never know what I'm going to come on. I feel like Sailor Time . . ." And although Miles never managed to dredge up the whole continent from that dilly-bag, it always contained plenty of proof that she was obsessed by that "deep infatuation" for Australia which she never ceased to demand that her fellow countrymen should share. Mixed up with odd bits of domestic shopping, lollies for any children she happened to talk to, photographs of various friends, a piece of cloth she had "promised to match for a very dear friend of mine," a doctor's prescription she had been "supposed to have had made up weeks ago," some bills "that will just have to be paid sometime," and other odds and ends, would be likely to be some very dog-eared notes for a novel, or a play, that she had "been trying to get down to for years," and a newspaper cutting that described, perhaps, the view from the top of Glass-house Mountains.
>
> . . . Also, and to Miles this was always the most important of all the contents of the dilly-bag, there would be a manuscript, worn thin from unfolding. It was never one of her own: at times it would even be by a totally unknown writer, who without a thought of the dozens of calls upon Miles Franklin's time, had sent it to her ostensibly for criticism, in reality in search of praise. Most often it was a poem: always it was something that Miles believed should be widely known. And at every opportunity she would "dive in my dilly-bag for it in preparation for doing my Ancient Mariner act." No matter what the time or place —tram, bus, train, restaurant, public meeting, business conference—it didn't matter to Miles. The slightly raspy voice, with what she proudly called "my Monaro accent," suddenly would exclaim, "That reminds me, there's something you must hear . . ." The latest skirmish in her battle for her protégés had begun.[6]

She worked to bring C. Hartley Grattan, the American publicist, to Australia and he proved a most stimulating critic with a continuing interest in Australian letters. She threw herself with enthusiasm into the short-lived Australian Book Society, being one of the adjudicators in its Australian Book of the Month scheme. It failed through lack of money. Miles talked well and wittily and was in demand as a speaker at all sorts of literary clubs and associations of writers.

In all this activity for literature something was missing. Miles was not writing. By the time she returned home in 1933 her great creative period was spent. She had dried up, written herself out. After 1933 she was only to write two books, *Pioneers on Parade* in collaboration with Dymphna Cusack and *Laugher, Not for a Cage*. The first was far inferior to her best work; the latter was not creative work. She put into shape the ideas and sentiments she had held for many years, adding little to them.

For years Miles had been asserting that a national literature to be valid must spring from the earth, adding as a rider that any man or woman who left his country broke that vital thread. Yet this was what she had done. For about two decades after her flight she was silent as if her muse were dead. Then came her *furor scribendi*, her fury of writing. By this time the only tie with her native land was the thick strand of a tenacious memory. By 1933 she was beginning to realize that her creativeness was slipping away from her. If anything would revive it a return to her native land would.

II *The Years of Drought*

She came back and there was no revival. There was always a streak of Celtic sadness in Miles; after all, she was half-Irish. With the fear that she could not write deepening into a certainty that her spring would not come again, despair overwhelmed her. Without the letters Miles wrote to Nettie Palmer between 1929 and 1952, which I have generously been allowed to read and to quote, I should have little real understanding of her feelings at this stage of her life. Like many others, she felt she could write freely to Mrs. Palmer and take refuge in her steadfastness.

In July 1931, while still in England, she was looking forward and full of hope, if not for herself, for Australian literature. "We are struggling with the very beginnings of a national school of literature, unforced, self-respecting, but of the soil as Russians are of their soil (I repeat this again and again and again) and we must nurture those who are indubitably of that soil, despite their blemishes." [7]

In 1935 she told Mrs. Palmer, "I am jaded into stagnation and retrogression, dry as dust spiritually and mentally, nothing left but the habit of character and that merely negative. I don't know whether it is the end or merely a phase." [8] And looking about she saw only darkness. "Australian life is nothing but animal mechanics." [9] She wanted "to hide for ever."

Ten years later the depression was still as heavy. She wrote "No, I cannot face this world. I am in a terrible mess because I can't quite make up my mind to depart like a black-fellow who has been boned." [10] This should not be taken as a threat to commit suicide. That would not be Miles's way. She meant rather a voluntary surrender of the will to live.

In 1947 Miles summed up her life:

I've had the flattest, respectabilist life, the only memorable thing about it (and that could not be made into news) is that though it was 100% frustration I am not internally frustrated but merely defeated. Any action in which I was involved was in a very humble way, never recorded and now with none to remember.[11]

Also, in another letter that year: "I have written nothing for six years. What's the use?;" and a year later: "Everything in my lifetime has been swept into minisculity by the oncoming of the atomic age ..."[12]

Miles's natural sensitiveness became exaggerated. Even friendship was a source of pain. "That way I lay up suffering—I care so deeply and miss my friends so desperately—despite tons of common sense and all the philosophy that can be applied."[13] Her disappointment in herself turned to bitterness against the world, especially the world of publishers.

The book trade is now big business, with ramifications and competition on a "global" plane. Caught in its coils, publishers seek a formula by which the novel can be assembled to belong nowhere so as to apply anywhere so as to facilitate standardization and mass production—and then on the level of a soft drink or chewing-gum, to be disposed of to a sequacious public by a bally-hoo of advertising and high-pressured salesmanship.[14]

At a Fellowship of Australian Writers meeting in January 1952 Miles said: "Nothing can be published nowadays but best-sellers. You have to write to a formula to get on ... Writers have told me it is easier for them to adapt others' work ... Adapting and adapting ... they'll run out of stuff, these fifth and sixth raters, then they'll need the creative writers."[15] Asked when she was "going to give us another novel," Miles said: "I haven't the time to write a novel and they only want best-sellers now."[16]

Harley Matthews, writing a tribute to Miles after her death, found another reason for her deep sadness. She was a "crusader" and all she strove for turned to dust in her hands.

In her lifetime she had seen what she had hoped for, pleaded for, worked for, come to pass. There had come into being a League of Nations, a United Nations, pacts outlawing war, all assuring Peace for evermore—Amen. She had seen the women of many countries presented with the Vote, and in nearly every country made independent of the male, and therefore presented with more leisure. Never before had the labourer been so sure of his hire, or so much of it, and he too had more leisure. And at last there were Australian publishers who published books by Australian authors and who found it paid because they kept on publishing them.

Yet today there are still wars and threats of bigger-than-ever wars; women are still women the world over, vote or no vote; the average man despite his high and sure wage and his plentiful leisure is still the average man with all the old lusts and appetites, still interested in anything but things of the mind, the Australian writer who must write something more than mediocre, still finds that he will not get even mediocre pay.[17]

This was true, and in her sleepless nights Miles's mind may well have filled with such thoughts. But I think that the core of her distress was her inability to write. Without husband or children her continuity was in her books. Part of herself was painfully amputated now she could no longer produce creative work. Any writer would agree with me.

Sad as she was at heart, Miles did not wear her grief upon her sleeve. She was too proud for that, and her "habit of character" kept the smile on her lips and the dancing light in her eyes.

CHAPTER 11

Everyone has a Philosophy

LIKE the man who, when he asked, "What is prose?" was amazed to hear that he had been reading, writing and speaking it all his life, we all have a philosophy of life. It is inescapable. We may never put it into words but it is there, it is the sum of our attitude to all the important experiences and situations in life. Miles Franklin, one of the least academic of people, had a well-marked philosophy.

At this moment in her story, when her life was at pause, it would be profitable to examine this creed under a few important headings. I promise to be brief, as much of the material is already scattered through this book in one form or another. I shall lean heavily on quotation, for I do not want to be like the schoolboy who began his essay "The poet means to say..."

I *Of Her Native Land*

Miles loved Australia. In all the years she spent overseas its beauty haunted her and its ghostly rivers sang in her memory. Her love was focused on the bush and within the bush on the mountainous, well-watered country where she was born, the Monaro.

There are many passages in her books praising the beauty of the scenery and its unique character. She went further. She saw Australia as the country of the fresh start where humanity could regenerate itself. Before the white man came to this fifth continent there were no diseases or pests. It was pure. Miles makes of this purity a moral quality. Miles reverses the "pathetic fallacy" in which nature is made to mirror the emotions of man so that for the young lovers it is springtime, for the despairing the sky is overcast, the landscape dark and forbidding. She substitutes another fallacy. For her the untainted land is a good influence upon the inhabitants, ennobling them.

Miles, after quoting Furphy who "under harassment or disappointment would remark with humorous philosophy 'Never mind, I still have Australia'," says:

Others have, and will continue to have Australia in spiritual or aesthetic satisfaction. Just to go abroad on her wide surfaces, to drink in the blue and dreaming distances, to soak in the haunting gone-awayness and mystery that enshrouds them, to breathe their freedom from exploding civilizations, is a more exalting nectar than the vintners can distil.[1]

It was from the Australian earth, not Australia the political entity, that Miles drew her strength. To it she gave her love. She had no illusions about politicians or politics, she recognized dullness and monotony in the Australian way of life. She knew her people had a long way to go. She was not a "my country right or wrong" woman. But for the artist and the writer there was, she felt, a Castalian fountain within, as Miles would put it, their "own bailiwick."

Literature is dependent on ideas for life, but irrespective of nationality it derives warmth from infatuation—an obsession as consuming as love or hatred—and will continue to draw deeply on attachment to native soil.[2]

To the earth Miles added the horse as an ennobling and liberating element.

Absence of backward breeds abolished the flunkey class; the transformations of the peasant element was the contribution of the horse. No man can remain a peasant and go a-horse. Willy-nilly the blood, saddle horse will limber him out of his peasant characteristics. This four-footed brother cannot supply what Nature omitted, and liven dunces into intelligence, but he can change their bovine peculiarities into those of jockeys or caballeros of sorts.[3]

Even women were freed by the horse.

Regardless of sex, the Australian bush child had a horse long before he was seven. Children went a-horse in their parents' arms before they could sit up. At an earlier age they rode with their indefeatable mothers to be born, for though property rights for women on the Murrumbidgee had not advanced far beyond Brehon Law, the exigencies of pioneering put women on horseback.[4]

Those valiant horses carried the burden of pioneering, as pack horses or harnessed to the plough. Their speed was the lifeline of the lonely, scattered homesteads. Then they were shipped to India in their thousands as army remounts, they went to war with the Australian Light Horse to Egypt and Palestine and none returned. At the end their riders shot them as the kinder fate. Their day is over now except for the few. Those that escaped to the bush and bred in the mountains, the brumbies, are being rounded up, trucked in terror and slaughtered to provide the pet food shops. What would Miles's comment be? Are Australians less free?

II *Of War and Wastage*

Miles saw war at first-hand, she had no illusions about its grandeur. She saw it in terms of the dead and maimed and realized its futility. For her World War I was "the great idiocy, the unforgivable betrayal."[5]

War was "the recurring lunacy"[6] that destroyed whoever took up the sword.

For the writer, too, war was disastrous.

Then for the second time within the same generation world war, by laying waste the present and mortgaging the future to disaster, baffled any of the senior novelists who were not stifled. How many potential juniors were destroyed, retarded or battered out of their bent cannot be computed. Some accepted the challenge of the immediate hour, but, with rare exceptions, novels written while the rage of battle lingers are inadequate or mere documentaries: none within the period reached the "world standard" which the academical firmly demand of Australian novels. The last decade of the half-century was ruined for many writers by the dearth of paper and tradesmen to produce books—if written. The present is the most difficult for novelists, major or minor, to portray with insight and balance . . .[7]

"But dead men write no novels."[8]

The Boer War is portrayed, off stage, in *Cockatoos*, World War I with considerable bitterness in *All That Swagger*. About World War II Miles did not write at all.

III *Of Heroes*

In turning our attention to Miles's delineation of male characters we are moving into an amusing field. Here the ardent feminist and the incurable romantic came into head-on collision. In her handling of all things masculine Miles is extraordinarily innocent for one who grew up in a mob of brothers, cousins, uncles. . . Her male characters fall into three main types.

There is the domestic tyrant of which Old Blastus (*Old Blastus of Bandicoot*) is the richest example. He is comic as well as tyrannous. He is an Uncle Sally. Old Mazere (*Up the Country* and *Ten Creeks Run*) throwing mustard pots at his daughter's suitors, is a more refined version. Old Healey (*Ten Creeks Run*) sacrificing his daughter to keep his property is a third.

Then we have the gentle, noble-hearted man who idealizes the woman he loves and asks nothing of her. Arthur Masters who quietly stands aside to let Ignez have her career (*Cockatoos*) is such a one. So is Sir Hugh la ffollette (*Prelude to Waking*) and Dick Mazere (*Back to Bool Bool*) the poet who loves Freda but knows that she is not for him, and Harry Delacy and his son Darcy, (*All That Swagger*). In a minor role there is Stapleton who adores and does not presume (*Up the Country*).

We come at last to the hero par excellence. Bert Pool dominates *Up the Country* and *Ten Creeks Run* and he has everything. He is, to begin with "singularly handsome" and "no deed of daring or chivalry was beyond him . . ."[9] He could "shoot the eye out of a mosquito" and was "only a shade less wonderful at bush lore than the aborigines." ". . . Bert and his black mare, reclaimed from the wild horses towards the Bulla Bulla Mountains, could perform feats beyond normal men."[10]

He was hopelessly in love with beautiful Rachel Mazere and had the anguish of seeing her wed another.

His full beauty bursts upon us:

He had changed perceptibly since the wedding. Boyish gawkiness had left him. He had gained poise and assurance and was lithe and sure in his movements. His silence made his beauty the more striking. He was six feet one inch in his socks, and straight and well-formed from his well-cut head to his long sunburnt hand with the filbert nails like Charlotte's [his sister], which all the hard work could not entirely disfigure in either of them. His black hair was straight with a crisp white parting. His brows were level and delicate, his nose well-formed and of dignified size. His lips firm and sweet and at present smudged by a small silky moustache, just to show what he could do, for clean lips and chins were the order of the day among Society leaders, the only hirsute garnish below the eyebrows being a little patch of lawn near the ears.[11]

All the girls adored him, of course. He had a wonderful way with horses and children. There was no coarseness in him at all. He could love unrequited with the best of them. He is rewarded at last by the love of an innocent girl, young enough to be his granddaughter.

Peter Pool is somewhat in his image but not so lush (*Gentlemen at Gyang Gyang*). He at least has the same ennobling purity of mind and handsome physique.

Villains are not numerous but where they occur they are cast as anti-heroes, as black as Bert Pool is white. Ced Spires is the most notable, a very nasty piece of work (*Gentlemen at Gyang Gyang*). Flash Billy is also a particularly low type (*Ten Creeks Run*).

There are a great many other male characters who do not fit into any of these categories. They are either stage properties or simply woman-fodder. They are created to admire and even sometimes to marry the heroines. Harold Beecham (*My Brilliant Career*), Henry Beauchamp (*My Career Goes Bung*) and Ernest Breslaw (*Some Everyday Folk and Dawn*) are obviously measured for this purpose. So are Ronald Dice (*Ten Creeks Run*), Simon Labosseer (*Up the Country*) and Malcolm Timson (*Cockatoos*). They can easily be picked out. Their role is like that of male dancers in old-fashioned ballets whose sole duty was to support the ballerina.

Miles is less successful in drawing men than women. They appear artificial because her treatment is either too romantic, even sickly, or she is too eager to score off them in the interests of women's rights.

IV *Of Heroines*

Hero and heroine are old-fashioned terms but then Miles was old-fashioned in many of her attitudes. She created heroes and heroines and no doubt believed them necessary to a well furnished book. She was deeply involved in all her people. Some she loved and on them she heaped praise and caresses. Others she disliked and treated with contempt.

Except for Bert Pool and Danny Delacy her affections centred mainly on the women in her books. They fall roughly into two categories, "a group of noble dames," inspired perhaps by her grandmother, and a host of beautiful young creatures, virginal and spirited.

Amongst the former are Mrs. Mazere (*Up the Country* and *Ten Creeks Run*), Rachel Labosseer (*Up the Country* and *Cockatoos*) Miss Jessie M'Eachern (*ibid.*), Mrs. Clay (*Some Everyday Folk and Dawn*), Maria Brennan, Charlotte Pool ... Johanna Delacy does not quite make the grade because first place is reserved for her husband Danny. They are all wise and competent, generous, noble-hearted, dignified and full of good works.

The beautiful young creatures might all be sisters. They are pure and spirited as well as exquisite. Miles loved to deck them out in their finery and show off their charms. Here is Emily Mazere at her coming of age ball:

> She was a fairy apparition in her tulle or jaconet, or organdie, or whatever it was, but it was white and diaphanous and virginal. Laces and frills billowed around her lovely young form on the hoops that Hugh had carried for her all folded in his valise. Her ringlets were like minted gold, her eyes blue as the skies above old Kosciusko, her cheeks

like England's lilies and roses. Gladness and youth and chastity enwrapped her.[12]

All these maidens were besieged by suitors but none of them would brook the slightest familiarity. Sybylla Melvyn slashed Harold Beecham across the face for wanting a kiss when he thought they were betrothed. Dawn threw dishwater over her Ernest for no reason at all except that she happened to be thinking all men were beasts. Rachel Mazere, when Simon proposed to her, threw a cabbage and the knife she had just cut it with, at him. Milly fought on horseback for her honour which was not really threatened and then rode ninety miles to safety, her escort left lying unconscious in a pit. This was not Milly's first experience. Donald and Ronald had both paid her attention and Ronald had snatched a kiss.

And now Ronald disclosed himself as of the same quality as Donald, whereas Milly had kept herself unspotted—but Ronald! Who can estimate the anguish of a high-spirited maiden when awakening to the electrifying passion of first love to find the reptile lust confronting her? . . . His one kiss had disturbed her considerably. Her first kiss from a lover. To her it almost meant betrothal.[13]

Ignez was friendly but did not even notice that Arthur loved her. Freda was an untouchable (*Back to Bool Bool*). Only Dot Saunders (*Cockatoos*) and Mabel Barry (*Old Blastus of Bandicoot*) ever fell and they spent the rest of their lives ruing their wickedness.

It is revealing to consider the fate of all these girls. Sybylla, surrounded by eligible suitors, will have none of them. Her recorded life ends in stalemate (*My Brilliant Career* and *My Career Goes Bung*). Dawn marries her Ernest, he is well subjugated and the story does not pursue them into the future (*Some Everyday Folk and Dawn*). Emily Mazere loves Bert Pool but she is drowned on the eve of her wedding (*Up the Country*). Jessie M'Eachern proposes to Bert, is gently refused and remains a spinster. Mary Brennan becomes a nun through unrequited love of Bert. Rachel marries Simon Labosseer, an honourable man who shortly dies and leaves her to fulfil her destiny as a matriarch. Bert loves Rachel but never wins her as maid or matron (*Up the Country*). Aileen Healey loves Ronald Dice but must marry a man old enough to be her father (*Ten Creeks Run*). Freda Healey loves Dick Mazere and he her, but they never come together, knowing it hopeless. Mollye Brennan, the prima donna, proposes marriage to Dick but he eludes her and she is left with her empty fame. Laleen Mazere loves Nat Horan, the pianist, but he is drowned. This group of frustrated lovers are all to be found in *Back to Bool Bool*. Zarl

Osterley mocks her suitors and goes on fancy free (*Bring the Monkey*). Ignez Milford loves no one and goes her lonely, disappointed way. Bridget Finnigan loves Wynd Norton but he is killed in the Boer War. Sylvia Mazere loves Malcolm Timson, but dies in the early years of her marriage (*Cockatoos*). Clare Margaret loves her cousin Darcy but he dies after a few short years of marriage. Della Delacy, embittered by spinsterhood, marries late a boy her junior (*All That Swagger*). Bernice Gaylord proposes to Peter Pool, the marriage actually takes place but Peter surrenders himself completely to her career (*Gentlemen at Gyang Gyang*). Larry Healey loves Milly but must marry Dot Saunders. Milly loves, proposes to and marries Bert Pool who is old enough to be her grandfather (*Ten Creeks Run*). Merlin Giltinane loves Nigel Barraclough but he only discovers his feeling for her too late (*Prelude to Waking*).

This is an extraordinary record of frustration, nor is it all. There is also a long string of disappointed wives and reluctant spinsters. There is many a slip between the lip and the loving cup.

V *Of Love and Marriage*

Miles draws a distinction between love, which hardly exists outside dreams, and what she calls *amour*. Amour is a snare and a delusion. It is sex, and "the quicksand of sex forever confronted the unwary." [14]

The young girl Laleen asks Freda:

"Isn't there any real and lasting love—not *ever*?" and Freda answers:
"One kind of love is only a delusion of animal magnetism, a *fata morgana*. Sometimes when its glow has diminished two people miraculously find themselves enjoying sweet friendship and continue in companionship—they are blessed." [15]

That is about the best that Miles can say for marriage. If her characters are married before the book begins, well and good. Life must go on. If they are not she has the greatest difficulty in getting them to the altar.

Dick declares:

"Marriage is for the heroic and I'm only a poor shy dingo craving to crawl into some secluded hollow log and be at peace;" and "marriage could be unresting purgatory. Someone always waiting to devour in the name of love." [16]

Ignez cries, "I don't believe that the kind of love that poets rave about is decent. How could it be?"[17] Freda Healey has "an incurable disgust for marriage."[18]

Even little Milly thinks:

> It was disgusting that the wonder of a lovely little baby of one's very own should rest upon such vulgar horror. Ugh! She would not marry at all, no matter what anyone said about old maids.[19]

The woman characters are all very vocal on the subject of love and marriage. What the men think is rarely revealed. They are the ravening wolves. The grand seduction scenes flop badly.

Arthur Ashworth has something to say about the war of the sexes in Miles's novels:

> And this is a most fascinating war, because one is beguiled into romance and sentiment, then shocked by the writer insisting upon realism at a point where a really romantic writer would consider it a most impossible intrusion. Romantic happiness is reserved for the lesser characters and a tragic frustration, allied with fortitude, is the lot of the chief personages. "Amour" is analysed with clinical objectivity, due tribute being paid to its glamour...[20]

Miles Franklin's outlook in her seventies was very much the same as it had been in her youth. Some but not all of her crudities had been shed. She changed less than most people do. Her outlook remained that of the 1890's. She went on fighting old battles.

It would be quite wrong to think of Miles as a tough feminist, a battle axe, because of her attitude towards marriage and her contempt, even loathing, for what she insisted on calling *amour*. She was neither tough nor hard.

She held in her heart an impossible ideal of human relationships and when she found it unrealizable, not so much for herself as in the lives of others, she was bitterly hurt and disappointed. All those lovely girls in her books deserved something better than the dull marriages of servitude to husband and children. She rescued them even if it meant drowning them. Or if marry they must it was to some cypher of a man, or there must be some unusual element in the marriage, a disparity in age as when Della married a boy nearly young enough to be her son and Milly married a man old enough to be her grandfather, and Clare Margaret married a cousin which was almost, in the eyes of her family, like wedding a brother. The dearest of her creations, Ignez and Freda, were out of bounds for any marriage.

Miles did not hate men. Her books make that clear. She did find it degrading to be a woman in a man's world. That love and marriage should put chains on a woman she found revolting. Freda often speaks for Miles and she cried: "I *would not* be a slave, a weak puling slave, to be undone and be fooled by such a simple weakness of the flesh, such as ignoble one." [21]

Miles, like her heroines, valued purity above all. Love should be spiritual. That it had another side she, rather unjustly, blamed on men.

Back in the 1890's, where Miles stayed, married women did not have careers, only in rare instances were their talents considered. They did not plan their families. Life often turned them into drudges.

Miles was involved in a love-hate relationship with life. Her writer's temperament and Irish blood led her to exaggeration. She was caught in a complex of love-fear-and-hatred. She turned it all into a crusade. She was a crusader, not a battler.

It was the same at seventy-five as it had been at twenty-one, but she had grown tired in the one-sided, profitless battle.

CHAPTER 12

Farewell and Hail

I *Death of a Writer*

ALWAYS fragile but with a great spirit, Miles in her seventies began to fail in health. She was depleted by insomnia, but that malady does not kill. She also had a heart condition that was getting worse. Her friends were often worried to see her looking ill but she rarely complained and did not welcome solicitude. She continued to live alone at Carlton. Miles had always feared death. Long ago in *My Career Goes Bung* she had written of the "awful silence which I hate and resent."[1] In 1941 she wrote to Nettie Palmer:

I have a great distaste for birthdays and for my middle-aged friends publishing their years, because once or twice I have been so happy in the companionship of elders whom I thought in the prime of life. Suddenly they announced a filthy birthday away up near the allotted span and I became nearly ill thinking that so much of their time had gone and they might leave me alone in this lonely world. The going of anyone I know, in any degree, makes me ill—there I am honest and publish my weakness. A person with such a mentality could never achieve anything in this life, except affection—and what good is that?[2]

As her illness progressed Miles grew very tired, so tired that even her fear of death was dimmed, too tired to do anything but let herself drift out on the tide.

Miles Franklin died on 19 September 1954. Her body was cremated and by her wish her ashes were scattered on the Jounania Creek at Talbingo. Miles had come back to the country where she was born and that she loved so dearly. Her lullaby was "the cool, familiar song of the river poured between day and night like eterity whispering Hussssssssssh to the mundane disharmonies of man."[3]

II *And After*

As long ago as 1930 Miles wrote to Nettie Palmer: "We do need in Australia those to mother us out of the caterpillar stage."[4] She was speaking of Australian literature and the need of writers for help. During her lifetime and even today, few creative writers could or can hope to live by their pens. They must work at something else to make a living and that leaves them little time or energy to write. A population of ten to eleven million people does not provide a large market for any but best-sellers. The Australian writer, Miles felt, needed patronage. The State, through the Commonwealth Literary Fund, helped by subsidy to keep writers writing. The value of this is not only financial; it is an assertion that writers are of value to the community, that what they have to give is of importance and has a right to public support.

Miles felt that it would have made a great difference to her if she had had help and encouragement. She wrote to Mrs. Palmer in 1933: "I am destitute and no one to push or encourage me as I have spent my life in doing for others."[5] In using the word "destitute" she did not mean that she was penniless, rather that she was destitute of ideas for a book and unable to write. Had she had more encouragement, she argued to herself, everything might have been different and she would have had the incentive to go on writing.

It was in these years that Miles decided that she would do something for her fellow-writers. If she could not write herself she could and would help others. To that end she began to save money, with the intention of endowing a foundation which would provide an annual prize for a novel which illuminated a phase of Australian life. It was to be called The Miles Franklin Award. Each year now a prize of £500 is awarded to the best novel submitted. It is the most valuable literary prize offered regularly in Australia and attracts a large field. The first time it was awarded the Prime Minister made the presentation and the Leader of the Opposition also made a speech. To be invited to the party is a coveted honour.

So long as this prize is given Miles Franklin's name will be remembered, but she has a more important claim to immortality. Hers is a very special place in Australian literature and in the Australian legend. It is not her style or her technique that is important; it is her subject matter.

In her novels she summed up for Australians their pastoral age, the day-to-day life of the squatter and the small farmer, in a way that it has never been done before or since. She knew it at first hand, though only in her youth. Her parents, her grandparents, her uncles and aunts had been pioneers. She had a great fund of memories, experienced and related, to draw upon. She recreated an era that has gone and will never come again. The future historian, the student of economics, the sociologist, will read Miles's books for the living pictures of a time and place that they present. Others will read them for their natural verve and the lively stories they tell.

To Australians, pioneers and the pastoral age have a very special significance. Our pride is rooted in them. The peaceful conquest of a continent is our saga and is, we think and feel, uniquely Australian. I have stressed Miles's ancestry, her early experiences and her bush background. Without an understanding of these the true value and historic importance of her work cannot be appreciated.

Miles Franklin, like her hero Joseph Furphy, was Australian to the core and gave back to her countrymen their own image in the most acceptable form. On that her immortality rests.

Notes and References

Chapter One
1. T. I. Moore, ed., *Australia Writes* (Melbourne, 1953), p. 278.
2. Quoted by permission of Miles Franklin's friend, Pixie O'Harris (Mrs. Bruce Pratt), the artist, from an address given before the Fellowship of Australian Writers.
3. Thelma Forshaw, "Stella and Miles," *Nation*, 10 Aug. 1963, p. 22.
4. E. Morris Miller, Frederick T. Macartney, eds., *Australian Literature: a bibliography to 1938*, extended to 1950 (Melbourne, 1956), p. 184.

Chapter Two
1. *Childhood at Brindabella* (Sydney, 1963), p. 23.
2. *Ibid.*, pp. 24–25.
3. Douglas Stewart, "Brindabella," *Meanjin Quarterly* (No. 4, 1962), p. 410.
4. From an unpublished manuscript by John Tierney.
5. *Gentlemen at Gyang Gyang* (Sydney, 1956), p. 15.
6. From an unpublished manuscript by John Tierney.
7. "Brindabella" (above, note 3), p. 406.
8. *Ibid.*
9. Danny Delacy.
10. *All That Swagger*, p. 73.
11. *Childhood at Brindabella*, pp. 118–119.
12. *Ibid.*, pp. 121–122.
13. *Ibid.*, p. 1.
14. *Ibid.*, p. 130.
15. *Ibid.*, p. 10.
16. *Ibid.*, p. 2.
17. *Ibid.*, p. 24.

Chapter Three
1. *Childhood at Brindabella*, pp. 19–20.
2. *Ibid.*, p. 20.
3. *Ibid.*, p. 20.
4. *Ibid.*, p. 107.
5. *Ibid.*, Publisher's note p. vi.
6. *Ibid.*, p. 72.
7. *Ibid.*, p. 69.

8. *Ibid.*, p. 18.
9. *Ibid.*, p. 120.
10. *Ibid.*, p. 85.
11. *Ibid.*, p. 84.
12. *Ibid.*, p. 138.
13. *Ibid.*, p. 96.
14. *Ibid.*, p. 141.
15. *Ibid.*, p. 142.
16. *Ibid.*, pp. 158–159.
17. *Ibid.*, p. 142.
18. *Ten Creeks Run* (Edinburgh, 1930), p. 44.
19. *Ibid.*, p. 36.
20. *Ibid.*, p. 33.
21. *All That Swagger* (Sydney, 1936), p. 362.
22. Blenkinsop appears in *Ten Creeks Run*.
23. *Up the Country* (Edinburgh, 1928), p. 33.
24. *Back to Bool Bool* (Edinburgh, 1931), p. 83.
25. *Ten Creeks Run*, p. 123.
26. *Back to Bool Bool*, p. 279.
27. *Gentlemen at Gyang Gyang*, pp. 51–52.
28. Preface, *Up the Country*, p. xi.
29. *Childhood at Brindabella*, pp. 52–53.
30. *Ibid.*, p. 57.
31. *Ten Creeks Run*, pp. 201–202.
32. Preface, *Up the Country*, p. xi.

Chapter Four

1. Frontispiece, *Childhood at Brindabella*.
2. *Laughter, Not for a Cage* (Sydney, 1956), p. 106.
3. Vance Palmer, *The Legend of the Nineties* (Melbourne, 1954), pp. 9–10.
4. *Ibid.*, p. 77.
5. Bernard O'Dowd, *Collected Works* (Melbourne, 1941), p. 35.
6. *Ibid.*, p. 208.
7. *Up the Country*, p. 20.
8. *Laughter, Not for a Cage*, p. 105.
9. *Ibid.*, p. 114.
10. Editor of *The Bulletin*.
11. *Laughter, Not for a Cage*, p. 99.
12. Preface, *My Career Goes Bung* (Melbourne, 1946).
13. *Laughter, Not for a Cage*, p. 119.
14. *My Brilliant Career* (Edinburgh, 1901), p. 21.
15. *Ibid.*, p. 24.
16. *Ibid.*, p. 26.
17. *Ibid.*, p. 27.
18. *Ibid.*, p. 47.

NOTES AND REFERENCES

19. *Ibid.*, p. 49.
20. *Ibid.*, p. 113.
21. *Ibid.*, p. 207.
22. *Ibid.*, p. 45.
23. *Ibid.*, p. 79.
24. *Ibid.*, p. 225.
25. "A Bookful of Sunlight," *The Bulletin*, Sept. 28, 1901, Red Page. [The Red Page of *The Bulletin* was traditionally famous for its reviews. This page has no number. The review in question is printed inside of the journal's cover.]
26. *Ibid.*, Red Page.
27. H. M. Green, *A History of Australian Literature*, I (Sydney, 1961), p. 640.
28. R. Mathew, *Miles Franklin* (Melbourne, 1963), p. 8, quoting from *Weekly Critical Review* (Paris), Sept. 17, 1903.
29. Mathew, p. 11.
30. *Ibid.*, p. 30.
31. Cecil Hadgraft, *Australian Literature* (London, 1960), p. 164.
32. *My Brilliant Career*, p. 162.
33. Mathew, p. 19.
34. "A Bookful of Sunlight," *The Bulletin*, Sept. 28, 1901, Red Page [see above].
35. *My Career Goes Bung*, pp. 37–38.
36. *Ibid.*, p. 55.
37. *Laughter, Not for a Cage*, p. 119.
38. Mathew, "Appendix II," p. 34.
39. *Ibid.*, p. 35.
40. *Laughter, Not for a Cage*, p. 119.
41. William Moore in *New Idea*, May 6, 1904, p. 998.
42. Serialized in *New Idea*, 1904.
43. Miles Franklin, "Rose Scott," in *The Peaceful Army* (Sydney, 1938), p. 91.
44. *Ibid.*, pp. 91–92.
45. *Ibid.*, p. 93.
46. *Ibid.*, p. 93.
47. *Ibid.*, p. 98.
48. *Ibid.*, p. 99.
49. Miles Franklin, *Joseph Furphy* (Sydney, 1944), pp. 95–96.
50. *Ibid.*, p. 97.
51. *Ibid.*, p. 97.
52. *Ibid.*, p. 125.
53. *Ibid.*, p. 99.
54. *My Career Goes Bung*, p. 211.
55. *Ibid.*, p. 204.
56. Hadgraft (above, note 31), p. 164.
57. *My Career Goes Bung*, pp. 226–227.
58. *Ibid.*, p. 120.

59. *Ibid.*, p. 110.
60. *Ibid.*, p. 76.
61. *Ibid.*, pp. 228–229.
62. *Ibid.*, p. 187.
63. *Ibid.*, p. 12.
64. *Ibid.*, p. 195.
65. *Ibid.*, p. 189.
66. *Ibid.*, p. 233.
67. *Cockatoos* (Sydney, 1954), p. 148.
68. *Back to Bool Bool.*
69. *Cockatoos.*

Chapter Five

1. *Cockatoos*, p. 249.
2. *Ibid.*, p. 249.
3. Alice Henry, *Memoir* (Melbourne, 1944), p. 89.
4. *Joseph Furphy*, p. 125.
5. *Cockatoos*, p. 251.
6. *Back to Bool Bool*, p. 64.
7. Preface, *My Career Goes Bung*, p. 7.
8. *Some Everyday Folk and Dawn* (Edinburgh, 1909), p. 2.
9. *Ibid.*, p. 337.
10. *Ibid.*, pp. 93–94.
11. *Ibid.*, p. 308.
12. *Ibid.*, p. 11.

Chapter Six

1. Alice Henry, *Memoir*, p. 89.
2. *Back to Bool Bool*, p. 137.
3. *Prelude to Waking* (Sydney, 1950), p. 7.
4. *Childhood at Brindabella*, p. 35.
5. *Laughter, Not for a Cage*, p. 140.
6. *Prelude to Waking*, p. 33.
7. *Ibid.*, p. 118.
8. *Old Blastus of Bandicoot* (London, 1931).

Chapter Seven

1. *Up the Country*, p. 20.
2. *All That Swagger*, p. 409.
3. *Ibid.*, p. 27.
4. *Ten Creeks Run*, p. 118.
5. This incident takes place in *Up the Country*.
6. This is evidenced in *All That Swagger*.
7. Vance Palmer and P. R. Stephensen.
8. *My Career Goes Bung*, p. 230.

NOTES AND REFERENCES

9. Nettie Palmer, "More Brent of Bin Bin," *Illustrated Tasmanian Mail*, June 18, 1930, p. 4.

10. E. Morris Miller, ed., *Australian Literature: a Bibliography*, p. 80.

11. Miles Franklin to Nettie Palmer in an unpublished letter dated July 22, 1929.

12. *Up the Country*, Preface, p. viii.

13. Ray Mathew, *op. cit.*, pp. 22–23.

14. *Up the Country*, p. 387.

1930, p. 4.

15. "More Brent of Bin Bin," *Illustrated Tasmanian Mail*, June 18,

16. *Up the Country*, p. 154.

17. *Ibid.*, p. 126.

18. *Ibid.*, p. 116.

19. *Ibid.*, p. 39.

20. *Ten Creeks Run*, p. 276.

21. "More Brent of Bin Bin," *Illustrated Tasmanian Mail*, June 18, 1930, p. 4.

22. *Ten Creeks Run*, p. 222.

23. *Ibid.*, p. 224.

24. *Ibid.*, p. 226.

25. *Ibid.*, p. 252.

26. *Ibid.*, p. 157.

27. *Ibid.*, p. 275.

28. *Ibid.*, p. 276.

29. *Cockatoos*, pp. 3–4.

30. *Ten Creeks Run*, p. 125.

31. *Cockatoos*, p. 4.

32. "Steele Rudd" (Arthur Hoey Davis), *On Our Selection* (Sydney, 1899).

33. *Cockatoos*, p. 2.

34. *Ibid.*, pp. 2–3.

35. *Ibid.*, p. 4.

36. *Ibid.*, p. 6.

37. *Ibid.*, p. 7.

38. *Ibid.*, p. 214.

39. *Ibid.*, p. 63.

40. *Ibid.*, pp. 231–232.

41. *Ibid.*, p. 236.

42. *Ibid.*, p. 1.

43. *Ibid.*, p. 1.

44. *Ibid.*, p. 270.

45. *Ibid.*, Preface.

46. *Gentlemen at Gyang Gyang*, p. 32.

47. *Ibid.*, p. 158.

48. *Ibid.*, p. 80.

49. *Ibid.*, p. 21.

50. This occurs in *Up the Country*.
51. This occurs in *Ten Creeks Run*.
52. Mathew, p. 7.
53. *Back to Bool Bool*, p. 235.
54. *Ibid.*, p. 55.
55. *Ibid.*, p. 98.
56. *Ibid.*, pp. 241–242.
57. *Ibid.*, p. 132.
58. *Ibid.*, p. 97.
59. *Ibid.*, p. 110.
60. *Ibid.*, p. 170.
61. *Ibid.*, p. 247.
62. *Ibid.*, p. 94.
63. Dawn appears in *Some Everyday Folk and Dawn*.
64. Dora appears in *Old Blastus of Bandicoot*.
65. *Back to Bool Bool*, p. 29.
66. *Ibid.*, p. 311.
67. *Ibid.*, p. 316.
68. *Ibid.*, p. 5.
69. *Ibid.*, p. 50.
70. *Ibid.*, p. 266.
71. *Ibid.*, p. 266.
72. *Ibid.*, p. 249.
73. *Ibid.*, p. 271.
74. *Ibid.*, p. 292.
75. *Ibid.*, p. 18.
76. *Ibid.*, p. 164.

Chapter Eight

1. *Bring the Monkey* (London, 1931), p. 151.
2. *Ibid.*, p. 164.
3. *Ibid.*, p. 38.
4. *Ibid.*, p. 11.
5. *Ibid.*, p. 12.
6. *Ibid.*, p. 98.
7. *Ibid.*, p. 186.
8. *Ibid.*, p. 185.
9. *Old Blastus of Bandicoot*, p. 15.
10. *Ibid.*, p. 181.
11. *Ibid.*, p. 18.
12. *Ibid.*, p. 106.
13. *Ibid.*, p. 16.
14. *Ibid.*, p. 37.
15. *Ibid.*, p. 114.
16. *Ibid.*, p. 62.
17. *Ibid.*, p. 47.

18. *Ibid.*, p. 78.
19. *All That Swagger*, p. 14.
20. *Ibid.*, pp. 26–27.
21. *Ibid.*, p. 63.
22. *Ibid.*, p. 29.
23. *Ibid.*, p. 30.
24. *Ibid.*, pp. 493–494.
25. *Ibid.*, p. 230.
26. *Ibid.*, p. 228.
27. *Ibid.*, p. 76.
28. *Ibid.*, p. 78.
29. *Ibid.*, p. 111.
30. *Ibid.*, p. 101.
31. *Ibid.*, p. 101.
32. *Ibid.*, p. 290.
33. *Ibid.*, pp. 267–268.
34. *Ibid.*, p. 266.
35. *Ibid.*, p. 131.
36. *Ibid.*, p. 217.
37. *Ibid.*, p. 75.
38. Menura is the scientific name for the lyrebird, so called because its tail, raised in courting display, is the shape of the musical instrument. The bird is also famous for its mimicry; the species is peculiar to Australia.
39. *All That Swagger*, pp. 125–126.
40. *Ibid.*, p. 413.
41. *Ibid.*, p. 412.
42. *Ibid.*, p. 394.
43. *Ibid.*, p. 395.
44. *Ibid.*, p. 412.
45. *Ibid.*, p. 22.
46. *Ibid.*, p. 270.
47. Hadgraft, pp. 165-166.
48. *Childhood at Brindabella*, pp. 53 ff.
49. *Ibid.*, pp. 53–54.
50. *All That Swagger*, p. 289.
51. *Ibid.*, p. 286.

Chapter Nine

1. Preface, *My Career Goes Bung*, p. 7.
2. Mathew, p. 17.
3. *Miles Franklin: a Tribute* (Melbourne, 1955), p. 25.
4. *Pioneers on Parade* (Sydney, 1939), p. 75.
5. *Ibid.*, p. 153.
6. *Ibid.*, p. 108.
7. *Ibid.*, p. 152.

8. *Ibid.*, p. 121.
9. *Ibid.*, p. 204.
10. *Ibid.*, p. 161.
11. *Ibid.*, p. 245.
12. *Ibid.*, p. 219.
13. *Ibid.*, p. 10.
14. Miles Franklin, *Joseph Furphy: The Legend of a Man and His Book* (Sydney, 1944), Prefatory Note.
15. *Ibid.*, Acknowledgement.
16. *Joseph Furphy*, p. 124.
17. Alfred Vincent, an artist.
18. *Joseph Furphy*, p. 82.
19. Phil May was a well-known cartoonist. His full name was Philip William May. He was born in England in 1864 and in 1885, when he had made a name for himself with his drawings, he was offered a post on *The Bulletin* in Sydney. In 1888 he returned to England and worked on *Punch*. He died in 1903.
20. Victor James William Patrick Daley was born in Ireland in 1858. In 1878 he emigrated to Australia where he worked as a clerk and as a journalist. Much of his poetry was published in *The Bulletin*. He won fame if not financial success. Most of his poetry may be read in two collections: *At Dusk and Dawn* and *Wine and Roses*. He died in 1905.
21. *Joseph Furphy*, p. 113.
22. *Ibid.*, p. 38.
23. *Ibid.*, pp. 2–3.
24. *Ibid.*, p. 3.
25. *Ibid.*, p. 3.
26. *Ibid.*, p. 3.
27. *Laughter, Not for a Cage*, p. 230.
28. *Ibid.*, p. 1.
29. Ruse, James (1760–1837). He was born in Cornwall, England. In 1782 he was convicted at Bodmin Assizes of a crime, the nature of which is unknown, and condemned to transportation. In 1788 he was sent to Australia in the first fleet. As he knew something of farming and was of good behaviour Governor Phillip, in 1789, set him up on a small plot of land. He supported himself and his family and, as a reward, in 1790 was given the first land grant to be issued in the colony. It was of 30 acres at Parramatta, a settlement 16 miles from Sydney. He prospered and died a man of some substance.
30. *Laughter, Not for a Cage*, p. 8.
31. *Ibid.*, p. 3.
32. *Ibid.*, p. 15.
33. *Ibid.*, pp. 125–129.
34. *Ibid.*, p. 31.
35. Henry Handel Richardson was the pen name of Ethel Florence Lindesay Richardson who was born in Melbourne, Australia, in 1870. In 1887 her mother took her to Germany to study music but the girl

found that her talent lay in writing. In 1895 she married Professor J. G. Robertson. She died in England in 1946. The book on which her international reputation rests is *The Fortunes of Richard Mahony* in 3 vols. 1917-1929.

36. *Laughter, Not for a Cage*, p. 150.
37. Late eighteenth century.
38. *Laughter, Not for a Cage*, p. 14.
39. *Ibid.*, p. 199.
40. *Ibid.*, p. 224.
41. *Ibid.*, p. 91.
42. *Ibid.*, p. 127.
43. *Ibid.*, p. 61.
44. *Ibid.*, p. 227.
45. Published by Angus & Robertson Ltd., Sydney.
46. Shakespeare Head Press Pty. Ltd., Sydney.
47. Woolloomooloo, one of the wilder, poorer waterside suburbs of Sydney.
48. *Sydney Royal*, pp. 83-84.
49. Mathew, p. 23.
50. *Prelude to Waking*, p. 224.
51. *Ibid.*, p. 221.
52. *Ibid.*, p. 66.
53. *Ibid.*, p. 30.
54. *Ibid.*, p. 19.
55. *Ibid.*, p. 184.

Chapter Ten

1. *Childhood at Brindabella*, pp. 54-55.
2. *Back to Bool Bool*, p. 153.
3. Miles Franklin to Nettie Palmer, private correspondence.
4. A short story.
5. Letter from Miles Franklin to Nettie Palmer, private correspondence.
6. *Miles Franklin: A Tribute*, pp. 16-17.
7. Letter from Miles Franklin to Nettie Palmer, private correspondence.
8. *Ibid.*
9. *Ibid.*
10. *Ibid.*
11. *Ibid.*
12. *Ibid.*
13. *Ibid.*
14. *Laughter, Not for a Cage*, p. 221.
15. Mathew, "Appendix II," no pagination.
16. *Ibid.*
17. *Miles Franklin: A Tribute*, p. 19.

Chapter Eleven

1. *Laughter, Not for a Cage*, p. 228.
2. *Ibid.*
3. *All That Swagger*, p. 123.
4. *Ibid.*, p. 125.
5. *Prelude to Waking*, p. 28.
6. *Ibid.*, p. 119.
7. *Laughter, Not for a Cage*, pp. 206–207.
8. *Ibid.*, p. 141.
9. *Up the Country*, p. 86.
10. *Ibid.*, p. 68.
11. *Ibid.*, p. 162.
12. *Ibid.*, pp. 215–216.
13. *Ten Creeks Run*, p. 197.
14. *Back to Bool Bool*, p. 151.
15. *Ibid.*, p. 94.
16. *Ibid.*, p. 223.
17. *Cockatoos*, pp. 163–164.
18. *Back to Bool Bool*, p. 170.
19. *Ten Creeks Run*, p. 219.
20. *Southerly* No. 4, 1951.
21. *Back to Bool Bool*, p. 139.

Chapter Twelve

1. *My Career Goes Bung*, p. 164.
2. Letter from Miles Franklin to Nettie Palmer, unpublished correspondence, 1941.
3. *All That Swagger*, p. 383.
4. Letter from Miles Franklin to Nettie Palmer, unpublished correspondence, 1930.
5. Letter to Nettie Palmer, 1933.

Selected Bibliography

1. Books by Miles Franklin, in order of publication:

My Brilliant Career. Edinburgh: Blackwood, 1901.

Some Everyday Folk and Dawn. Edinburgh: Blackwood, 1909.

Up the Country: A Tale of the Early Australian Squattocracy by Brent of Bin Bin. Edinburgh: Blackwood, 1928.

Ten Creeks Run: A Tale of the Horse and Cattle Stations of the Murrumbidgee by Brent of Bin Bin. Edinburgh: Blackwood, 1930.

Back to Bool Bool: A Ramiparous Novel with Several Prominent Characters and a Hantle of Others Disposed as the Atolls of Oceania's Archipelagoes by Brent of Bin Bin. Edinburgh: Blackwood, 1931.

Old Blastus of Bandicoot: Opuscule on a Pioneer Tufted with Ragged Rhymes. London: Palmer, 1931.

Bring the Monkey: A Light Novel. Sydney: Endeavour Press, 1933.

All That Swagger. Sydney: Bulletin Co., 1936.

No Family, in *Best Australian One-Act Plays.* Sydney: Angus & Robertson, 1937.

Pioneers on Parade, with Dymphna Cusack. Sydney: Angus & Robertson, 1939.

Joseph Furphy: The Legend of a Man and His Book, with Kate Baker. Sydney: Angus & Robertson, 1944.

My Career Goes Bung: Purporting to be the Autobiography of Sybylla Penelope Melvyn. Melbourne: Georgian House, 1946.

Sydney Royal: Divertisement. Sydney: Shakespeare Head, 1947.

Prelude to Waking: A Novel in the First Person and Parentheses by Brent of Bin Bin. Sydney: Angus & Robertson, 1950.

Cockatoos: A Story of Youth and Exodists by Brent of Bin Bin. Sydney: Angus & Robertson, 1954.

Gentlemen at Gyang Gyang: A Tale of the Jambuck Pads on the Summer Runs by Brent of Bin Bin. Sydney: Angus & Robertson, 1956.

Laughter, Not for a Cage: Notes on Australian Writing, with Biographical Emphasis on the Struggles, Function, and Achievements of the Novel in Three Half-Centuries. Sydney: Angus & Robertson, 1956.

Childhood at Brindabella. Sydney: Angus & Robertson, 1963.

2. Short articles by Miles Franklin:

"Novels of the Bush," *Australian Mercury*, I (July 1935) 51–54.

"Literature," *Culture in War Time*, Central Cultural Council, Sydney, 1941, 40–44.

"Is the Writer Involved in the Political Development of His Country?" with L. G. Ashton, *Australian Writers Speak*. Fellowship of Australian Writers, Sydney, 1942, 21–32.

"Our Best Poets," *Southerly* (Sept. 1942) 23–26.

"Henry Lawson," *Meanjin Papers*, No. 12 (Dec. 1942) 17–20.

3. Books and articles about Miles Franklin:

Baker, Sidney J. *Australian language*. Sydney: Angus & Robertson, 1945, pp. 312, 315.

Barnard, Marjorie. "Miles Franklin," *Meanjin Quarterly*, XIV (Dec. 1955), 469–487.

Berkelouw, Book dealers, Sydney. Miles Franklin Manuscripts and Typescripts. 125 items described in 74 lots. Issued to commemorate the one hundred and fiftieth anniversary of the firm Messrs. Berkelouw, 1812–1962, with an illustrated brief history of the firm and biography-bibliography of Miles Franklin. Sydney, 1962.

Brockman, Henrietta Drake-. "Miles Franklin," *Australia Writes: An Anthology*. Edited by T. I. Moore. Melbourne: Cheshire, 1953.

Dutton, Geoffrey, ed. *Literature of Australia*. Adelaide: Penguin, 1964, pp. 186, 188–190.

Ewers, John Keith. *Creative Writing in Australia*. Melbourne: Georgian House, pp. 66–68, 89–90.

Green, Henry Mackenzie. *History of Australian Literature*. Sydney: Angus & Robertson, 1961, pp. 242–3, 635–643, 785–6.

Green, Henry Mackenzie. *Outline of Australian Literature*. Sydney: Whitcombe and Tombs, 1930, pp. 133–5, 223–5.

Hadgraft, Cecil. *Australian literature*. London: Heinemann, 1960, pp. 163–8, 282.

Mathew, Ray. "Miles Franklin," *Australian Writers and their Work*. Melbourne: Lansdowne Press, 1963.

"Miles Franklin:" A Tribute by some of her Friends. Melbourne: Bread and Cheese Club, 1955.

"Miles Franklin." (With portrait.) *The Australian Women's Sphere* (April 1904), p. 429.

Miller, E. Morris, ed. *Australian Literature from its beginnings to 1935* [a bibliography]. Melbourne: Melbourne University Press, 1940, V. 2, pp. 504–6, 683, 769–70.

Miller, E. Morris and Macartney, Frederick T. *Australian literature: a bibliography to 1935* by E. M. Miller *extended to 1950* by F. T. Macartney. Sydney: Angus & Robertson, 1956, pp. 80–1, 184–5.

Palmer, Nettie. "More About Brent of Bin Bin," *Illustrated Tasmanian Mail*, June 18, 1930, p. 4.

Index

Aborigines, Australian, 5, 7, 114, 116, 117; place names, 13-14, 78, 113
Archibald, John Feltham, 41
Arlen, Michael, 137
Ashworth, Arthur, 154
Auchinvole, Mr. (first teacher of Miles Franklin), 25, 30
Austen, Jane, 133, 135
Australia, foundation, 5; Miles Franklin's attitude to, 3, 39-40, 132-135, 144; penal settlement, 5, 9, 117; Sesqui-centenary, 123-128; settlement, 6-9
Australian Book of the Month scheme, 143
Australian Book Society, 143
Australian language, 7

Baker, Kate, 129-131
Bin Bin, 12, 75
Boake, Barcroft, 40
Bramina river, 13
Brarina, 12
Brent of Bin Bin (pseud.), 73-105, 112, 119, 122, 137-139
Bridle, Martha, *née* Smith (great-grandmother), 10
Bridle, R. F. (cousin), 99
Brindabella, 12, 14-15, 17-19, 20-33, 37, 74, 88, 115, 120
Bulletin, The (journal), 41, 46, 52, 107, 112, 130
Burrabinga, 15, 113, 114, 115, 120

Caine, Hall, 37
Carlton (Sydney suburb), 140-141, 156
Chesterfield, 37
Chicago, U.S.A., 62, 64, 71
Clyne, Dan, 99
Collins, Tom, *see* Furphy, Joseph
Commonwealth Literary Fund, 3, 132, 141-142, 157; lectures, 46, 131-132, 142

Convicts, 127, 132, 134-135
Corelli, Marie, 37
Cusack, Dymphna, 99, 123-124, 143

Dickens, Charles, 37, 134
Drake-Brockman, Henrietta, 1

E. *see* Fullerton, Mary E.
Ellis, Havelock, 47
Endeavour Press, Sydney, 107
Eucumbene river, 13, 40

Fellowship of Australian Writers, Sydney, 132, 141, 145
Flea river, 13
Franklin family, 21-22, 50, 120-121
Franklin, Donald (cousin), 35
Franklin, George (uncle), 12, 18
Franklin, John Maurice (father), 1, 12, 23, 36, 60, 99, 120, 140
Franklin, Joseph (grandfather), 12, 21, 30, 75, 120
Franklin, Miles, animals, love of, 23-24, 26, 42, 63, 105, 106-107, 117, 137; appearance, 1-2, 24, 25, 37; as Brent of Bin Bin, 73-105; as critic, 122, 128-131, 132-135; as journalist, 52; as lecturer, 63, 131-135; as maid servant, 52; as nurse, 53; Australia, criticism of, 142, 148; Australia, love of, 40, 74-5, 134, 143, 147-148; autobiography, 22-35, 44-45, 50, 51, 52, 88, 120-121; birds, love of, 32; birth, 12, 17, 20; character, 2, 34-35, 36, 60-61, 104-105, 154-155; characterization, 51, 96-97, 103, 109-110, 111, 115, 126, 137, 149-153; childhood, 4, 12, 15-16, 20-33, 35, 100; children, love of, 26, 143; collaboration, 76, 98, 122, 123-131; courage, 70-71; death, 156; death of sister, 19,

35; despair, 144-145; diary, 4, 22, 99; education, 4, 21, 24, 25-26, 34, 36, 133; egalitarianism, 63, 77, 105, 116; feminism, 2, 36-37, 43, 59-60, 75, 82, 104-105, 110, 135, 138, 149, 154; gardens, love of, 32-33; health, 24, 35, 64, 71, 122, 156; homesickness, 4, 33, 64-65; horses and riding, 2, 20-21, 23-24, 26, 30-32, 148; house at Carlton, 140-146; humour, 77, 89-90, 107, 119, 124-128; in exile, 3, 61, 62-68, 143-144; legend, 3-4; literary earnings, 46; literary qualities, 28-29, 48-49, 67, 75, 78-79, 80, 83, 94; manuscripts lost, 65-66, 122, 129; marriage?, 69; move to Stillwater, 26, 34; musical ambitions, 37, 41, 53, 60, 62, 64, 91; *nom de plume*, 73-105; on Australian literature, 144, 156-157; on publishers, 145; on the peace 1918, 71-72; on war; 71-72, 149; pacificist, 4, 63, 71-72; paradoxes, 28; philosophy of, 147-155; productivity, 122, 123, 143-144; prose style, 73-74, 80, 81, 82, 98, 116, 123; rebellion, 27, 33, 36, 37, 49, 58; relatives, 34-35, 49-50, 76; religion, 24-25; return to Australia, 140, 144; river motif, 13-14, 44, 67, 75, 80, 104, 112-113, 147, 156; romanticism, 61, 98, 104, 107, 109, 149; secretiveness, 3, 4, 27, 76-77; sensitive nature, 3, 51, 145; social crusader, 2, 40, 62-68, 70, 104-105, 145; vocabulary, 44, 58, 66, 74; visits to Australia 1924, 1930, 72; war service, 70-72; wit, 4, 109, 119

WRITINGS OF:

All That Swagger, 3, 30, 52, 73, 74, 75, 111-121, 122, 149, 150, 153;

quotations from, 15, 74, 112, 113, 114, 116, 117, 118, 148

Back to Bool Bool, 61, 74, 77, 95, 97-105, 124, 150, 152;

quotations from, 31, 65, 70, 100, 101, 102, 103, 104, 140, 153

Bring the Monkey, 49, 74, 106-107, 122, 153;

quotations from, 106, 107

Childhood at Brindabella, 22, 27, 30, 120;

quotations from, 15-16, 16-17, 18, 21, 22, 23, 24, 25, 26, 27, 28, 32, 71, 120, 140

Cockatoos, 62, 73, 74, 75, 77, 88-95, 96, 99, 111, 119, 122, 149, 151, 152, 153;

quotations from, 61, 62, 65, 88, 90, 91, 92-93, 94, 95

Gentlemen at Gyang Gyang, 74, 77, 95-97, 122, 150, 153;

quotations from, 14, 31-32, 96, 97

Joseph Furphy, 128-131;

quotations from, 55-57, 64-65, 128, 130

Laughter, Not for a Cage, 42, 69, 132-135, 143;

quotations from, 37, 40-41, 42, 51, 52, 133, 134, 135, 147-148, 149

Ministering Angel, 53

My Brilliant Career, 31, 41-52, 57, 58, 60, 74, 75, 76, 90, 94, 99, 122, 151, 152;

quotations from, 42-45

My Career Goes Bung, 41, 57-61, 65, 74, 94, 99, 122, 128, 151, 152, 156;

quotations from, 41-42, 50-51, 58-60, 65-66, 76

No Family, 136-137

Old Blastus of Bandicoot, 74, 107-111, 122, 149, 152;

quotations from, 108, 109, 110, 111

Pioneers on Parade, 124-128, 143;

quotations from, 125, 126, 127, 128

Prelude to Waking, 49, 75, 122, 137-139, 150, 153;

quotations from, 71, 138, 139, 149

Some Everyday Folk and Dawn, 37, 66-69, 74, 99, 105, 111, 151, 152;

quotations from, 66-68

Sydney Royal, 136-137;

quotations from, 137

INDEX

Ten Creeks Run, 30, 74, 77, 83-87, 88, 98, 149, 150, 151, 152, 153;
quotations from, 31, 75, 85, 86, 87, 89, 152, 154
Up the Country, 30, 73, 74, 75, 77, 81-83, 95, 98, 122, 149, 150, 151, 152;
quotations from, 32, 73-74, 79-80, 81, 82, 150, 151-152
Franklin, Stella Maria Sarah Miles —*see* Franklin, Miles
Franklin, Susannah, *née* Lampe (mother), 1, 10, 18-20, 24, 25, 30, 32, 35-36, 60, 75, 120, 140-141
Franklin, Thomas (uncle), 12, 18, 21, 25
Fullerton, Mary E. (friend), 72, 76, 98
Furphy, Joseph, 51, 55-57, 128-131, 132, 134, 142, 147, 158

Gillespie, Mary Ann Elizabeth, 34
Gilmore, Dame Mary, 73
Goldstein, Vida, 61
Goodradigbee river, 12, 13, 14, 29
Grattan, C. Hartley, 143
Green, Henry Mackenzie, 47

Hadgraft, Cecil, 48, 58, 119
Hebblewhite, T. J., 42, 132
Henry, Alice, 62-64, 70
Herlihy, Mrs. Dan, 20
Homesteads, 11, 18-19, 81, 86, 114-115
Horses, 13, 20, 21, 30-31, 83, 84-85, 87, 114, 148

James, Henry, 134, 135
Jounania creek, 44, 156

Lampe family, 21, 22
Lampe, Altmann (grandfather), 10, 11, 35
Lampe, John (uncle), 11
Lampe, Sarah, *née* Bridle (grandmother), 10, 11, 20-21, 24, 26-27, 34, 50
Lampe, William (uncle), 11, 20
Lane, William, 39-40
Lawrence, D. H., 134
Lawson, Henry, 37, 45, 132

Mathew, Ray, 47, 49, 52, 80, 122, 137
Matthews, Harley, 145
Micalong river, 13
Miles, Edward (ancestor), 9
Miles Franklin Award, 157
Miller, E. Morris, 3, 79
Mitchell Library of Australiana, 3
Monaro *district*, 12, 13, 29, 49, 74, 78, 88, 89, 90, 95, 147
Moore, Tom Inglis, 136
Moore, William, 136
Mudie, Ian, 143
Mungee river, 80, 103, 104
Murrumbidgee river, 13, 15, 29, 107, 112

New Idea Magazine, 51

Oakdale, 12
O'Dowd, Bernard, 39-40
Ogilvie, Will, 37
O'Harris, Pixie, 1, 23
Outside Track, The—*see* Franklin, Miles, writings of, *Cockatoos*

Palmer, Nettie, 78, 81, 84, 142, 144, 156
Palmer, Vance, 38, 76, 142
Pastoral Age, 8, 77-87, 158
Paterson, A. B., 37
Peaceful Army, The, *Memorial volume*, 123
Penrith *district*, 37, 66, 74
Pioneering in Australia, 4, 5-19, 29-30, 78, 111-121, 124-128, 157-158
Port Jackson, 6
Prior Memorial Prize, 52, 112, 129, 131

Queen Victoria Hospital for Women, 63

Reiby, Mary, 123
Richardson, Henry Handel, 134
Royal Easter Show, Sydney, 136
Rudd, Steele, 90
Ruse, James, 133

Scott, Rose, 53-55, 62, 63, 99, 123
Scott, Sir Walter, 134

Scottish Women's Hospital Unit, 53, 70, 71
Shaw, Molly Scott, 99
Singleton, Mabel, 72
Smith, Susannah (ancestor), 10
Snowy Mountains, 13, 40
Southerly, No. 4, 1957, quotation from, 154
Spence, Catherine Helen, 63, 133, 142
Squatters and Squattocracy, 6-9, 12, 29-30, 74, 75, 77-87, 97, 157
Stephens, A. G., 46, 50, 132
Stephensen, P. R., 76
Stewart, Douglas, 13, 14-15
Stillwater, 26, 27, 33, 34, 37, 74, 88, 90
Sydney, Australia, 6, 103-104

Talbingo, 10, 11, 12, 17, 20, 21, 27, 30, 33, 35, 37, 156
Thackeray, William Makepeace, 37, 134
Thornford, *district*, 26, 28, 74
Tierney, John Lawrence, 13
Trade Unionism, 64
Trade Union Woman (journal), 64

Votes for Women, 40, 63, 66

Walgrove, 12
Women's Trade Union League, U.S.A., 64

Yarrabongo river, 75
Yarrangobilly river, 13